# AT ANY COST
## LOVE, LIFE & DEATH AT SEA

# AT ANY COST
## LOVE, LIFE & DEATH AT SEA

An Autobiography by Peter Tangvald

**CRUISING GUIDE PUBLICATIONS**

Dunedin, Florida

Cruising Guide Publications is a special interest publisher of sailing guides to cruising in various areas around the world and other publications of nautical interest. CGP endeavours to provide comprehensive and invaluable materials to both inveterate sailors and less experienced seafarers seeking vital vacationing tips and navigating information relative to the journey to and the enjoyment of their prospective destinations.

Library of Congress Cataloging-in-Publication Data

Tangvald, Peter, 1924-1991
        At any cost: love, life & death at sea / Peter Tangvald


ISBN # 09-44428-07-X (hardcover)

Library of Congress Catalog Card Number: 91-77857

Edited by April Manning, Nancy Scott, Rose Grant

Printed in the United States of America.

# Dedication

*I dedicate this book to my son, Thomas, who did not make it to the hospital in time and thus was born "on the high seas," and to my daughter, Carmen, who made it to the hospital with 45 minutes to spare!*

"Qui vit sans follie,
n'est pas aussi sage
qu'il croit."

— Whoever lives without folly
is not as wise as he thinks.

*(author unknown)*

# Contents

# Introduction

*N*ear the end of 1957, when sailing to the Canary Islands, I anchored in Las Palmas. From a neighbouring yacht, a lanky figure sculled over and introduced himself as Peter Tangvald. Like me, he was bound singlehanded across the Atlantic and wanted to arrive in Antigua for Christmas. Time was getting short, so we decided to make a race of it. The prize: *one dollar*. Peter won and the dollar, suitably framed, was hung in the saloon. Thus started a long lasting friendship.

Throughout the ensuing years, we have never been long out of touch by mail and we have met up again in the Western Hemisphere and the Far East. I sailed with him on occasion, knew his last three boats and several of his wives.

*L'Artemis de Pytheas* was Peter Tangvald's dream ship—designed and built by him as a labour of love in French Guiana. When fitting her out afloat in Kourou and expecting me from across the South Atlantic, he called to a friend heading down river for a sail, "Have a look out to sea—I believe my friend will be coming."

I arrived that very afternoon. This was my first sight of *L'Artemis*—long, low and rakish—a refreshing change from the mass-produced, plastic boxes one sees nowadays. However the rig was a bit odd. To my queries Peter airily explained that it was "just a jury rig to get me to Martinique." He was still saying that 15 years later.

It is not easy to find a rig suitable for both deep sea sailing and for the light conditions and calms that can be experienced on entering port. Peter never considered installing an engine. His previous boat, *Dorothea*, had an engine when he bought her, but he soon threw it overboard and went on to sail around the world.

Peter Tangvald's extraordinary sailing adventures were rivaled only by his extraordinary matrimonial adventures, but his reputation for discarding women like matches was quite unjustified, as any reader of this book will agree. There are many instances of his love for his wives and children. After Lydia's death, Peter was completely shattered, putting his cherished boat up for sale and going on with his life only to look after his son, Thomas. Having heard about the state he was in, I flew across the Indian Ocean to Malacca to join him and managed to infuse enough enthusiasm into him to persuade him to refit his boat and plan further escapades.

This honestly written book is a tribute to both Peter Tangvald's spirit of adventure and his chosen lifestyle.

—Edward Allcard
Andorra

# 1

# The Year 1985

What should I do now? At 60 years old I was alone with two small children. Suddenly my 50-foot sailboat seemed much too big. I had lost all interest in it and I was feeling so tired. Perhaps the best thing to do would be to follow my family's advice and return home to Norway. I could sell the boat. Perhaps it would pay for a small house where I could live in safety with the children.

I tried not to think about how I would stand the long, cold and dark Norway winters after 36 years in warm climates. Finally I found the courage to set the course north, but, instead of sailing directly to Norway, I steered for the States where I expected to get a better price for the boat. Perhaps also, subconsciously, I hoped to find a good life there despite the fact that I would have no relatives to help me as I would in Norway.

We were in the center of the ill-famed Bermuda Triangle when Thomas asked me hesitantly, "Tomorrow I'll be eight years old, Papa, but I suppose I won't have any birthday, now that Mama is no longer with us."

He seemed so sad I had difficulty holding back my tears. I had promised to bake him a birthday cake with eight candles on it. I was glad he had reminded me about his birthday in time, because I'd completely forgotten all about it.

Fortunately, I did find eight candles in the box in which we'd saved last year's Christmas lights, candles and stars. Although I tried my best, the cake was a complete failure. When I put it on the table,

Thomas looked at it apprehensively. There it was, all crooked and three times as high on one side as the other. We had been closehauled and heeling over heavily, causing the unevenness in the cake which was overcooked on the thin side and undercooked on the thick side. At the first bite, we both realised that I also must have made a mistake with the recipe, as the cake was quite inedible. Quietly Thomas pushed his plate away, mumbling that it was not quite as good as those Mama made.

He was clearly disappointed about his birthday because I was not able to have a birthday present for him. But what hurt me most was the realization that his sadness went much further than just the disappointment of a poor cake or the lack of a present. After the loss of Ann, our whole life had become so sad and empty—not just for me, but for Thomas and perhaps also for little Carmen. She was too small to understand what had happened but, certainly the sudden interruption of her breast feeding and the sudden lack of motherly warmth, replaced only by my clumsiness and the bottled milk must have affected her.

We missed Ann desperately.

# 2

# Adolescence

For the last 30 years I have lived on a sailboat. Even if sometimes I long to settle down, it's most likely that I will continue to live my free and vagabond lifestyle until the very end.

When I think back to try and figure out what started me in this way of life, I fear I have to put the blame on my father, or perhaps I should say, he deserves the credit.

I was born in Oslo, Norway, on the 27th of September, 1924. My father was a well-known skier and airplane pilot but, not long after my birth, he abandoned the air force because of family pressure and became a businessman. He first established himself in Drammen, where he imported Spanish oranges (he was the first ever to do so in Norway), and then in Switzerland, where he imported Norwegian ski equipment. My brother, Odd, was born while the family was in Switzerland.

In 1931 we moved to Paris, where my father started a ski factory. We were to stay there for nine years until rumours of World War II prompted our return to Norway in 1940. In the beginning my brother and I had a difficult time in Norway, because everything was so different from Paris. It took time for us to overcome the language barrier for, although our parents were Norwegian and always spoke Norwegian at home, French was our first language. We spoke Norwegian with a very heavy French accent and poor grammar, which made everyone laugh. At that time, there were practically no foreigners in Norway and no one spoke broken Norwegian as we did.

Fortunately for my brother and me, we were young enough to learn quickly, and it didn't take long before we were as fluent as the natives. Yet, for children raised in a large and sophisticated city like Paris, it was quite a change to suddenly find ourselves in an austere country like Norway. It was not all for the worst, though—in fact, it proved to be far better because we children were able to get much closer to our father than we might have otherwise.

While Father was in Paris, he had been much more interested in his factory and his social life. When I think back to our apartment in Neuilly, which is one of the best districts of Paris, I can't even remember how our living room looked, we were permitted in it so seldom. We spent nearly all our time in our rooms, supervised by a strict, uniformed nanny. On the rare occasions when we were permitted to have our meals in the dining room, we were not allowed to talk, because "Nice children should be seen but not heard."

In Norway everything was so much simpler—we had no servants—and family life became much nicer. We rented a small house on Nesodden by the fjord, not too far from Oslo.

One day my father saw my mother giving me a sleeping pill half an hour before bedtime and asked if I was sick.

"No," said Mother, "he's not exactly sick, he's just taking his usual sleeping medicine."

"Sleeping medicine!" exclaimed Father. "Sleeping medicine for a 14-year-old boy? What kind of nonsense is this? How long has this been going on?"

"But, dear," said Mother, "you must know that Peter has very fragile nerves and that for four or five years he's needed special medicine to calm him down at night so he can sleep. His psychiatrists, both in Paris and here in Oslo, have been taking good care of him and know best what kind of medicine he needs."

I will never forget the expression on my father's face when he learned that not only was his son getting sleeping tablets, but he had been going to psychiatrists for years!

Father did not care much for doctors in general, but I suspect he considered it directly harmful for anyone to get involved with psychiatrists. He himself was so strong and healthy that he never had to consult any type of doctor (except for one operation after a bad ski accident) and had difficulty seeing his own son in doctors' and psychiatrists' offices. But I remember he refrained from any further comment except to say that, in his opinion, all I needed was healthy food, fresh air and enough exercise. I feel sure, though, that he must have had a serious talk with Mother behind closed doors after I had gone to bed: The next morning my usual breakfast of strong coffee with white bread and jam had been replaced with a big glass of milk and brown bread with cheese. I never got another sleeping pill and I never saw another psychiatrist after that day.

My father's decision for me to lead a healthy life would change my life forever. That same day a mooring buoy was laid out in front of our house, and that evening I saw a beautiful sailboat tied up to it. I saw my father onboard the sailboat with a man I did not know.

"This is my alternative to psychiatrists and sleeping pills," explained Father to me as he came ashore. "I just bought this boat and I have hired this man as your skipper and sailing instructor. You shall obey him in everything he tells you, so you'll learn as quickly as possible. He's going to live with us all summer and you're going to sail from seven in the morning 'til seven at night every day, regardless of the weather. I have hired him at a regular salary," he added, "but I've promised him a good bonus if he succeeds in teaching you enough before the end of the season so that you'll be able to handle the boat by yourself in any kind of weather and pick up the mooring under sail with no help."

I never found out how big that bonus was, but it must have been tempting enough, judging by the way the instructor made me work. He had me reef and unreef hundreds of times. I anchored and got underway again and again. He let me know in no uncertain terms when I wasn't successful in making the manoeuvres exactly as he directed me. He laid out small floats to simulate anchored boats, docks or reefs and had me manoeuvre between them. If I didn't place the boat exactly where he directed me, I was in for it.

"No, no, and again, no! Can't you see that you anchored much too close to that boat on your starboard side? Get the anchor up again and be sure to break out the anchor with the wind on your starboard side, otherwise you'll ram that boat, but get your speed up so you can tack again before hitting those reefs on your port side. OK, you did it. Now try to anchor again and do it right this time. Not too close to that boat, but not too close to those reefs."

All the practice using buoys to simulate anchored boats and other dangers was, of course, to make sure I could manoeuvre the boat correctly and not damage our boat or cause any accidents with other boats. But during that summer, I am sure I must have reefed, tacked, gybed and anchored more times than most sailors do in a lifetime. At the season's end, my instructor got his bonus with no arguments. Never had I felt in better shape. I had gained weight and become stronger and, after 12 hours on the fjord, I certainly didn't need any sleeping tablets to fall asleep!

But surprisingly, even though I had been doing all the hard work and otherwise shared the same life, my instructor had lost weight and looked tired by the end of the season. Mother noticed it too and, on the last evening, mentioned it to him.

"Is that so surprising?" he answered angrily. "Who wouldn't get tired after having to work 12 hours a day without a single day's respite for two solid months?"

I had shared the same life, the same food and the same hours as my instructor but, after thinking it over, I didn't need to be a psychiatrist to see what the difference had been. For me it had been play—for him it had just been work.

Father had been very successful in getting me healthy, but had he realized to what extent sailing would affect my life, he probably would have chosen another sport. It proved no advantage to my schooling. I just sat through my classes and daydreamed about next year's sailing.

A couple of years later, in 1942, when everyone thought the war was almost over, I succeeded in convincing Father to take me out of school. My plan was to go to sea and get enough sea time to be eligible to get into the naval academy as soon as the war was over. I wanted to become a naval officer in the Norwegian navy.

My first assignment was the Coast Guard vessel stationed at Einervika, which was skippered by Captain Farsted. Einervika was a desolate little bay just south of Namsos, not far from the Arctic Circle. The vessel was one of the famous Colin Archer sailing vessels, 58 feet long with a 15-foot beam, built at the end of the last century. Despite their huge beams, these ships had a reputation as good sailers and were surprisingly graceful, thanks to the genius of Colin Archer.

I had been so excited at the thought of sailing on one of his vessels that, on boarding the boat, I was very disappointed to see that it had been "modernized" with a huge diesel engine and a wheelhouse. The big, slow-turning motor had a huge propeller which, to my mind, was nothing but a horrible sea anchor. The deckhouse had necessitated the raising of the boom, with consequent sail reduction. In fact, since most sailing workboats never bother to sail anymore in light air, the crew had taken down the topmast, as well as removed the bowsprit altogether. Only the reduced boomed sails and the staysail were able to be set instead of the five original sails: main, mizzen, staysail, jib and topsail. The boat was nothing more than a motorsailor and, in my eyes, had lost all interest. Nevertheless, I needed the sea time, so I stayed on.

We were four men on board: the skipper, the first officer, the machinist and the cook. I was the cook. I didn't realize I was to be the cook until I came onboard, for if there's something I didn't know then and still don't know today, it's how to cook. But perhaps those who suffered the most were the three others who had to content themselves with what I was able to serve!

Norwegian Coast Guard vessels, which are stationed all along the coast of Norway, have no police authority, unlike those along the coasts of most other countries; they are there solely to assist vessels who need help. With the enthusiasm of youth, I had visualized us flying through storm-swept waves to go to the rescue of sinking steamships. Reality was altogether different for, although these lifeboats had occasionally rescued crews from sinking steamships, our main duty was simply to lay hove to on the fishing banks to watch over the fleet of small fishing boats. We represented security to the smaller boats which, without our presence, would not often have dared go as far from land as is required for the best fishing.

This was before the days of the big commercial fishing vessels. Each man fished for himself in the family boat. There were just two men and one pair of oars in each boat. The boats were beautiful and easy-rowing. They looked like small Viking ships with very low freeboard amidships and high ends, and were clinker-built out of wood. These small boats would row far out from shore, sometimes out of sight of land, and the men would fish for big codfish by hand until their freeboard became so low that they dared not catch any more. They then rowed back to shore to clean and dry the fish. The boats were fast-rowing and surprisingly seaworthy.

But there is a limit to what any pulling boat can do against a strong headwind. Over the years, many lives had been lost when unforeseen storms blew up from the shore, blowing the boats far out into the cold northern sea. Our job was simply to stay on watch and take all the boats in tow on a long line should such a wind hinder them in getting back to shore.

Today it sounds like a lot of wasted manpower, but in those days motors were expensive and had to be paid for in cash, making them all but impossible for those poor fishermen to acquire. And since it was during the war, only a few boats were given fuel.

Since then, all that has changed. The government encouraged the big, factory-like fishing boats and paid the small fishermen high bonuses to destroy their boats. The fishermen were offered steady jobs with high pay as workers on the big fishing boats. Financially the government has made a success of it and, certainly, the fishermen are much richer today than they were. But, socially, I'm not so sure it is the best. I suspect they were much happier in the days when they were free men with no bosses over their backs.

For me at that time, it was a dull routine just to patrol those fishing grounds. It was the same day after day, and it was cold and dark. Being close to the Arctic Circle in the middle of winter meant the sun just barely came over the horizon around noon. Besides, I was not much liked by the others onboard. They didn't appreciate that they had to suffer from my lousy cooking so that I, "the privileged kid from Oslo," could get enough sea time to be admitted into the Naval Academy.

One day after the fishing fleet had just reached shore and we were on our way back to port, a sudden storm blew up with such ferocity that the skipper was later to write it down in his log as "a hurricane force storm, force 12 on the Beaufort scale"—something he had never in all his life written down before. The huge boom carrying just the small, cut-down sail broke like a matchstick and the sail, which was as thick as a sheet of plywood, was flogging so wildly that the whole boat was shaking despite its weight. At long last we succeeded in getting it down to the deck, where we all had to crawl so as to avoid being blown over the side.

I considered it a good day because I didn't have to cook, as everyone was too busy trying to get the boat safely to harbour. When we finally did reach port, we discovered we had sprung two serious leaks, one by the bow and one by the stern. The ship had to go on the slip for repairs. The whole crew got a leave of absence for the time of repairs and I took the first train back to Oslo.

I'd discovered that pleasure sailing had very little to do with commercial seafaring and my love for the sea suffered a serious setback. I had no desire whatsoever to return to the lifeboat and confessed to Father that my idea of becoming a marine officer had all been a mistake; his idea to send me to study in Switzerland after graduation from high school in Oslo had been the right one. He was easy to convince and made the necessary arrangements to free me from the Coast Guard and put me back in school.

But although I was relieved to have gotten out of the hard and dull life in the north of Norway on that lifeboat, I did not like school any more than I ever had. All too often, I was skipping classes and spending most of my time running around with girls. When I finally had to take exams, I failed miserably. I got F's, not in just one subject, but in Norwegian, German and English, as well as in history and chemistry. Father was annoyed, but I flatly refused to go back to school for another year.

By 1945, Germany had surrendered, but the war still went on with Japan. One day an ad in the paper came to my rescue. The air force had just been given a new air force base in England and needed volunteers to sign up to become pilots to be sent into action against Japan. My father, a reserve officer in the air force who had just been called back into service, could hardly object to my applying, especially after I reasoned that the war with Japan surely would be over before my training would be finished. But at the enrolling office, instead of being accepted on the spot, as I had presumed with a youth's naivete that I would be, I was informed that only 30 men would be accepted among the more than 100 applications and that they would let me know in due time.

In the meantime, summer had arrived. Our boat was ready to sail and I had a girlfriend, Reidun, who was most willing to go cruising with me. So with the irresponsibility all too common to young people of that age, we sailed away without letting anyone know where we were going. We wanted to get to Sweden, for now, with Germany defeated, we saw no reason why we couldn't sail there, even without passports, visas or any papers whatsoever.

We were not the only ones with that same idea about Sweden, which had escaped the war. For most of us in Norway, Sweden represented "God's promised land," with all kinds of food and merchandise available with no restrictions to anyone. As we approached the border, we were met by a long line of boats coming back, which had been stopped by patrol boats.

"Can't we try to get through without being seen?" I asked.

"No, it won't work," they all answered. "There are lots of patrol boats, and even warships, patrolling back and forth watching the border very carefully."

Reidun was barely 17 and I was not all that much older, but I wanted her to look up to me as a man, and I didn't want to give up that easily on the golden voyage to Sweden I had promised her.

By studying my school atlas, which was all we had to navigate by, I decided that, instead of following the coast adjacent to Sweden and then crossing the border—which is what everyone did because it was the most logical route—we could sail down the opposite side of the fjord, then along the southwest coast to Kragero and lay the course straight across the open sea to somewhere around Goteborg, way beyond the border. Surely no warships would be looking for a small, illegal yacht coming from Norway.

We got a fresh breeze and became a bit seasick, but after a star-studded night we saw land straight ahead. It had to be Sweden and we saw no warships anywhere. On the other hand, we were far from sure of our exact location. We also didn't understand what all the beacons meant because they were of a different type from those used in Norway.

Should we keep to our right or left? Should we go the east or the west of them? With no proper charts and no knowledge of how to negotiate these beacons, we would soon risk going aground among hundreds of islets and rocks.

Fortunately, we spotted a small yacht which we easily overtook in our fast racing boat. The owner was surprised to learn that we had come from Norway and offered to guide us to port—a good thing, as we never would have been able to find the way ourselves among all those rocks. When we finally arrived in the beautiful tiny harbour of Smogen, two other yachts were there. Their crews soon came over to greet us, as we were the first Norwegians they had seen for years.

This was my first trip out of sight of land in my own boat, and the first time I had sailed to any foreign land. It was a great adventure for both of us but, by the next day, it was to end.

A man came running towards us from a neighbouring house and asked if I was Tangvald from Oslo.

"Yes, I'm Tangvald," I replied, a bit surprised that anyone here would know who I was.

"I have your father on the phone," he said. "It's very important!"

Reidun was in a panic. At that time, moral standards were quite different, much more conservative than what they are today, so Reidun had lied to her parents that she was going on a bicycle trip with a girlfriend and staying with her friend's parents. As for me, I had said I was going to sail with a classmate, which was technically true. We did go to the same school, but I had conveniently omitted the fact that the classmate was a girl.

I followed the man back to his house and took the phone. It really was my father. He said I had to come back to Oslo immediately because the air force had called me in to be sent to England. If I didn't show up, I not only would lose my chances of becoming an officer and a pilot in the air force, but also would face punishment for not answering the draft.

I promised to sail immediately, but I didn't dare ask Father how he could have known I was there in that tiny harbour so far from home. Perhaps he simply had called every little place along the coasts of both Norway and Sweden until he finally happened to find us.

In any case, I hoisted the sails without delay and didn't lower them again until we reached Oslo, even though I was nearly falling asleep at the end. In the strong following wind we had, I dared not let Reidun take the tiller for fear she could have let the boat gybe, something which easily could have dismasted my slender and delicate boat. It had been designed for around the buoy racing in smooth water, not for open sailing in heavy weather. In the last part of the voyage up the fjord of Oslo, the seas did flatten out, but the wind remained fresh, so I stayed at the tiller the whole way.

When I returned, I got into battle dress and was sent to England to the little airfield base of Winkley, not far from Exeter, in the southwestern part of the country. But to my great disappointment, I was soon to realize that there had been a complete lack of understanding between the head office in Norway, this new base in England and the old Norwegian base in Canada, which was called "Little Norway." Apparently, unknown to the headquarters in Oslo, "Little Norway" had just been transferred to Winkley which, due to its small size, was already overcrowded. There was no need for new recruits from Norway. In fact, there was hardly room for us!

After a few weeks, those of us from Oslo had nothing to do and just drifted around until we finally were assigned jobs. I was to be kitchen helper! A far cry from the promised pilot and officer training I had been promised—and for which I had volunteered. I felt badly cheated and demanded to be sent home immediately. But I never saw the commanding officer. Surely he had more important things to do than to listen to dissatisfied new recruits. On the whole, the others just laughed at me. I'd been in uniform for only a few weeks and already I wanted to be released. Didn't I realize that many of them had been in uniform for years and still didn't see an end in sight? The war was still on, they reminded me.

"If you want to become a pilot, don't you think those who have waited their turn for years in Canada should get their chance before you?" they demanded.

"Of course, I can see your point, but I don't think it's right to have made me volunteer to become a pilot so they could use me as kitchen help," I answered angrily.

"You have to complain to the office in Oslo where you signed up."

And that was the end of it, as far as they were concerned. So I mailed many letters to Oslo, but never got a single reply.

My esteem for the Royal Norwegian Air Force sank pretty low. However, since I was apparently stuck in England, I tried to make the best of it. I bought myself a motorcycle, a 1934 Norton 630cc model monocylinder, which was to give me much pleasure.

Thanks to owning the bike, it was easy for me to get off the base when I was off-duty, and I soon learned more English in a few months than everything my teachers had tried to hammer into my head during my long, boring school years. So my time in the air force had not been completely wasted and the day finally arrived when I was sent home to Norway and discharged.

I found Reidun again and discovered that we were still as much in love as ever. I was now 21, she 18. Perhaps just to prove that we were adults, one day we stopped by City Hall and got married.

Mother cried; Father got mad. "What are you going to do for a living?" he wanted to know. Well, we hadn't given it that much thought. A few days later, I got a message to come and talk to Father at his office.

"I hear that your father-in-law has found an apartment for you," he began. "He must really have the right connections. It's almost impossible to find any kind of housing, not to mention a brand new apartment in a good district! You really are lucky. I also want to participate in helping you get a good start with a belated marriage present: I'll pay your rent, including electricity, water and heat for the next four years, provided you follow the plans I have for you."

I didn't interrupt, waiting anxiously for the rest of what he had to say as I felt that this would determine the way of life awaiting me.

"So far, you haven't done very well in life," he said. "You didn't take advantage of my offer to go to college in Switzerland—one of the best colleges in Europe—which would have made life easy for you later on. You didn't even bother to study enough to pass high school. Your own idea to become a navy officer failed even before you fulfilled your sea time to be accepted at the naval academy, and you didn't do much better in the air force. Since you didn't take advantage of gaining entry into an adult's world through the big gate when you had an opportunity to do so, you're going to have to start at the bottom and gradually climb as you prove yourself. I have made the necessary arrangements for you to start as a tool and die apprentice in one of the largest factories here in Oslo."

I wasn't quite sure what a tool and die maker was, but guessed that it was some type of blue-collar worker. I couldn't understand why my otherwise snobbish family now wanted me to become an ordinary working man.

Father smiled when he saw my surprise. "I must admit that I would have preferred you to become an engineer, and then, later, a doctor of engineering, but times are changing and will continue to do so. The social classes will equalize more and more, and so will salaries. It's no shame for you to be an "ordinary working man," as Mother says. On the contrary, if you succeed in becoming a tool and die maker, you will be a valuable man to society because they are the basis of all industry.

"However, the main reason I want you to become a tool and die maker is that I need a tool and die department in my factory. It would be more efficient to have the department in my factory instead of farming out my tools and dies. I'd like you to be in charge of it as soon as you have finished your apprenticeship in four years' time and know about the trade."

He paused for my reaction, but I couldn't think of anything to say. He ended the meeting by saying that I was to start the next morning at seven and not to be late.

Reidun wasn't too happy at the prospect of having a tool and die maker for a husband and reminded me that I had talked about becoming a photographer, which would have been far more exciting. We talked it over, but how was I to become a photographer when we didn't have a cent to buy a camera? Besides, four years of paid rent was nothing to frown about. In fact, how were we otherwise going to pay the rent at the end of the month? So we decided to try, at least for a while. If I became too tired of it, I could always quit and then try to switch over to the photography after having saved some money.

I arrived the next morning at seven. The building was dark and dirty. They led me to my bench, which was equipped with a vise, a drawer containing a few tools, a stool to sit on and a small closet. One of the other apprentices was to be my leader for the first few days to show me how all the machines worked. There were seven or eight apprentices in addition to about 20 "old boys"—the name we gave to the full-fledged tool and die makers, some of whom really did look old and tired.

The first day I felt like fleeing. It was primarily thanks to Reidun that I returned the next day at all. She encouraged me not to give up so easily and to at least wait until our first month's rent had been paid. Strangely enough, it wasn't long before I started to like my new life. Everybody was nice and friendly to me and they all seemed to enjoy explaining how everything worked. Soon I was able to saw, plane, mill, and pierce slabs of steel. I was fascinated by it all. The foreman not only gave me permission to walk around the shop and see what the old boys were doing, but even encouraged me to do so.

"By looking at what the old boys are doing and by following their progress from day to day," the foreman said, "you'll learn much faster than you could from me teaching you; the sooner you learn the trade, the sooner you'll become a useful man to us."

Those were wise words, but he didn't know to what extent I was going to take advantage of the situation. Each time a new drawing came from the engineering office and was given to one of the tool and die makers, I would rush over and study the drawing with him while the foreman explained how he wanted everything done. I never hesitated to ask extra questions if something wasn't clear to me, and the foreman always answered patiently. Every day I would follow up with what the tool and die maker did, so it wasn't long before I felt capable of making a whole die on my own, instead of just making odd pieces for the old boys, and I said so.

The foreman just smiled at me and said that, while he had noticed I was learning much faster than he had ever seen anyone do before me, I shouldn't overestimate my capabilities. No apprentice was ever given a complete die to do before the end of his second year of apprenticeship. When he saw how hurt and disappointed I must have looked, he added hesitantly, "Let's at least wait until you have 18 months of experience behind you, and then I'll see if I can find a simple one for you to try on your own."

Not long after that conversation, I overheard my father tell a business friend that one of his dies had broken down and it was going to cost him a lot of money to have the pieces redone. He was told he wouldn't be able to get a new die for nearly a whole year because it was just after the war and tool and die shops were overbooked and completely submerged with work. Listening to the conversation gave me an idea, and I asked Father if the die was complicated.

"No," said Father, "it's a very simple one, but it doesn't matter how simple it is, because I'm not equipped to make any types of dies. I'm just stuck. Now you see why I wanted you to learn the trade."

"One of my friends in the shop has some machines at home," I lied without a qualm, "and can take in some extra work in his free time. Perhaps he could do it for you rapidly if you give me the drawings for it." My plan was to try to make it myself when the foreman wasn't looking and thus make some extra money.

"I have no drawing," said Father, "but an experienced tool and die maker should be able to make it from a sample. That I can give you."

Tentatively I asked him how much he expected to pay for such a die. Today, I can't remember the amount he said, but I do remember that it sounded like a small fortune to me at the time.

When he gave me the sample, he added that he would be willing to pay quite a bit more than the usual price if he could get it back rapidly. Back in my apartment, I lay awake trying to figure out how to make the die. It looked very similar to some of the dies I'd seen made in the shop. Before long I felt confident I'd be able to do it.

I worked on that die for several hours each day, usually when the foreman was in the engineering office. Less than two weeks had elapsed when I called Father and said that "my friend" had finished the die, but he had no presses at home and had asked me if I could try it for him in Father's factory.

I hadn't dared take the chance to try it at work; it would be too easy to get caught trying out a complete die. Making the die had been far less risky because I made only one part at a time and then assembled the whole thing at home in my apartment.

I was a bit apprehensive as I adjusted the die in Father's press, wondering if it was going to work properly. But seeing Father watch me almost respectfully, without saying a word so he wouldn't disturb me, filled me with pride. At long last, I could show him something I understood and he didn't.

He had always said that he was a businessman and couldn't do anything with his hands. In fact, I can still remember the times when he'd bought a new painting and would ask one of his workers to come more than 20 kilometers to the suburbs to hang it. The worker would hammer in the nail while Father and one of the servants held the painting in the right place. After verifying that the painting was indeed hanging correctly, the man would take the long way back to the factory, all on the factory's time! Yet, at that time, I thought there was no other way.

But now, when everything was adjusted properly and the pieces were flying out to perfection, I had trouble hiding my pride. To my great relief, Father refrained from asking any questions regarding my invisible "friend" and gave me the money to pay him—in cash. My conscience wouldn't let me take the extra money he had offered for quick delivery. I assured Father that my friend, who was operating on a very small scale and wasn't overbooked, didn't want any more than the normal price.

I also felt proud when I showed Reidun all my newly earned

money. For despite having our rent paid, my apprentice salary hardly covered anything more than buying food. There wasn't much left for luxuries.

After my first success, I didn't feel like stopping. I put a small ad in the paper, advertising dies made by a small shop with short deliveries. Customers were a bit surprised to see the address, a private apartment in a good residential district, but I explained that I was just starting in business and rented time in various small shops. Since all shops were overbooked, prospective customers refrained from asking too many questions and seemed all too glad for the short delays I quoted them.

Since I needed about two or three weeks' time to make each die, only the first customers were getting a short delivery time. It wasn't long before I had to ask a couple of the old boys to work with me and thus get better turnover. Since they seemed to have no idea about how much dies were bringing on the market, I never had to pay them more than a fraction of what I was getting. Yet, they seemed satisfied because it didn't matter to them if they worked for me or for the boss. And what I gave them was straight extra cash that they didn't have to tell their wives about and could spend on themselves!

Because I had to decline all the jobs where the dies seemed too complicated for me, I lost a lot of money and soon realised that it was the more complicated dies that were bringing in the most money.

In the public library I found an American book showing how to make complex dies and studied it until, little by little, I could do more of the complicated ones. I also hired more and more of the old boys. It wasn't long before half the shop was working for me!

One day, a year and a half later, the foreman called me into his office and declared with a friendly smile that this was the big day and he was going to trust me to make a complete die all by myself.

"I think you'll be able to manage it, but if you have any difficulties, don't hesitate to come and ask me and I'll help you," he said. He then explained to me in detail how it was going to work.

The die was an extremely simple one and there was a lot of laughter in the shop after the foreman left for one of his usual visits to the engineering office. Everyone laughed to see how little the foreman knew had been going on right under his nose for more than a year. And we weren't ever going to get caught.

I was able to buy a huge old luxury car, which weighed two and a half tons even though it was only a two-seater. It was a Minerva, which, in its heyday, had cost more than a Rolls Royce. I was able to get it fairly cheaply because the factory had gone bankrupt and there were no spare parts available for it. But I was madly in love with that car. It was in immaculate condition and never needed the least bit of overhaul or repair. In all the time I owned it, it always started and ran to perfection. Today I would not be able to afford even the 12-quart oil changes which were recommended every 1,200 miles.

As my two-week summer holiday approached, I dreamt of driving to Paris, where I had been raised. It would be fun to see the city as an adult. The war was over, but Germany still lay in ruins; gasoline was restricted in most countries, and even food was still partly controlled and rationed. Clearly, it was not the most sensible thing to play tourist on a long car trip, especially in a car which probably couldn't be repaired if it broke down.

In order to avoid any arguments from our families, Reidun and I told them we were leaving for a trip to neighbouring Sweden, which was true except that the trip didn't stop there. We took the ferry over to Denmark and then drove through the desolation of Germany. We traveled over makeshift bridges, built where the original ones had been bombed, and got lost trying to bypass the streets filled with ruins of collapsed houses. We finally reached Belgium and then, eventually, Paris.

I'll never forget the thrill of driving that big convertible, day after day, on the nearly deserted roads of that time. Old luxury cars, even as far back as 1928 (the year mine was built), were far more sophisticated than most people seem to think today. The big wheels attached to the heavy weight gave us a smooth ride; the big, slow-turning motor was so silent that, at first, I had trouble knowing when to change gears. The car even had what were called servo-assisted brakes. The power could be adjusted from zero to 10 with a knob on the dashboard. At zero, I had no assistance and really had to stand on the brake pedal to stop those two and a half tons. But at 10, the assistance from the servo system was so powerful that just a light touch to the pedal could lock all four wheels.

In Paris, I visited my old childhood friends, and together we made up for all those dull years when all I saw of Paris was my room, my school, or the Bois de Boulogne, always accompanied by either the nurse or my mother.

The weeks soon turned into months, as I completely disregarded the two-week limit of my vacation. We probably would have stayed there forever, or at least until my money ran out, had it not been for a telegram from Father, saying, "Come home immediately for voyage to America. Have purchased tickets for you and Reidun."

By now I was old enough not to have to obey my father, but a trip to America sounded exciting, and we quickly decided that we shouldn't let the chance get away.

At that time, speed restrictions were not severely enforced; in fact, I'm not sure they even had any, except for the requirement to be "reasonable." In any case, we drove so fast that, on the entire trip from Paris to Norway, we were not passed by a single car. Admittedly there weren't many cars on the roads at the time, but nevertheless, we were pretty proud of our old Minerva.

When we returned, Father refrained from reproaching us, even though we had been away nearly four months instead of the two weeks to which I was entitled. He even managed to greet us with a welcoming smile and asked if our vacation had been pleasant before he started to explain his telegram.

"I have the impression that you have learned all you'll ever be able to learn in the shop where you are now," he began. I was starting to feel uncomfortable wondering if he knew about my illegal "business" within the shop, but he went on. "I'd like you to become a real top man in the trade before we start a tool and die department together. Therefore, I want you to go to America to see how they work there. In a way, I'd like you to do some industrial espionage. The Americans are producing both better and cheaper dies than any other nation in the world.

"I want you to apply for jobs over there, and try several shops," he continued. "Don't say you are still an apprentice. I suspect that you know enough to be able to pretend that you are a full-fledged tool and die maker. As soon as you think you have nothing more to learn in one shop, just quit and go to another. Go all over the country, because techniques may not be the same everywhere. Open your eyes and try to learn all the tricks, so when you come back here, we should be able to have the best tool and die company in Norway, far above our competition.

"As you must realize, your boss here did not appreciate your long absence—especially since you didn't even bother to notify him. But I've had a long talk with him, and he agrees to forget the irregularity. Not only will he grant you a legal leave of absence so you can learn in America, he has agreed to count the time you work there as part of your legal apprenticeship. When you come back, your time will be practically complete and he'll give you the official certificate saying that you are a full-fledged tool and die maker."

"The certificate is very important," Father went on. "According to the government's new regulations, no one can start a business without being a professional. In our case, I would not be permitted to start a tool and die shop, but you will be, so we'll start the new department in your name only."

Unfortunately, things were not going to be as easy as Father had hoped. We were to learn that the tourist visas he had arranged for us would not allow us to work in the United States. Immigrant visas would be necessary, so, despite Father's many connections, we were required to wait several months to get new visas and had to cancel our tickets.

Finally in March 1949, we at long last waved to our families and friends from the deck of the old ship *Stavangerfjord*. The trip took all of 11 days to sail directly to New York and to a new life.

# 3

# A New Life Begins

*E*verything was going to work out as Father had planned, with one big exception. I was going to like it in the States so well that I didn't want to return to Norway.

In the beginning, I had a difficult time because my English was very poor and the American tool and die makers were far more advanced than any I had seen in Norway. In fact, I was fired from my first job within a week, because I didn't meet my boss's expectations. My second job lasted nearly a whole month which, in my eyes, was an improvement. Most important was the fact that, during those two jobs, I had time to correct most of my shortcomings. From then on, I did well enough to be considered equal to the others.

I was enthralled with my salary, which had nothing in common with the old world's apprentice salaries. Tool and die makers in America were the prima donnas of the industry, and commanded its highest salaries, allowing them to live in fancy houses and drive Cadillacs if they wished.

We tried many of the states: Connecticut, New Jersey, Ohio, Colorado and, at last, California with its wonderful climate. By then, secure in each of the jobs I had taken, I purchased a brand new car and rented a comfortable apartment. For the first time in my life, I felt completely free and independent of my father. Although I loved my parents, it was such a wonderful feeling that, when six months had elapsed and, according to our plan it was time to return to Norway, I wrote home, saying that I hadn't learned as much as I should and

I proposed to stay another six months. My father readily agreed, but poor Reidun was disappointed. She didn't like the states much and was getting more and more homesick for Norway and for her family. Nevertheless, she agreed to stay another six months, "but not one day beyond that," she threatened.

Those next six months went all too fast, and I was becoming more and more infatuated with the U.S. Even the prospect of becoming a factory owner in Norway could not tempt me. To gain further time while avoiding family pressure, I enrolled in a three-year program in a technical school which, upon graduation, would grant me the title of Industrial Engineer—perhaps not as fancy a title as the doctorate of engineering diploma my father had planned for me if I had studied in Switzerland, but an engineer, nevertheless.

But if ever I thought my father would give up his plan of being in partnership with me, I was sadly mistaken. When he realised I had no intention of ever coming home, he sold everything he had—the business, his house, the log cabin in the mountains, the boat—and came over to America with Mother and my brother, Odd, to start the tool and die shop with me.

Reidun kept her promise and left on the very last day of the second six-month period. She returned to our old apartment and later sued me for divorce. She married an architect and is still living in Oslo today.

In 1951, we built a factory in Van Nuys, California in the San Fernando Valley, just north of Los Angeles. We called it Tangvald & Son, Tool, Dies and Manufacturing Company (although with Father's sense of humor, he thought we should call it Tangvald & Father because he still knew nothing about tools and dies). Ever the business-man, he ran the office while I was given the title of Plant Manager on my calling cards, although in reality I was merely a foreman.

My brother, Odd, who had interrupted his studies at law school, was our sales manager. I hired a Norwegian friend as an engineer to make our drawings, and two of my fellow workers from my apprenticeship came from Norway to work as tool and die makers. This was during the Korean War, when tool and die shops were overbooked and it was difficult to find tool and die makers. When the workers arrived, I very strictly pointed out that I wanted no more illegal work from them, and we all laughed, thinking back to the old days during my apprenticeship in Norway.

Everything went well for four years until we made a bad decision to import Norwegian office chairs on a large scale without having properly checked the market. We were so sure that the chairs had perfect features and an advanced design. I don't remember how many chairs we eventually had in stock before we realised that we would never obtain the expected price for them. We finally sold them to a wholesaler at such a ridiculously low price that we never recovered and, after a month of struggling, we finally declared bankruptcy.

In the meantime I had married a French-born woman named Helene. We had a beautiful home in a good district not too far from Beverly Hills and Los Angeles. I drove a Lincoln; Helene had a Chrysler station wagon. On weekends, we would take long rides to Palm Springs, Las Vegas, Newport Beach, Carmel, and even Mexico. We had a good life. I had a good wife and many friends. Or so I thought—until the day of the auction. It was sad for us, my father and me, to see the greediness of people all trying to take advantage of our misfortune. Even our friends had eyes only for the auctioneers, and hardly acknowledged our presence.

I will never forget the expression on my father's face, a mixture of sorrow, disappointment and anger. As for me, I was disappointed because Helene had not been willing to stand by my side and give me moral support during the ordeal. But the worst was yet to come. The telephone rang. It was Helene's attorney. She had filed for divorce. She said she'd realised I was not the right man for her, after all.

Although Father knew that Mother would stand by his side no matter what, the bankruptcy was still much worse for him than for me. He wasn't young anymore, and had no capital to start a new business. I had attained my engineering degree, in addition to being a tool and die maker and, just two days after the auction, I found a very good and well-paying job in an engineering shop developing new ideas and new inventions. In fact, it was much more pleasant than the struggle of having to run a shop. I was making enough money to buy a new car, but perhaps, just for spite, I bought the ugliest old jalopy I could find, and in large letters on the back of the car I wrote, "JUST DIVORCED."

Several people laughed, but not everyone shared my sense of humor. Some of my "friends" asked me to park my car further down the street, rather than in front of their houses. On the whole, I soon got the impression that my old friends would prefer not to see me anymore, now that I was just a wage earner and no longer at their social level. I soon lost all contact with them.

Then, in my bitterness, I remembered my old teenage sweetheart, Lillemor, who had often repeated to me, "Remember, Per, no matter what happens, no matter where you are, you can always count on me." On a sudden impulse, I called her long-distance from the office.

"Is it you, Lillemor? It's Per. I've gone bankrupt and my wife has left me. Would you like to come over and marry me?"

She still had the same young girl's voice I remembered so well, and she hardly even sounded surprised at my call. She made up her mind during the last three minutes of our conversation. She said yes, I bought a new car, and a few weeks later she arrived.

We soon married but, regrettably, the marriage broke up just a few years later. Having been teenage sweethearts didn't necessarily mean that we would be suited to each other in our thirties. To my great disappointment, during the years we had lived our lives apart, she had become very fond of "taking a drink now and then"—something which irritated me endlessly. I hate alcohol and what it stands for. Besides, the bitterness of the bankruptcy and my divorce had probably made me into a poor husband—intolerant and disillusioned. I had lost interest in making money for the sake of money and, most of all, just longed for a vacation away from it all.

Then one day I got a wild idea while reading a yachting magazine, in which I noticed that prices on yachts seemed much lower in England than in the States. Why not go to England, I thought, buy a yacht at their favourable prices, and then sail it to Los Angeles, where I should be able to sell it with sufficient profit to cover all my expenses? I'd be able to get the most fantastic vacation any yachtsman could desire—for free.

Lillemor didn't share my enthusiasm. "I really can't understand you, Per," she said. "Why in the world should we expose ourselves to all the inconvenience, hazards and strains that such a long voyage would entail, when we're so comfortable here in a nice apartment with a large swimming pool and a fancy car? Let's enjoy life here with your good salary, and forget this ridiculous idea of sailing halfway around the world for no reason."

But she did come with me after all, and in the spring of 1957 we visited friends and family in Norway before traveling to England to buy the most elegant 45-foot yawl, *Windflower*. She was built out of teak and, as far as I could see, was in perfect condition.

Our first sail was not a success. Halfway over to Dover from West Mersea on the North Sea side where we had bought the boat, the winds blew up to a gale force 8 on the Beaufort scale. It seemed like a full-fledged storm to me, because I hadn't sailed for many years. I was so seasick I felt like dying.

While Lillemor didn't get seasick, she was so frightened that she was unable to utter a word and sat paralyzed in a corner of the cockpit looking at me—the only person onboard who could bring her to safety—so sick I could hardly move. To make matters worse, water was rising above the floorboard. A leak apparently had developed due to the storm. I'm not sure how I managed to get the boat to port.

But once we were safely anchored in the inner basin of Dover Harbour, Lillemor saw how discouraged I was and tried to comfort me. "Don't feel so distressed, Per," she said. "It's better to realise our limitations now in the beginning of the trip than, perhaps, in the middle of the Atlantic. We have enough money to ship *Windflower* over to California by steamer and we can still get a lot of pleasure with her along the coast when the weather is good."

I jumped up in dismay at the thought of going back to California on a steamship. "Anyone can get seasick in such weather when they're not used to going to sea," I objected. "I'll get over it after a while. I'd regret having to abandon this great adventure for the rest of my life if I gave up just because I got seasick the first day."

Lillemor could hardly believe her ears. Obviously we couldn't sail all the way to Los Angeles when we'd gotten in distress the very first day close to shore.

"OK, keep on sailing since you can't see reason," she said. "But if you want to drown, you'll have to do it without my company. I'm going back to Norway." And leave she did.

After she left, my first job was to get the leak repaired. I'd learned how to sail a boat, but I knew nothing about maintaining a boat. The yards in Norway had always done that work for me. I found a couple of shipwrights who located the leak close to the bobstay in the stem, and repaired it by recaulking the planking. I discovered later that the proper repair would have required much more than that. It was to become a constant source of worry for me in the beginning of the trip.

I took off alone and made good time along the shore in short hops until I finally arrived in Falmouth, the last possible stop in England before the long trip over the Bay of Biscay to Spain.

According to the world atlas, I had covered an insignificant distance compared to the distance which remained to get to California, yet the long hours at the tiller had already worn me out. I felt I needed a crew to relieve me at the tiller and help sail the boat, at least down to Spain. I put an ad in the local papers, but received not a single reply; it was October and the sailing season was over. At the yacht club, they told me it would be folly to try to cross the Bay of Biscay during October, and I should wait until next summer, when I would have no problems finding a crew.

Frustrated at the obstacles preventing me from realising my dream, I disregarded reason and, on the 3rd of October 1957, hoisted sail early in the morning for the open sea, firmly determined to reach Los Angeles or bust.

I knew I couldn't sit at the tiller the whole way to California, even though self-steering gears were unknown at that time. As soon as I got far enough from shore, I started to experiment, adjusting the sails and the tiller to try to get the boat to hold an approximate course on her own. After a few hours, to my great joy, she did keep a steady course roughly in the right direction, even if it was at a slower than normal speed. Trimming the sails for self-steering was quite different from the proper adjustment for best speed.

But I was overjoyed and didn't mind the slow pace, as long as I didn't have to sit at the tiller. I had time to cook, rest, sleep and even read. The first book I wanted to read was the navigation book I had found just before leaving. I needed to learn how to use my sextant, otherwise I would have to rely on my dead reckoning to find Spain.

During the days that followed, I continued to find new tricks for holding the boat on a steady course, and soon it became mere routine for L'Artemis to keep course on her own, whether the wind was light or strong, and regardless of its direction.

It took me seven days to reach Vigo, if I remember correctly. What I remember most as I walked down the picturesque streets of that little town was that I was the happiest man on earth and, perhaps, even prouder of my achievement than when I had sailed from Norway to Sweden many years before.

The next stop was Las Palmas in the Canary Islands, where I anchored next to a 36-foot ketch called *Sea Wanderer*. I could hardly believe my eyes. It had to be the boat of Edward Allcard, a famous British yachtsman and singlehander. I had enjoyed reading his articles and books for many years. It indeed was Allcard, and he invited me onboard. As he talked to me on equal terms, I realised that I had graduated to that select band of ocean traveler I'd only read about until then.

Allcard's main income came from writing newspaper articles, and in the interests of getting a good story, he proposed we race across the Atlantic to the West Indies. The winner would receive one dollar. I arrived just before Christmas 1957, a couple of days before Allcard.

The *London Times* ran a big story about the event. Singlehanded sailing was very rare at that time, and a race between two such boats meant big headlines. Today hundreds of boats cross the Atlantic each year, many of them singlehanded, often with no mention made in the press.

I framed my winning dollar and I've still got it. It hangs on the bulkhead in the saloon of my present boat. Allcard was a good loser and never got sour on me for having snatched the dollar from him. In fact, he has become my best friend.

When Lillemor learned that I had reached the West Indies safely, she said that she had regretted not staying with me. Perhaps walking in deep snow in Norway was not as pleasant as the prospect of warm tradewinds in the West Indies. I was glad to see her again, but it quickly became all too obvious that she had not lost her fear of the sea. She did her best and traversed the Panama Canal with me, but when we reached the other side of the peninsula and Costa Rica, we agreed that it would be best if she disembarked again. She went to Los Angeles to my parents' apartment to wait for me.

I had a wonderful trip along the coast, despite getting mostly headwinds. I visited many exciting places in Mexico before arriving in Los Angeles just after Christmas 1958. Everything had worked out as I'd planned, except for Lillemor's dropping out and the fact that the trip had taken a year and a half instead of just a year.

I sold the boat at a price which not only paid for all my expenses, but also left me with a fair profit. What I hadn't foreseen was that, after the freedom I had experienced on my wonderful trip, I wasn't going to be able to stand the old eight-to-five routine anymore. Nevertheless, I returned to my old job, where my boss received me with open arms and a big smile. He even transferred the old man sitting at my former drawing board to another place so that I would immediately feel at home.

But as soon as I'd arrived, I felt like choking from the cigarette smoke. I looked out at the 50 or 60 men leaning over their boards in that huge, hangar-like office and instantly regretted giving up my freedom as a skipper running down the tradewinds. How could I let myself be locked up in that smoke-filled office? I could return to England, bring back another boat and earn money on the deal. Why not do it while I still had the cash from the sale of the *Windflower*?

By quarter past eight, I had made up my mind. I went into the boss's office and quit, this time for good. It was to be the last "proper" job I was ever going to have, except for two years I later spent as technical adviser in Taiwan, Republic of China.

I bought the 32-foot *Dorothea*, a Marconi-rigged cutter, in England. Although she was not as elegant as *Windflower,* she was very strongly built of teak and pitchpine, and much more seaworthy.

Unfortunately, Lillemor just couldn't get used to the sea and, after a rough crossing of the Bay of Biscay from England, she disembarked, this time for good. She later sued me for divorce. A few years later she married an architect, just as Reidun had done. She, too, still lives in Oslo.

I set off alone again, first to Casablanca and then to the Canaries before crossing the Atlantic to celebrate Christmas in Antigua among old friends. Edward Allcard was still there; he was making money chartering, carrying paying passengers up and down the chain of islands from Antigua to Trinidad.

I was planning to do the same until I met Simonne, a French physical education and yoga teacher working in Martinique. She proposed that we sail together to Tahiti, where she expected to be transferred. Or, perhaps, I was the one to convince her; I don't remember for sure. In any case, we sailed together just after New Year's Day 1961, first to Panama, then to the Galapagos, and from there to the Marquesas and Tahiti.

In Tahiti, Simonne was disappointed to learn that her application for a job transfer had been refused and she was ordered back to Martinique. I stayed on alone for a while, enjoying the charms of the fabled Tahiti until the day came I had to leave, partly because my six-month visa was expiring, and partly because of pressure from my parents. They were living in San Francisco, and told me it was high time I came back to a "normal" life.

In any event, I was running out of money, and the easiest and fastest way to replenish the bank account would be to go back to California where I had many connections and where I could easily get a new job. It would be nice to see my parents again, and I wouldn't have to keep the job forever; perhaps just six months would be enough to enable me to go cruising again.

On the way to California I made a stop in Honolulu, arriving in 28 days from Papeete. The newspapers carried a big article about my trip, because single-handed sailing was still unusual.

Helene, whom I hadn't seen since that auction day many years earlier, had moved to Honolulu and had become a manager in one of the fancy restaurants for which Honolulu is so famous. She saw the article in the paper and came to visit me. I was standing on deck, unconcerned with the fancy sports car which pulled up alongside. But I could hardly believe my eyes when I thought I recognised the elegantly clad woman who came toward me with an outstretched hand as one of my ex-wives. She looked older, had gained weight and lost the nice figure I remembered, but her smile was still the same. In any case, all doubts disappeared when she greeted me in French, "Bonjour, cheri, content de me revoir?"

We spent the day together. First she drove me around the island, which was truly beautiful, and then took me to her fancy apartment. I had a view of the whole harbour and could even see my boat. She dished up an exquisite meal as only a French woman can do. After living for 28 days at sea on bachelor meals, I really appreciated it. But when she proposed to come back to the boat the next day, all the bitterness of that auction day came back to me and I declined curtly without even trying to find an excuse.

On the other hand, it was with great pleasure that I received letter after letter from Simonne, who said she missed me and hoped we could get together again. I stayed longer than expected in Hawaii making repairs and, just before I was to leave for California, a new letter arrived from Simonne. She suggested I forget about looking for work; she was saving up enough money for us to sail together to France. She could get a year's leave of absence from her job before transferring to a new job in France. She even added that she hoped my pride wouldn't prevent us from having a nice voyage together.

She said I shouldn't be embarrassed to have a woman pay all the bills—it hadn't bothered her when I paid all the bills on the way to Tahiti when she was broke, and it was only fair that she take a turn, now that she had money and I was broke.

I made up my mind at once. I had no desire to go back to work, and getting back to France for a while sounded nice. I wrote two letters, one to Simonne saying that I was taking off immediately for Tahiti and would wait for her there, and one to my parents saying that I had changed my mind and hoped they would not be too disappointed that I had planned a trip to Europe and was not coming back to California after all.

Had I known then that I was never going to see Father again, I probably would have gone to California. Father died shortly thereafter, at barely 65 years old.

Mother had to deal first with Father's death and then with problems with my brother. He had been beaten by the Gestapo during the war and suffered constant back pain. He finally decided to try a risky back operation the doctors had suggested. The operation wasn't successful and he became much worse. The doctors then admitted he needed a second operation to get things right. The second was no more successful than the first, and a third left him worse still. He couldn't bear it anymore and committed suicide.

Mother, tired and full of sorrow, chose to return to Oslo where she still had some family, rather than stay alone in California. She, too, died just a few years later.

Having mailed my two letters, I bought food for the trip at the local supermarket and took off for Tahiti. I had better winds on the return trip and arrived in 22 days. Tying up at the dock in downtown Papeete, it was wonderful to be greeted by all the friends I had made there during my previous visit. I can still remember how good the loaf of bread they gave me as a welcoming present tasted after several weeks at sea on my bachelor diet.

In August 1962, Simonne joined me and we sailed together towards France on the other side of the earth. First we stopped in New Hebrides, and then across the Indian Ocean and up the Red Sea to enter the Mediterranean through the Suez Canal. Next we sailed to the Greek Islands before arriving at the French Riviera the following summer.

Simonne was hired by a school in Cannes, not far from the world-famous port where we spent the winter. While she was at work, I wrote a book about our circumnavigation called *Sea Gypsy*. During the summer, we took a quick round trip to England through Gibraltar and across the Bay of Biscay to bring *Sea Gypsy* to a publisher.

In addition to writing the book, I studied naval architecture, or rather yacht design, in the hopes of breaking into a new field. I had grown tired of the tool and die trade and never wanted to go back to that again.

We stayed another year in France, but when money started to come in from the book, I became restless. I decided to build a new boat, based partly on my practical experiences as a sailor and partly on my studies, as well as on all the information I had gained from writing to famous designers like Francis Herreshoff, Phillip Bolge, Thomas Colvin, Howard Chapelle and others. They had patiently answered my letters with long replies to my many questions.

I had good teachers and spent every spare minute studying the fascinating subject of designing the perfect boat. I hoped I would be able to make a living designing boats. To start, I decided to become my first customer and build myself a dream boat, which later would serve as my calling card.

The plan at first was to build the boat in Brazil, where some of the world's best timber was available at ridiculously low prices. But

Simonne couldn't continue to take leaves of absence if she didn't want to hurt her records with the French school system. She suggested that we could build the boat in French Guiana, which was just next door and certainly had the same trees. Because Guiana was a French territory, she could probably get a transfer from her job in Cannes.

The idea pleased me only halfway, because I knew that life in any French possession would be very expensive and would cost much more money than in Brazil. But Simonne easily talked me into it, assuring me that her high salary would more than compensate for the difference in prices, since she wouldn't have been allowed to work in Brazil. She was granted one last leave of absence, provided she promised that afterward she would faithfully stay at her job.

During that last year of freedom we were able to take it easy along the way and really enjoyed the trip, stopping in Majorca, Spain and the Canaries before crossing the Atlantic again over to South America, the location of French Guiana.

In Gibraltar, Simonne started to press me for marriage, even though I had told her from the very beginning that I would never marry again.

"It's not fair," she said. "You've been willing to marry three women who all left you as soon as it suited them, but you don't want to marry me, the one person who has always followed you wherever you wanted to go. You saw yourself how embarrassed my whole family is to see me living with a man I'm not married to. And now that I'm going to start a new job in a small place like Cayenne, where everybody knows each other, it's going to be most embarrassing for my students to see me living with a man!"

Thus it was that, in the fall of 1965, I married again.

My faithful boat *Dorothea*, which had carried me all around the world without a single mishap, was to suffer a tragic end in February 1967. She sank about 55 miles from land to westward of the West

Indies headed to Ft. Lauderdale. I'd been planning to sell her since I didn't need her anymore, now that I was building a new boat. She hit some wreckage in the dark, which holed her heavy pitch pine planking, and she sank rapidly.

The fact that I was able to cover those 55 miles in a seven-foot plywood dinghy and I'm still around is a miracle, when you consider that poor *Dorothea* lies 2,000 fathoms below the Atlantic.

# 4

# Cayenne

*M*ost people, when they imagine Cayenne, St. Laurent and Devil's Island in French Guiana, think of the movie *Papillon* and the forced labour penitentiary. But that time is past; today French Guiana is just a little piece of France, down in the tropics. Its official title is "department," although some claim "colony" would be more accurate.

I was to build my dream ship in French Guiana entirely by myself, using my own ideas and drawings. It was a different life from sailing around the world but, perhaps, just as great an adventure.

In French Guiana I could choose among the world's best timber, better even than the famed teak which comes from Asia, and at prices cheaper than what crate wood costs in the States or Europe.

I rented a big house in the suburb of Cayenne to live in while the building went on. Just next to the house, I built a large shed, 60 feet long by 40 feet wide. Here I would build the boat and lodge my tools and machines. I love the tropics, but prefer to be shaded from the broiling sun and the frequent, violent downpours.

French Guiana had all the wood I needed, but nothing else. There was no labour, no tools, no machines, no hardware and no fittings of any kind for boats. And, although the trees were plentiful, they had to be cut down and sawed into planks before I could use them. There were local sawmills, but they kept a minimum stock and would only cut the trees to order. It was, therefore, out of the question for me to expect to find seasoned lumber. I would have to wait for the freshly cut wood to season while I did the building.

To reduce the drying time as much as possible, I redrew my construction plans from the planned heavy single planking to much thinner planks to be laid in two layers. The thinner planks would season more quickly. I chose a double-diagonal system, held together with copper rivets, an old, well-proven method which makes for a very strong, light hull. The timber would have ample time to dry because the construction took much longer than I had anticipated.

To build a nearly 50-foot long boat is a huge project, the immensity of which can be appreciated only by those who have actually done it. Just the preparations to get started took forever. After I found a house suitable for the building site and constructed the shed, I had to hunt around for all the materials to be ordered in Europe or in the States, and redraw the plans to suit local conditions. It all took so long that it was spring of 1967 before I finally could start working on the boat itself.

Although I had a big job ahead of me, at least all the preparations were complete. After years of thinking and studying, I had detailed drawings of my dream ship. I had designed the boat to, first and foremost, have a soft and comfortable motion at sea to reduce seasickness. I also wanted a boat with a shallow draft for convenience, and one that was fast, yet easy enough to handle so I wouldn't have to depend on a crew. Most of all, she had to be beautiful.

It took me several months to finish the double planking, a much slower job than single planking. The job would have gone even slower, had I not built the boat upside down, which put me on top of the planking. If the boat had been standing upright, I would have had to work overhead. But after finishing the planking, I had to pay for that convenience by having to turn the ship the right way up.

For one lone man with no special machinery to turn such a large ship weighing several tons would seem an impossible task; yet, with time and a little ingenuity, there are practically no limits to what a man can do. Archimedes did not exaggerate when he declared that he could lift the world if only he had a lever long enough and a solid point on which to rest it. I would claim that a lone man could build a pyramid if he lived long enough, say, a few thousand years.

In my case, I decided the easiest way to bring the boat upright would be to roll it over. For that I needed more room than I had in the shed. The first thing I did was to drag the boat out in the open. I built a simple cradle under the boat over a makeshift "railroad," made out of greased planks laid flat on the ground. My two-cylinder French pickup truck pulled the boat along the track. Of course, my little truck would not have been able to pull that heavy load had I tied it directly to the cradle, so I used two sets of double blocks, each giving a purchase of four-to-one, thus giving a total of 16-to-one.

The truck was now able to pull, but what I had gained in force I had lost in distance (and time), for when the truck went 16 feet forward, the boat moved only one foot! Then I had to stretch out all my purchases for a new "trip" because, by then, the blocks had been pulled block to block and could go no further. Yet, by evening, the boat was out of the shed where there was plenty of open space. All that remained was to turn it over.

I started by digging the sand out from under one side of the boat, causing it to heel over more and more. When it was heeled over as much as possible, I rigged up my purchases again, this time athwartship to the boat. The blocks were tied from the boat to a tree, while the end of the rope was again tied to the truck. Before I pulled the boat over its balance point to let it fall down on its keel, I made a huge mattress out of about 20 large truck tyres and more than 100 automobile tyres. The boat fell on the mattress with a surprisingly slow motion and then kept bouncing on it back and forth for a short while, as if already at sea. What an exciting moment! At long last I could admire the ship in its proper perspective, instead of upside down, and she was even more beautiful than I had expected.

Now all that remained was to get the boat out of the broiling sun and back into the shed. First I pulled out all the tyres from underneath the boat by simply tying each tyre to the truck and jerking them out one at a time. I leveled the boat, using a hydraulic jack, and built a new cradle to fit her in the right-way-up position. I used the truck to slide her sideways until she lined up with the shed and then finally pulled her in again.

The whole operation had taken an entire week, but I had been able to do it all by myself without it costing a cent, other than gasoline for the truck. (All the tyres were free from the junkyard, where they would have been burned.) I enjoyed seeing the look of surprise on my friends' faces when they came to visit me and all of a sudden they saw the ship right-side-up. When they asked me how I had done it, I casually replied, "Oh, I just did it by myself with block and tackles."

As far as anyone could remember, no one in French Guiana had ever built a boat before (except for the natives' canoes), and consequently I had many visitors curious to see my progress. One day I had a visit which was going to change my life altogether, although I could not have suspected it at the time. Two shy, young girls with pigtails and flat sandals came to visit. They introduced themselves as Lydia and Agnes Balta and said they were our new neighbours. They had just moved with their family into the house next door and wondered if they could see the boat under construction which they had heard so much about.

They even said that we knew each other from before, from the time we had laid anchor next to each other in Martinique. But, try as I might, I could not remember either of the girls. Since I was getting too many such visits, which were delaying my work and the launching day, I soon found an excuse to end the visit and lead them to the door. Little did I suspect that one of those young girls was going to become my wife and the mother of my son Thomas.

After they left, I suddenly recalled the boat they had been on which they called *L'Aviateur*—"The Pilot"—rather a strange name for a boat. We had indeed anchored next to each other in Martinique, but that was nine years ago when these young girls could hardly have been more than 6 or 7 years old. I do like young women, but there are limits, so it was not so surprising that I didn't remember them. But I remembered the boat very clearly. Like mine, she had no engine, but solely trusted her sails. It must have required first-class seamanship of her skipper, for the boat was very large, over 70 feet, with a great beam and heavy displacement. And now that I remembered the boat, I also remembered the girls. They were among the six or seven siblings playing together on the deck and had been headed to the South Pacific with their parents and a crew of strong men. The father had been a missionary there in his younger days and wanted to return with his family in his own boat.

While we had been at anchor next to each other, one of those small girls had decided that she would marry me when she grew up and we would sail around the world together! (I was a singlehandler at the time). But history should show that we should not always laugh at young girls' dreams. Although our paths separated shortly after that time, we were to meet again now. Not only did both our boats anchor in the same port again, but we both moved ashore to houses, and next to each other at that!

Lydia was to tell me later that she had not been surprised to see me there, as she was so sure that our paths would cross again and that heaven would fulfill her prayers for me to become her husband. She had been deeply disappointed that I had not waited chaste for her but, far from giving up, she considered that the time was not ripe yet. She would wait.

She got a chance the following year, when I purchased a fancy motorcycle capable of speeds in excess of 100 miles an hour which made a frightening noise. Instead of taking the school bus, she waited for me to pass on my bike. She hid in the bush by the road and, as soon as she heard the roar of the bike, sprang out on the road with her thumb up. Trying to look desperate, Lydia explained that she had missed the bus and was late getting to school. Could I *please* take her to school? How could she have known that I was going to drive to town that day? (Perhaps she had tried in vain several days before and just waited until I drove to town.)

As we stood in front of the school, she apparently panicked at the thought of entering class so late and declared that she would rather I take her to Kourou, where I was headed. She had never been in that town before, she said, and besides, she would *so* love to ride with me as she just *loved* big motorcycles and had never ridden one before.

I hesitated a bit, thinking about what her missionary father would say should he learn that I had taken his daughter on a long drive through the bush country while she should have been in school. Besides, I was a married man, and doubted Simonne would much appreciate it, either. Not that she mistrusted me, but she would worry about what people would say.

But then, I remembered an ashtray which had so troubled my strict childhood with its inscription of "Qui vit sans follie, n'est pas aussi sage qu'il croit"—Whoever lives without a little folly is not as wise as he thinks. So I set off with Lydia.

I knew the road by heart, having raced on it many times, and I knew exactly the maximum speed at which I could take each turn. To drive fast on a big motorcycle is always exciting, but to be in the tropics with an attractive young girl wearing a thin blouse and hanging on tight was especially exciting. In the tropical heat, one doesn't wear the heavy, protective leather garments worn in other countries. As we were banking in the long fast turns, I could feel her flat tummy and hard, small breasts against my body as clearly as if we were naked. I felt as if we were making love from all the sensations rushing through my body on that motorcycle, the sexiest machine man ever invented.

From that day on, Lydia came to the shed every day after school to help me with the boat. Neither Lydia's father nor Simonne appreciated it very much. I was falling more and more in love with this beautiful young girl who was not yet 18 years old. Simonne grew more and more tired of the situation and finally asked for a transfer back to France, "so I could get the girl out of my system."

You would think that Lydia would feel guilty for trying to break up an apparently happy marriage, especially since she was a fervent Christian, but, far from feeling guilty, she never ceased to reproach me for having gone and married another woman, instead of waiting for her as she had done for me! Woman's logic is sometimes hard to follow. This was to remain a delicate issue between us for as long as she lived.

But far from quickly tiring of her as Simonne had gambled, I fell more in love with her than ever before, and lived in a permanent state of ecstasy until one day when disaster struck.

Lydia's mother died and her father decided to return to France with all the children. Lydia was just barely 18 years old and still had three years to go before she was legally an adult and free from the jurisdiction of her father. Her father would not even consider the possibility of her staying on in French Guiana, with or without me.

We were in despair, for my boat was far from ready and I could not follow them to France. And we could not stand the thought of being separated for several years until she became a legal adult, so we decided to do what so many couples have done throughout the ages: We eloped! Lydia wrote a letter to her father saying that she had fallen in love with a man in French Guiana and, consequently, didn't want to leave the country. They would have to leave without her. Then we found a safe hiding place for her and waited.

As soon as her father got the letter, he naturally suspected me, and sent his oldest daughter over to fetch her back. Because she was much older than Lydia, she had always acted like a second mother to her. I pretended to know nothing about it all and, seeing her wrath, I didn't try to hinder her from searching the shed as well as the house.

The family asked for the assistance of the police and postponed their departure, but they never found her and eventually had to leave without her. Half an hour after the roar of their plane had disappeared on its way to France, Lydia openly moved into the house with me—much to the outrage of most of my friends.

Despite the disapproval of our friends, I felt like I was in paradise. Our whole existence centered around our love and our boat. Our nights were the most wonderful any lovers could dream about. Lydia also brought me happiness during the day. The hard work of building the boat was so much more pleasant now that we were two doing the job. Her enthusiasm made me enjoy building the boat even more.

We were going to sail to the end of the world with this boat. This boat was going to be our home, a home in which our children would grow up. Our whole world would have been perfect, except for increasing money worries.

Neither of us had any revenues. My first book, *Sea Gypsy*, had practically stopped bringing in money. As a foreigner, I was not permitted to work and Lydia was just out of school. The money I had left was rapidly disappearing despite our thriftiness. We knew we had to do something before it was too late. We decided to launch the boat as soon as possible, even though she was far from ready to go to sea. If we could camp in her, we could move out of the house and no longer have to pay rent.

Launching day soon came and, according to tradition, no ship should ever be launched without being properly baptised. This is generally done by a designated godmother breaking a bottle of champagne against its bow. This bottle should not be of inferior quality or of lower price than one serves the guests, less we risk attracting the wrath of the sea gods. I usually respect old traditions but, in this case, I dared make a small change insomuch as I neither like champagne (nor any other alcoholic beverages for that matter) nor do I like to waste money or think about that expensive champagne flowing down to the ground. I also never liked the brutality that the broken bottle represents in my eyes so, instead, I picked one of the many coconuts growing on my property, which during the long building years had so often quenched my thirst. Opening the nut, the designated godmother gently poured its water against the bow while her clear voice proclaimed, "I hereby baptise you *L'Artemis de Pytheas*. May luck and happiness go with you over all oceans."

Only now was the name revealed, as tradition declares it bad luck to let anyone know the name before the official baptism. I had chosen the long name in memory of Pytheas, that great astronomer, mathematician and navigator, whose story I had read during the vessel's construction and whom I admired so much. Three hundred years before Christ, he knew the earth was round and he had been able to calculate its size fairly accurately—something Christopher Columbus had failed miserably to do. Columbus thought he had already arrived in India when he had just reached the West Indies.

Pytheas wanted to verify his astronomical calculations by making additional observations from the "top of the world"—the North Pole. He calculated that he should be able to make the trip within the summer half of the year and he succeeded until he was stopped by the ice, something he, as a Mediterranean, had no knowledge of. He left Marselia, which today is called Marseille, early in spring in a square-rigged ship manned by a crew of 44. He was also equipped with oars for auxiliary power when becalmed. He did come back six months later with the same full crew and entered the port under "parade stroke," or full speed, which showed that the crew was still fit. Columbus couldn't measure up in this area, either, as he had countless dead. Pytheas had failed to reach the Pole, which had been his objective, but his voyage was, nevertheless, remarkable for such a distant past. When he had been stopped by ice, he turned eastward and reached Norway where he did some trading. He exchanged his silks and wine for amber, which he sold upon his return at a sufficient price to cover the cost of the entire expedition. There was no plundering or fighting, much in contrast to Columbus's voyages.

Besides admiring Pytheas, I saw something symbolic in his voyage, linking France, where I was raised, to Norway, where I was born. Therefore, I named my boat after Pytheas's ship, *Artemis*.

When the boat was finally lowered into the water, I felt a new chapter of my life beginning.

# 5

# Back to Sea at Last

*B*y Christmastime 1973 the boat, while not completely finished, was finally seaworthy. So the day came when we at long last sailed down the river while our friends waved us goodbye. What a thrill it was to see the brown, muddy waters of French Guiana gradually change to the beautiful blue of the open sea as land disappeared behind us and the open, endless horizon appeared in front of us.

The boat handled nicely and moved effortlessly through the waves. She seemed to be very fast. At long last I was profiting from the long building years and all the planning I had put into the boat. It was very satisfying for me to see everything work out to my expectations.

The whole world lay open to us now with the exception of a few political trouble spots. We decided to stop first in Martinique in the West Indies, where Lydia expected easily to get a job in one of the fancy tourist hotels. As for me, I hoped to be able to start a career in photography, having equipped myself with an expensive new Linhoff 4 x 5 plate camera.

Just two days after our arrival, Lydia got a well-paying job as a receptionist in one of the four-star hotels, thanks to her good looks, good manners and probably most of all, her ability to speak several languages including French, English, German, Dutch and even Creole, the native language. In addition to her salary she was given all her meals free but, of course, this didn't include meals for me. So she asked permission to have her meals served in a lunch box, which was readily granted. She made friends with the cooks and had them fill her pots to the brim, which was more than enough food for both of us. We were able to save not only the cost of my food, but also the wasted time to shop for and cook it.

We laid anchor only about 100 yards from the hotel in a beautiful little bay called Anse Mitan. While Lydia was working on replenishing our empty bank account, I did photography and worked to finish the thousand and one things which always remain to be finished on a new boat.

We were happy and thought we nearly had found paradise when things suddenly began to go wrong. The girl on the night shift was expecting a baby and quit. The new girl hired in her place soon tired of the night shift and demanded to exchange her shift for Lydia's— who, as a stranger to the island, shouldn't be given priority. Thus Lydia was given the night shift, which was to change our lives entirely, and not for the better.

Even though we were just a few hundred yards from the hotel, it was out of the question for a girl to walk alone that lonely path, especially at midnight, and again early in the morning when she finished her work. I accompanied her but, even together, we didn't feel safe. More than once, gangs of ten or more men had knocked down a woman's companion and all had taken turns raping the girl.

We soon tired of the situation and decided to move on. Why not sail back to France for a while, we thought. Lydia was French, we had both been away from France for a long time, and we thought it would be nice to go there for a while.

It would be no problem to cross the Atlantic in the new boat, except for one thing. Our main mast, which was really a makeshift telegraph pole, had been bending alarmingly whenever it had been breezing up. We decided, therefore, to play it safe and get a new mast.

It was easy enough to buy all the materials at the Fort-de-France local lumberyard, where I bought 2-by-10-foot pitch pine planks and enough glue to make the mast out of five layers glued together.

Finding a suitable place to work was not as easy. While searching for the right place, we happened to see a postcard in a newsstand which showed what seemed like the perfect spot—a beautiful, tiny harbour, complete with a small dock, yet apparently nearly deserted. On the back of the postcard was written "Gustavia, St. Barthelemy, West Indies." I knew that the island was a free port with no authorities whatsoever, so we made up our minds immediately. We loaded all our timber on the deck, temporarily transforming our elegant yacht into an overloaded workboat, and took off downwind to St. Bart's under easy canvas.

The place proved to be every bit as beautiful as the postcard, and we tied up to the very dock we had seen in the photograph. (That was in 1974—today there are hundreds of boats crowding the harbour and overflowing into the bay outside of it.) As I was practically alone in the port, I made myself at home, unloading all my timber right on the dock, and went to work. I hadn't bothered to ask permission of anyone, yet nobody ever reproached me, nor did I have to pay any fees. Those were the days!

The island was a barren one with not much going on, but I did manage to find a small workshop with a planer, who rapidly planed down smooth timber for a reasonable fee. Next to the boat, it was an easy matter to glue the boards together. I could only glue one plank at a time, then had to wait for the glue to set before proceeding with the next one, so it took some time to scarf the planks to make up the 40-foot length. I glued up the five layers to obtain the full thickness and, after a few weeks, I had a square column which now needed to be rounded down.

With my adze, a wonderful, nearly forgotten tool from prehistoric times, which resembles an ax with the shaft turned at 90 degrees to the blade, I rapidly trimmed the big pole to accurate size, still just square, but straight and to the exact dimensions the finished diameter would be. Guided by a long, tight string, I drew lines and cut the corners to make it into an eight-sided column. Afterwards I repeated the operation to make it 16-sided. It was easy enough then to smooth it up with a long plane and make it perfectly round.

In the meantime, Lydia had found a job as a waitress in a small restaurant nearby, so we didn't have to worry about running out of money on our trip to Europe.

It is an exaggeration to say that there were no authorities of any kind on the island. Two French gendarmes were stationed there with their families, but they gave us no hassles and didn't even bother us with the usual red tape. They contented themselves to come everyday to "inspect" my work, often staying for a long while to chat.

On the last day, they shook my hand and congratulated me on my work, saying they never in their lives would have thought it possible to transform that pile of lumber I had on my deck into a slender and smooth mast with just hand tools and the dock!

Since there were no cranes on the island, I'd planned to build a temporary crane, but on the day I was to start making one, a small Norwegian freighter came into the harbour to unload a couple of cars. I rushed over to see if the captain would be willing to step my mast. He smiled and reminded me that this was the 17th of May (the Norwegian equivalent of the American 4th of July), and they had a celebration planned at their next stop. He had no more than half an hour to spare before they would have to steam out of the harbour. I assured him that we could do it in that amount of time and rushed back to the boat to warp it alongside.

About 20 men gathered quickly; volunteers picked up the quarter-ton mast, threw it in the water and floated it alongside the boat. I came alongside with my yacht and they carefully lowered it, through its partner and into its mast step on top of the silver dollar I had remembered to put there for good luck. In the same instant, my lines were cast loose from the steamship, which lost no time in leaving for the planned celebration. I happily tied my boat to the little dock on the opposite side of the harbour where I had been before.

During the following days, I rerigged the vessel to prepare for the long trip to France. We intended to make the trip nonstop, as the season was advancing and the summer season in Europe is very short.

St. Bart's had not been just a beautiful and convenient place for us to build our mast—it was also an interesting small country. The all-white population there is quite unusual for the West Indies, whose population overall is mostly black, with just a small percentage of whites.

The island is barren and infertile, so it is generally considered very poor—so poor that the French tax collector had never bothered even to go there. The population showed no exterior signs of wealth and contented themselves with modest clothes, modest food, modest houses, and practically no cars.

When the time came for the islanders to exchange old French money for new bills as they had done in France, the French authorities were in for a big surprise. The civil servant sent over to deliver the new bills had his little suitcase emptied in no time at all. It's said that he had to return as many as six times with a bigger suitcase, full of bills each time, before the demand was exhausted!

Where did all this wealth come from? An explanation is simple—smuggling. As a free port, St. Bart's population could import liquor tax-free. They then "exported" it to the neighbouring islands at great profit. They had this revenue for many years, if not for generations. Because they never had to spend much money, it stands to reason that the money accumulated. And it all accumulated in cash, as most inhabitants didn't trust banks and preferred to keep their cash hidden in their homes. Needless to say, the following year the taxman did come to collect his share of all that wealth. This caused such an uproar among the population, who were infuriated that they would have to share the "income" they considered their right, that the poor taxman finally fled for his life in a small private plane. To my knowledge, neither he nor any of his kind has ever returned to the island!

A fellow yachtsman from Martinique who "swallowed the anchor" after getting married and starting a small business, decided to move to St. Bart's when he felt the French taxman in Martinique was taking too big a share of his hard-earned money. Today he has a real factory in St. Bart's, apparently harvesting big money, without paying a single cent to the taxman. As for myself, I'm not so business-minded and just enjoyed the place for its own sake.

Now we were ready to go to sea without having to worry about the integrity of our mast. Our route took us first through the ill-famed Bermuda Triangle, as we wanted to gain northing as quickly as possible. North of Bermuda we would get favourable winds towards Europe. But as we approached Bermuda, we were hit by a violent, ice cold wind from the northwest. Although the direction was favourable for us as we headed eastward, the wind was so strong it forced us to heave to while we hid below in bed, tight against each other to try to keep warm. And this was June! How would it be in wintertime and how would it be further north? I love sailing, but I hate cold weather, which just makes me ache everywhere.

I lost all ambition to get up to the western winds. As soon as the gale blew itself out, we made sail again, aiming for Gibraltar's latitude, and contenting ourselves with the light, irregular winds of the "horse latitudes" of that region. (The area got its name for the many horses which had been thrown over the sides there. Early settlers sailing with horses sometimes suffered such long periods of calm that, running out of water, they had to sacrifice the animals.

Our boat was better able than heavy cargo carriers to take advantage of very light winds, so the light winds were not as bad for us as they would have been for them. In any case, we were more than willing to accept the slow speed in order to gain the good climate and warm sun of the lower latitudes. After a few weeks, we saw the high mountain peaks of the Azores in the distance, but we were impatient to see Europe again, so we kept on sailing.

Whale hunting has been going on for years in the Azores and, apparently, whales do live in that region. Suddenly one surfaced just a few yards from us, its huge bulk frightening us nearly to death. It must have weighed many times that of our boat, and kept us company for hours, swimming alongside and, sometimes, diving under us to reappear on the other side. It never touched us, but kept us on edge for hours as we tried not to think about what would happen if it gave us even a flick of its tail. The whale finally passed on around midnight with no damage except, perhaps, to our nerves.

About a week later, we entered the Straits of Gibraltar. Luckily, a good following wind made the tricky strait easy for us. The wind got much stronger than we had bargained for, however, gradually forcing us to reef down. Finally we had only our small jib up and nothing else, yet we continued at top speed.

It was in all this turmoil that we got our first fish since leaving the West Indies. Lydia got so excited at the prospect of getting fresh meat after the long trip that she screamed at the top of her lungs, "Per, a fish! A tuna! Get it, Per, don't let it get away!"

I was also keen on fresh food but, most of all, I would have felt embarrassed if Lydia thought I was not capable of getting the fish on board. Despite my repugnance in such work, I plunged my fingers deep into its gills as soon as it broke the surface to avoid having to rely on a thin line to lift it onboard. Thanks to the very low freeboard, it was easy enough to reach the fish by leaning over the side. I was rewarded for my effort by the nicest meal of the whole trip, which Lydia was able to cook despite the strong winds.

The Mediterranean proved tiring to sail. We had to keep a constant vigil against the dangers of collision, due not only to the heavy traffic, but also to the constantly shifting winds, which continually required us to readjust our sails. Yet boats of all sorts have sailed back and forth in the Mediterranean for thousands of years, so it can't have been worse for us than for all the others. Indeed in the end we arrived at our destination in Port Grimaud, that fabled little city built from a swamp just a dozen or so years before. It looked like a genuine old fishing port! Two or three hundred years ago the small towns along the south of France must have looked just like this charming village. On closer inspection, we saw not the traditional small fishing crafts of old, but super, modern yachts, most of them serving as second homes for the wealthy, and worth fortunes.

We were going to be able to stay in this rich man's resort because one of my friends, who had been doing well in business, had purchased one of the houses as one of his many "second residences". Since his own boat was in the West Indies, we were invited to use his dock. We were going to be able to live in a millionaire's dream town without having to pay for it.

But even if each house did cost a fortune and had a private dock, we were soon to see the drawbacks. It's not surprising that they cost a fortune—someone had to pay for all the filling in of the swampland and for digging and dredging the canals. But I wonder if the buyers here were really getting their money's worth, compared with what they might have gotten elsewhere. After a while each house seemed awfully narrow and too close to its neighbours. Each house was only 12 feet wide, leaving a dock just wide enough so that each boat was fender-to-fender with its neighbour.

Shopping was limited and prices were high. We soon felt like we were in a tourist trap with the houses merely theatre mock-ups. Being in a tourist centre, we found that we could take advantage of it by selling the handpainted silk scarves Lydia had been making as a hobby in her spare time. She got enough orders during the summer months from a local gift shop, but when fall came, most of the inhabitants left to return to their normal lives in Paris, London, Germany and elsewhere. Most of the stores closed for the winter, leaving the impression of a ghost town—and no more customers for Lydia's scarves. I didn't make any money, either. I didn't sell any of my photos, nor could I find any customers to charter my boat. Something had to be done or we'd run out of money altogether.

"Why not sail over to the Amazon River, take photographs of that fascinating region and write articles about it," suggested Lydia.

"The Amazon is far from here," I said. "We don't even have enough money to buy much of the expensive film for the large format camera I have. If we wanted to sail the Amazon, we should have done it while we were next door in French Guiana. Now we're in Europe. Let's try to make the best of it."

"In that case, we should go to Paris and try our luck there," insisted Lydia. "In Paris everything is possible. We have a safe spot for the boat here without it costing us a cent. Let's spend the winter in Paris and see what comes out of it. Then next summer we can come down to the boat again on vacation if we've made good in Paris. But if we fail in Paris, then we'll come back to the boat to leave for another country where we may have more luck."

# 6

# Winter in Paris

We took the train to Paris to hunt for a place to stay with all our belongings in suitcases and paper boxes. Rents were awfully high and most landlords wanted as much as three months' rent in cash in advance and, furthermore, wanted to see our last paychecks to assure themselves that we would be able to continue paying. Certainly the big city didn't lay out any red carpet for us.

Finally we found a *chambre de bonne*, a servant's room in one of the better districts, where the woman in charge was content to get just one month's rent in advance and never asked where we worked.

I was shocked when I saw the number on the door—number 13. But the shock got even worse when the door opened onto a tiny room with no windows but for a small glass trap in the roof. We could see if it was raining or if the sun was shining, but nothing else. The room was sparsely furnished: one bed (the narrowest I have ever seen, even for just one person), one closet, one small table and a chair. The Turkish-type toilet, which we shared with all the other tenants of probably about 20 rooms, was out in the corridor and equipped with neither bowl nor seat. There were just two cement pads where you put your feet and a hole which you crouched down over. An efficient system, but not a very luxurious one.

These *chambres des bonnes* are common in buildings built before the war, when all well-to-do families considered it a must to have a maid. All the apartment buildings had their upper floors reserved to lodge all the maids, so the masters had full privacy when the help wasn't needed. The maids were not allowed to use their master's toilet, even during their working hours; instead they were required to take the service staircase to the top floor to use their own toilets.

As a child I had been curious as to what was going on on that mysterious top floor, but my parents had never permitted me to have the slightest peak. Little did I suspect at that time that fortunes are not necessarily permanent and, one day, I would have occasion to get to know the top floor in a much more intimate way than I would ever have dreamed possible.

We didn't share our floor with any maids, because no one could afford maids anymore. Some apartment holders just kept these rooms for additional storage, but most subleased rather than leave them unused. Even though we were in an excellent district of Paris, the cream of the crop didn't rent these rooms, so our neighbours were all hard-up people like us. Most had not found proper jobs, and a good many were blacks or Arabs freshly arrived to the "Great City."

I had always heard my parents talk about Paris as one of the seven wonders of the world and, no doubt, they were right. But what had been true for my father as a factory owner, who could afford all the luxuries Paris had to offer, wasn't true for me, living with Lydia in a maid's room which was too small for a single girl.

Lydia found work within a few days as an office girl but, fresh out of school, she had to start at rock-bottom wages which were just enough for us to survive on. We had absolutely no money for any-thing else besides the rent, our food and our subway fares.

I persisted in my new profession as a photographer without realising I wasn't good enough for a field already too competitive, especially in Paris, where the world's best photographers operated. I remember Paris now as the town where I got one door after the other slammed in my face. Then one day, I came to a door far more friendly than any of the others. It was the Rapho Photographic Agency and

Monsieur Grosset, the director himself, received me with a friendly smile. He looked at my work and listened carefully to what I had to say. He spent nearly a whole hour with me, which was extremely unusual in a society where every second counts and where most others had spent only a few minutes before getting rid of me.

He didn't offer me a job, much less any promised salary, but he did give me some advice. And in the years to follow, we made quite a sizable amount of money together.

First of all he advised me I was on the wrong track with my fancy 4 x 5 planfilm camera. "I can assure you that you are wasting your time and money with that big camera," he said.

"But I want to take the best pictures possible," I protested, "and the quality of my Linhoff far surpasses any 35-millimeter camera."

"Don't think that I'm not aware of the 35-millimeter camera's shortcomings," he replied. "For pure art's sake, certainly the big format still may have its *raison d'etre* but, quite frankly, although you do take good photographs, you don't measure up to the top photographers here in Paris using those cameras. I'm afraid that you'll never be able to make a living selling your pictures for their own merit. But I have read some of your articles, and I'm sure you could sell your pictures to illustrate your articles. And for that kind of work, spontaneity is far more valuable than the technical perfection you are expecting out of your big camera. Perhaps it will give you technical superiority, but how can you expect any spontaneity with such a big, cumbersome camera, which is too heavy to drag along, too slow to operate and too inhibiting to put into people's faces?"

"I bought the camera brand new and paid a lot for it," I said. "I hate to lose money on it now."

"You already lost your money when you bought an unsuitable camera for your needs. Listen, take my advice. I have about 40 years' experience in this business. Sell that camera and buy a Nikon or a

Leica with three lenses. That's all you need, although if you can afford it, it would be better to have two bodies, so you can have black and white in one and color slides in the other, or in case of trouble with one, you would have a spare. Get one wide-angle, say, a 35-mm lens, one normal 50-mm lens, and either a 90 or 135 long-focus lens. Then sail to a place which hasn't been covered too much—like the Indian Ocean, for example. Write me some articles from there and illustrate them generously with 35-mm photos, which aren't going to cost you much, and I'll bet we'll both make some money together."

I followed his advice, and we were to make some money together but not on the type of articles he had in mind.

That night, Lydia and I shared a modest evening meal, which we'd cooked over a single-burner gas camping stove. I sat on our only chair, Lydia on the corner of the bed, as I told her Monsieur Grosset's advice on how to handle the articles and photographs about the Indian Ocean and its shores. Lydia was all for it. After all, whether we went to the Amazon, as she had dreamed about, or the Indian Ocean, it would be the same life—the adventurous life of true travelers and reporters—and we would profit fully on our boat, rather than living in misery in Paris. We would again enjoy the tradewinds and the freedom of the boat.

"What kind of life are we having here in Paris?" she said. "We are so poor that we cannot even enjoy seeing your old childhood friends."

"Well, we did see several of them," I protested.

"Sure we saw them," she continued, "but you know yourself, we can't just go and ring their doorbells when it suits us and expect to have a nice chat together like we can do in most of the tropics, where life is so much more casual. We have to telephone first and then agree on a date. Invariably they would invite us to dinner and they would receive us in their three-piece suits, and serve us sumptuous meals with crystal and real silver. You would talk about your childhood memories together, and then what? They've all inherited their fathers' businesses or factories, they all live in luxury and they have their own lives—and no doubt their own worries. What more do you have in common today?

"Furthermore, you say that you feel like a freeloader if you accept their hospitality too often without reciprocating. And how could you possibly reciprocate? Certainly not in this awful maid's room! So, to a restaurant? One evening's bill would cost us more than what we spend to live for a whole month! No, we just don't belong among them anymore, while, on the other hand, I must admit we don't have much in common with those of our present income, like our neighbours on this top floor.

"In the tropics, it will all be different. There we'll be in our element again. Please, Per," she pleaded, calling me with the name she liked rather than Peter, "please, let's abandon the idea of making good in Paris. Don't think back on your childhood days. They're gone. Let's look forward. On our own ship we'll be happy in the tropics."

I felt she was right. I even wondered why I had wanted to get back to Paris. Maybe it was just a primitive craving to return to where I'd lived my childhood. Next day, Lydia gave her notice at work and I decided to sell my big, fancy camera. The task proved more difficult than I had expected because, although it was still the Rolls Royce of cameras, it was a very specialised camera which appealed to only a very limited type of photographer. Despite going from one store to the next that had advertised they purchased and sold second-hand cameras, I could find no one interested in mine at any price.

Finally, just before closing time, I found a shop that was interested. It was a store in a rather bad district of Paris, but I couldn't be too choosy and it made no difference to me who bought it, as long as I got my money. A lone salesgirl told me she was sure that her boss would be interested, as he had just had an inquiry from a customer who was looking for such a big camera. Unfortunately the boss was out of town on business, but she said she would see him later that evening. If I let her have the camera overnight against a proper receipt, she would show him the camera and all the equipment that went with it. I could come back the next day and she would give me the money; if he did not purchase it, she would return my equipment.

That sounded fair enough, but I was surprised next morning when the girl apparently didn't recognise me.

"What can I do for you, Monsieur?"

"I came to see if your boss agreed to buy the camera," I said, a bit surprised, but still with no suspicion of any foul play.

"I don't know what you are talking about, Monsieur."

"*Mais, enfin,*" I insisted, "you can't have forgotten me. I was here yesterday. I talked with you and left my camera for your boss to approve of its purchase. Look, here is the receipt you gave me."

She looked casually over the receipt and declared, "I don't know how you have gotten our printed receipt forms, but that signature certainly isn't mine and must have been forged."

Completely dumbfounded and outraged, I started to raise my voice, "Are you trying to steal the camera from me? In that case I'll go and file a complaint at the police station."

"Suit yourself," she answered calmly, ringing a bell. To the two rough-looking men who immediately appeared she said, "Please show this gentleman the way out."

There I stood in the street with neither my money nor my camera, but just a piece of paper which might prove useless. I could hardly believe my eyes and even began wondering if the fault were mine. Had I been confusing the store and the salesgirl with another place? But, no, the printed form and its address checked with the name and address of this store. I was not dreaming; I was being taken for a ride and plainly cheated, but I wasn't going to give up that easily.

At the police station, they sourly told me that I was not a victim of a crime, and if I felt I'd been victim of a dishonest transaction, that was none of their business. Again I was shown out to the street.

I remembered that one of my childhood friends was now a prominent lawyer and would surely be able to help me.

"Mon cher ami, what is the name of the store?"

When I told him, I heard a discouraged breath and he replied, "I'm afraid you've lost your camera. That outfit has been cheating people for years and nobody can do anything about it. The daughter of the owner is married to a high official in the police department. No judge will ever let you win a case against him. In fact, no lawyer will want to take your case. Not even me. I can assure you in advance that your case is lost and would, furthermore, put me and my business in trouble for the future. No, I'm sorry. Nothing can be done now. You should have checked on the honesty of that store before trusting them with your equipment."

I could hardly believe such a thing could happen in a civilised country. Relating the story to Lydia when she came home from work, I felt like a perfect fool, although she shared my indignation and did her best to soften the blow. For several nights I was unable to sleep, trying to figure out one plan after the other to get my camera back, but all was in vain until, suddenly, I hit upon a brilliant idea. The man had power within a crooked police setup, but if his daughter were married into the police, surely she couldn't be married into the customs department!

Customs—I had had plenty of trouble with that organization in various countries, with their paperwork and countless regulations that had always scared me. Their excessive power, run completely independently from the regular police, now, at long last, would be useful to me. I felt sure my plan would work and that I would get my camera back. I could hardly get back to sleep with my impatience for dawn to arrive.

I took the subway to the customs main office and told the man at the entrance that I came to surrender myself for a crime I had committed—selling contraband. I was immediately led into a high officer's office and invited to confess in detail what I had done.

"I am a foreigner and I had a very expensive camera bought outside of France. As I no longer needed the camera nor its equipment, I set it up for sale with a merchant without remembering that I should have checked with customs first to pay whatever duty was due. Having realised my error, I went back to the merchant to get the camera back, but he refused to give it to me, so I came here to surrender myself."

"So you aren't French. What are you?"

"I'm American."

"Hmph! I never would have guessed it by the way you speak."

"I was raised in France," I said.

"So that explains it, and that could mean that the buyer is of good faith. The fault is solely yours."

"Yes, I know," I said.

"What is the name of the store?" he said.

When I told him, his face changed and he thought for a while before replying, with what I thought could be a faintly malicious smile, "Go back to your merchant and tell him that I have told you I want that camera and all its equipment in my office by 12 o'clock tomorrow. Tell him that if he doesn't either bring it here himself or give it to you so you can bring it here, it will be my pleasure to send a squad car so we can pick it up ourselves."

I had the distinct feeling that he already knew the man and that this would be a matter of personal revenge for him.

I had hardly opened the door to the store when the boss shouted,

"Didn't we tell you not to bother us anymore?"

"I know," I said, undaunted. "But this time I'm coming with a message from the customs officer. He says that it will be a pleasure for him to come with a squad car and look for my camera himself if the camera isn't in his office for inspection before 12 noon tomorrow. The duty has not been paid, and I'm a foreigner."

"What? You're a foreigner? How come you didn't tell me?"

He looked pale, all his self-confidence gone. He told me to wait a second and went into the back room to telephone. I could only hear a word now and then; it sounded like he was calling someone for advice. A lawyer, maybe. When he came out, he said that he had already sold the camera but, due to the unfortunate circumstances, he would get it back within the hour.

I waited in a cafe on the opposite side of the street and, within an hour, a small van pulled up and a man entered the store with my shiny aluminum case in his hand. I went over to the store and had to surrender my receipt and sign a paper admitting I had never told him I was a foreigner and so he was in no way at fault as he had no reason to suspect that customs hadn't been paid on the camera.

I walked triumphantly out of the store with all my equipment and rushed back to the customs officer as the last part of my plan.

"He returned the camera to me," I informed him as soon as I entered his office.

"I was sure of that," he replied with a faint smile. "Now, let me see what papers you have for all that equipment," he said, glancing down at the papers I showed him. "But don't you know that French Guiana is part of France? These papers are perfectly in order and whether you are French or not has no bearing on this case."

"Oh, I'm so glad to hear that. I'm sorry to have troubled you for no reason," I said hypocritically.

"Are you really?" he asked me as he followed me to the door. This time his faint smile made me wonder if he hadn't seen straight through my scheme, especially when he added, "Next time you're in Paris, check beforehand whom you are dealing with."

Ever since that time, I have wondered if customs officers are really as dumb as some of us think. In any case, I will be forever grateful to this one for helping me get my camera back, not just for the money it represented, but for all the frustration I would have suffered for years to come, thinking back at what a fool I had been.

A few days later, I was able to sell the camera through a classified ad. I used the money to follow Monsieur Grosset's advice and bought the two Leica bodies and three lenses he had suggested.

We leased a car, which was the handiest way for us to get ourselves and our belongings back to the boat. It cost us no more than the train or taxis, and we didn't have to pay for round trip, but could leave the car down in the south of France next to the boat and pay for only the actual miles we drove.

Paris had been a disappointment and we were glad to leave. As we entered the southbound freeway, it was a joy to see a sign reading, "You are now entering the freeway going towards the sun." Indeed, it was with no regrets that we left the smog of the city behind us.

# 7

# The Mission

We were so overjoyed to find our boat again that we just couldn't understand how we could ever have left her—how even the glitter of Paris could have tempted us. We were now more tolerant of the faults of Port Grimaud, which we thought was a pretty good place after all. Summer was coming with all its transients, and Lydia was able to sell a few of her scarves while I worked full time to prepare the boat to sail to the Indian Ocean.

In Port Grimaud, in addition to the tourists and transients, were many of my old friends. These yachtsmen had each been able to find enough money to buy one of those houses with its own private dock right in front of the living room. Such homes fulfilled the dream of so many sailors—to have the security of a house and also the freedom a boat represents, with its ability to take the owner to the other side of the earth if he so wishes.

Claude was one of my old friends who had realised this dream. He'd bought not one house but two in which connecting doors had been cut, thus increasing the houses' small size and at the same time doubling the size of the dock. He was in partnership with a small yacht yard, but spent most of his time designing boats in the office he had made out of the living room of one of the houses. We often visited him and discussed the two projects he was working on. One was a 52-foot ketch for Monsieur H., a private owner, the other an 80-foot schooner for Monsieur S., a businessman planning to build a charter fleet of 12 such boats to be based in the West Indies. Claude was very interested in my boat, which had proven herself a good sailing vessel on the way from South America. My underwater lines were very similar to those of the 52-footer he was designing.

Lydia had become pregnant and we decided not to wait too much longer before setting sail for the Indian Ocean so that we'd have time to get settled there well ahead of the birth. I had a long talk with Claude, a talk which was to change our lives.

It looked like the boats were to be built in Sri Lanka, the island just south of India previously called Ceylon, the same general area I was planning to sail. A designer's job is not just to draw up the plans; in most cases he is also supposed to supervise the construction and be available for consultation should the builders run into problems or difficulties. This was the part of the job Claude hated. He liked designing; he was happy with his wife in a beautiful and comfortable house and had no desire to travel to Sri Lanka. I was headed that way anyway, so it gave me an idea.

"Since you hate the idea of having to fly over there on countless trips during the construction time, why not give me that part of the job—you do the plans and I'll do the supervising," I said. "It will also be in the interest of the owners inasmuch as I can stay there full time. If you take care of it, you could only be there on short visits."

"It would be a relief for me," admitted Claude, "but I'll have to talk with the two owners to see if they agree."

Both Monsieur S. and Monsieur H. readily agreed for me to take over that part of Claude's job. They both had admired L'Artemis and said that, if I could get the workers to do as good a job for them as I had on my own boat, they would be very happy. They were also very relieved to get a man who would be there permanently on site, rather than having to content themselves with Claude's short visits because of his other responsibilities in Port Grimaud.

We ran into a bit of an argument concerning my salary—they

didn't consider the job full time. I finally accepted their offer when they agreed that I would be permitted to take extra work on the side should I find some. Because we would live on the boat and would have no housing expenses, and knowing that the cost of living was extremely low in that part of Asia, we felt we were still getting a good deal. And how could we go wrong? We were headed that way in any case. They even agreed to pay me travel expenses and gave me the equivalent amount of a round-trip airline ticket. I thought that was fair enough, but Lydia felt hurt to be ignored and thought they should have given me the price of two tickets.

Everything would have been fine except that we had to wait for the contract to be signed between the yard and the two owners. Disagreements crept up, so while they were negotiating, they were also shopping around in other countries hoping to get a better deal. For a while it looked like they would settle for a yard in the Philippines. But the weeks dragged into months, Lydia was getting heavier and summer was soon over. We were beginning to regret the whole arrangement. If we'd been on our own, we would have sailed long ago while the weather was good and would probably have arrived already in the Indian Ocean. Then one day Claude came over and triumphantly announced the big news.

"This time everything is all set and the contact has been signed," said Claude. Both boats will be built in Taiwan. We're giving you a farewell luncheon tomorrow at the restaurant. We'll sign our contract with you and we'll pay you the travel money at the same time, and then you can sail immediately afterwards."

My enthusiasm was rather mixed, I must admit. January had arrived with its cold and all its winter gales, and Lydia was now five months pregnant.

"I had planned on going to Sri Lanka," I grumbled. "And where is Taiwan?"

"I'm not too sure myself," admitted Claude. "But what difference does it make? Asia is Asia. One place is much like the other."

We were all too soon to discover that one place in Asia is not necessarily the same as the next.

# 8

# Towards Suez

*I*t didn't take me long to realise that Taiwan was much farther away than Sri Lanka, which had been our original destination. In fact, Taiwan was twice as far from Suez as Sri Lanka! But Claude's enthusiasm made us forget about the drawbacks of leaving in the middle of winter; on January 5, 1976, we sailed out into the open sea headed directly for the other end of the Mediterranean to Port Said at the entrance of the Suez Canal.

The farewell party and the food had been excellent, as were all the speeches wishing us a good voyage on the long trip to Asia. Monsieur H. paid us his share of the agreed-upon travel expenses with no arguments, but Monsieur S., complaining that some of his creditors had failed to pay him, said he would have to send our money later on. He added very logically that, in any case, we wouldn't need any money at sea. He said he'd send us one-third of the money in Suez, one-third in Singapore and the last third upon our arrival in Taiwan. I was a bit annoyed, but thought it fair. Lydia was furious.

"They are sending us to the other side of the world with no other guarantee than a piece of paper—a paper which gives you more obligations to them than what they have to you," she pointed out. "They didn't give us one cent in advance money and, in fact, one of them even managed to avoid giving us the promised travel expenses."

Of course she was right. I should have taken it as a warning of what to expect in the future, but I was keen on the job and we were headed that way in any case. As we slid slowly into the calm waters of Port Grimaud towards the open sea, we crossed one of the small ferries taking tourists on sightseeing tours through this "Venice of France." I could hear the guide's voice through his loudspeaker.

"Ladies and gentlemen, take a good look at that sailboat crossing in front of us. This sailboat is not on an afternoon sail inside the harbour or in the bay within close reach of a port should a sudden storm spring up. No, ladies and gentlemen, this boat is now leaving for a voyage to China and intends to sail nonstop to Suez as the first stop on the way."

We heard some choked exclamations from people horrified at the prospect, but we also heard a good many laughs from people who must have thought it a joke. Most tourists know the Mediterranean Sea from their summer vacations when the sea is flat and calm. But when summer is over, the Mediterranean changes completely. It can get very cold despite its reputation of eternal summer. In fact, dew forming on the boat at night would freeze and transform our deck into a skating rink that was so slippery we could hardly walk. Admittedly, the morning sun would soon melt it, even though it was low over the horizon and gave little warmth.

The Mediterranean's well-known blue skies can give a false impression about the temperature, but even worse, sudden violent gales can spring up with no warning, whipping up the seas under a clear sky. Such storms can be violent enough to pose danger, even for large, modern steamships. In Pytheas's time, long before Christ, a general ban on all navigation had been imposed during the six-month period surrounding winter. During that time, all ships had to stay in a safe harbour or be put ashore because the shipwrecks which occurred during the winter months had become too much of a burden on the various nations along the Mediterranean shores. Regulations and customs have changed during the centuries, but the weather and its storms probably have remained much the same.

Yet, we had put to sea on the appointed day, heading clear across towards Egypt without even having listened to a weather report. Social and business reasons often make us disregard the most elementary rules of good seamanship. Certainly it couldn't be considered good seamanship to suddenly take to the sea in the middle of winter without even checking the weather, especially with no other crew than a pregnant woman.

We were lucky, though, and enjoyed beautiful weather day after day, although we were quite cold the first days. But the cold didn't concern us much. We had warm clothes and we knew that each day as we were gaining towards the south, the temperature would improve. The second day at sea, we still needed our thick fur coats, and Lydia insisted that we take a portrait of ourselves with the camera set on automatic, partly for us to keep as a souvenir and partly with the thought of illustrating a planned article about crossing the Med in winter.

I did write the article and sent the photo with it, but it was never published and just lay in the agent's files. Little did we suspect that, three years later, the photo would be enlarged and published in many of the world's newspapers, not to illustrate any of my articles but to announce Lydia's tragic death. Perhaps it's best that we can't foresee the future—it would often only spoil the present.

After passing Malta on the fifth day, we congratulated each other for the good weather for, according to the weather charts, the most dangerous part of the Mediterranean was behind us. From here to Port Said there was much less chance of gales and the weather should have been much milder. But we have since learned never to take anything at sea for granted until having reached a safe port. The next day, the sky was filled with dark, menacing clouds and the cold, biting wind from the north began to pick up.

Lydia, because of her pregnancy, became violently seasick as the sea rapidly became very stormy with short, steep and vicious waves.

She was so sick she threw up blood, and we worried that she would miscarry from her violent convulsions. I tried to soften the savage motion of the boat by reducing canvas, then by heaving to and stopping the boat, but no matter how much I tried to ease the motion of the boat in the gale, we could never get comfortable. As I watched Lydia suffer, I bitterly regretted ever getting involved in this job. If not for the job, we could have been at our destination, quietly awaiting the arrival of our baby under better and less strenuous conditions.

The storm lasted three full days. Heaving to during that time not only made life somewhat more bearable for Lydia, but also made it much easier for me. Otherwise I would have had to keep watch 24 hours a day all by myself, which was far less necessary with the boat at rest.

Many think that we shouldn't worry about keeping watch in a sailboat because sailing vessels are supposed to have the right of way over all motor-driven ships, and that the danger of colliding with another sailboat on the open sea is so small as to be disregarded. But in practice this theory doesn't work so easily. First of all, the lights on a small sailing vessel are never strong enough to be spotted from very far away, so a large, high-speed ship would have little time to take avoiding action. Also, there are so few sailboats compared to steamships on the ocean that the officer on watch is not geared to that eventuality. Normally all he has on his mind is the general rule that he only has to give way and to worry about traffic coming from his right. A boat coming at full speed from his left could easily hit a sailboat whose captain was not keeping proper watch.

In addition, it isn't quite accurate to claim that sailing vessels *always* have the right of way. Ships displaying difficulty in manoeuvering, fishing vessels at work, tugboats with long tows and surveying vessels at work will generally consider that they need not give way to a sailboat (and especially not for a yacht, as many of them feel that they are working and shouldn't be hindered by someone at play).

Neither can the overtaking vessel expect the right of way. This does happen at times. A sailboat like mine can reach speeds of close to 10 knots under favourable circumstances, while some commercial vessels may go at slower speeds. Chances of collisions are far reduced when hove to as when standing still, or nearly so. All I can hope for is that no ship will blindly run down on a light or on a ship not moving through the water.

During the storm, Lydia, a fervent Christian, asked me to reread the passage in the Bible about St. Paul's shipwreck, to try and find out how long his storm lasted and to see what time of year it was. We knew that he had been washed up on Malta in the general location we were in, but I was unable to find out any more than that it must have been during the winter months.

But we were to have more luck than St. Paul. We survived the storm with no damages. After three days, when the storm subsided, I set the boat back on course and we arrived at Port Said on January 23. We thought we had reached paradise. Even after the storm had abated, the seas had remained rough and uncomfortable the whole way. In the safety of the harbour, we found a beautiful mild climate. On shore we were impressed by the open-air market with its myriad fruits and vegetables of excellent quality sold at a fraction of France's normal cost.

At the yacht club, we were welcomed with open arms by the commodore himself, and invited to remain as long as we wanted and to use all of the facilities of the club free of charge. (That was in 1976!) There were two other yachts there, both waiting to pass through the Suez Canal, the shortcut to the east. The canal goes through the Lake of Ismailia, the Big Bitter Lake and the Small Bitter Lake, for a total length of about 80 miles. Unlike the Panama Canal, the Suez Canal presents a minimum of navigational difficulties.

The canal was built during the years of 1859 to 1869 by the French and administered by them for many years. After the war, when the Allies withdrew from Egypt, it seems like the canal could have been declared international waters, having more than paid for itself. Instead it was given to the Egyptians, who promptly tore down the statue of Ferdinand de Lesseps (who had built the canal), and then devised a schedule of fees for boats to pass through.

Part of the money, of course, goes to maintain the canal (this is done by Japanese firms who didn't hesitate to tow their equipment all the way from Japan), but the great majority of it has become Egypt's main source of income. They neither built the canal nor do the actual maintenance work, yet they gather its fruits. Granted, the passage goes through their territory, but does that justify the high fees charged to make it the main income producer for the country?

They charge not according to the cost of running the canal but, rather, charge slightly less than the cost for ships to sail the long way around the point of South Africa. And this explains why authorities include the "airdraft" (i.e., the height of the vessel above the water and its windage). I couldn't understand the logic of this, as there are no bridges to open across the canal, until a skipper of a towed oil rig with its sky-high towers explained it to me.

"They know what a job it would be to try to tow something with all that windage in the stormy region of South Africa," he said. "They know we'd rather pay quite a bit extra to be able to take the easy way through their canal, so they charge accordingly. In this case, they charged me over half a million dollars! And that's not counting all the *baksheesh* ["small presents," a custom prevalent in all Arab countries]. I have to pay *baksheesh* to the myriad of petty officials. If not, they will find all kinds of reasons not to sign the necessary papers and delay my transit when they know each minute costs my company too much money to allow any unnecessary delays."

But I suppose that's what we call business and, after all, they don't force us to go through their canal.

All these exorbitant charges didn't overly concern us. We were now glad to have arrived in a safe port after that last stormy passage, and we fully enjoyed the very mild climate, the sun, and the large, well-provisioned open-air market, where we could get all kinds of beautiful and very inexpensive fruits and vegetables. The Arabs fascinated us with their long robes, exotic air and customs that were so different from our own.

But we also had our problems. The promised money was not waiting for me at the consulate as I had expected and, in fact, the consul had never heard of either me or Monsieur S. Lydia, who had never liked Monsieur S., was furious.

"I'm not a bit surprised," she said. "I told you so even before the start, when he suddenly was so broke that he couldn't pay us in Port Grimaud as promised. This is a breach of contract. If he doesn't pay us as agreed, we no longer have any obligation towards him. Let's forget about him and stay here. We'll have the baby here and then push on when it suits us, rather than be pushed by Monsieur S. whenever it suits him."

"Well, we're still obligated to the other man who did pay us," I said meekly. But she countered immediately.

"So let's contact Monsieur S. and tell him to get us the money. Failing that, we'll consider our contract canceled."

She was right, of course, but I thought that the missing money might have been caused not by bad will but, perhaps, by a forgotten bill which seemed minor to an important businessman. On the other hand, it could serve as an excuse for us to stay in Egypt until the baby was born. It would certainly make life easier and safer for Lydia and the baby to live in a pleasant country with many doctors, rather than putting to sea for a long voyage far from help should any trouble arise.

Lydia, having heard that Moslem doctors performed internal examinations of women only in extreme cases, suggested that perhaps she should see a gynecologist after all, something she had refused to do until now. The thought of another man, even a doctor, touching her intimately was repugnant to her.

The doctor she found turned out to be a very charming man who listened carefully to what Lydia said. As he guided her into the examination room, he insisted that I be present. Lydia lay down on the bed fully dressed and the doctor put both his hands on her tummy on the outside of her thin dress. He soon declared with a smile that he could feel the baby's feet, behind and head, and assured us that the baby was lying in a normal position. After listening to a sort of microphone he laid on Lydia's tummy to hear the baby's heartbeat, he assured us that we had nothing to fear, but added, "I strongly recommend you remain here until after the birth—and don't tire the mother with a rough sea voyage."

Much as I always hate to abandon my plans, this was one occasion when I had to admit that we'd started much too late. The delays in reaching suitable agreements with the shipyards on the other side of the world had changed the situation for us. Although we had successfully survived the winter gales of the Mediterranean Sea, the long delays had made Lydia much less adaptable to travel. I began to weaken and consider abandoning the job in Taiwan. We were nearly broke, but life was so cheap in Egypt that, I figured, if I could do just one single good report on that exotic country, then we'd have enough to carry us over until the birth of the baby. We could then sail over to the Indian Ocean as originally planned.

We were about to make plans to stay, when the money finally arrived from Monsieur S., together with all his apologies for the delay. It would have been so much easier for everybody if he'd given us the money before our departure from France, but perhaps it was true that he'd been short of cash. More likely, he didn't want to give any cash to a sailor who could travel only a few miles and enjoy all the money with no intention of doing the job.

I could understand his side of the situation and didn't feel that he'd treated us unfairly. But now that the money had arrived, we had less of an excuse to remain in Egypt. Lydia was the first to admit it.

"I was discouraged the first few days here because I was weak from having vomited so much from the gale, but now I feel fine. I'm sure I won't start to vomit again from now on. It's only in the first few months of pregnancy that women vomit so easily. Now I've passed that stage, so I should be all right, especially since we have warm weather in front of us. In fact, I rather look forward to sailing again. After just a few days' sail from Suez, we should be halfway down the Red Sea, which is one of the hottest places on earth and we'll be in swimsuits. My, how nice that will be. In fact, I'll be much better off than if we'd stayed in Paris. Granted, we may have had better hospital facilities there, but I'd be breathing all that polluted air for our baby. Now we'll be in the sun with completely unpolluted air and all the freedom and lack of stress our life onboard affords us."

I was smitten by her enthusiasm and we decided to set sail as soon as possible. Fortunately, we didn't have to worry about paying a half million dollars to transit the canal. In fact, to try and promote tourism, the government had decided to let all yachts transit free of all charges. Free, that is, except for a few government stamps, the usual *baksheesh* and, of course, the fee for the agent, without whose services we had been assured we would never find our way through the spider web of Egyptian paperwork.

When the agent's fee proved to be about $200 U.S., Lydia volunteered to try to deal directly with the officials, despite all warnings that it would be fruitless. Never underestimate the power of a woman. Lydia did get through all the offices and, after a bit of waiting here and haggling there—and four full days of running around, she came back triumphantly with the permit and the date of transit. The whole thing had cost only $15 U.S., which was split evenly between the legal government stamps and some *baksheesh* she hadn't been able to bypass.

She told me that she could have taken care of the formalities in probably half the time had we been equipped with a motor. Although it is very feasible to transit the canal under sail alone, as had been done for about a century by the natives' dhows, this was no longer permitted. We would have to go through under power; those having no power would have to hire a tugboat. The catch was that, although it had been easy to find a fellow seaman willing to tow us through at a minimal charge, the authorities insisted that only a licensed Egyptian tugboat would be given permission to tow us. Of course, a sizable *baksheesh* to the right man would have smoothed all the difficulties. Lydia finally succeeded in getting permission to be towed by an ex-yachtsman who had just bought a 120-foot trawler, *The Dauntless Star*, on speculation and was also due to transit.

I paid Dick, the owner of the *Star*, $40 U.S., making the cost of our transit a total of $55—quite a bargain compared to the $200 for the agent plus $500 the Egyptian tugboat would have cost, with the very likely prospect of having to pay another $500 should the tugboat not find a customer for the return trip.

When the day came, I wasn't quite so happy when the skipper and the pilot insisted on towing me side-by-side, rather than behind on a long rope. I hate being towed on the side: unless you're on a perfectly flat sea, the two boats are being slammed against one another in a most frightening way, even when using big and numerous fenders. And, of course, the water was flat only in theory. Each time we would cross a ship, we would also have to suffer its bow and stern waves. Dick in his large steel boat didn't have to worry, and the pilot worried even less.

Being on a small wooden boat, I was the loser.

I became especially unhappy when the pilot, under the pretense of keeping on schedule, ordered maximum speed, which was 9-1/2 knots. No doubt he just wanted to get home sooner. Being towed put tremendous strains on my small ship, as could be witnessed by the tripled, one-inch nylon line, which was as tight as if made out of steel.

Fortunately by the end of the day, we arrived at the halfway mark, Lake Ismailia, with no damage, and were ordered to anchor for the night.

Next morning we were boarded by our new pilot, who was to guide us to Suez and the end of the canal to the Red Sea. He lost no time in asking where his *baksheesh* was, and became furious when both Dick and I said we had nothing for him as we had already paid all our lawful dues to the canal authorities and had been informed we would have nothing more to pay.

"If that's the way you feel about it," he burst out, "we'll see who of us has the most power. We won't move from here until I get my *baksheesh*."

"We're due to Suez before nightfall," said Dick calmly. "You can't hold us here without good reason."

"I'm the one to decide if I have good reason to hold you here," he barked back. "I'm telling you, you'll both sit here a fortnight if you each don't give me one carton of cigarettes and one bottle of whisky or the equivalent in cash."

"You're out of luck, as neither one of us drinks or smokes. We have neither cigarettes nor alcohol on board and, in addition, we're also pretty broke."

He sat down without uttering another word until he said that it was lunchtime and he was entitled to lunch. Dick said that, indeed, we were just going to the table and we could all share lunch together.

Lunch consisted of English tea, bread, a few sardines and nothing else. Our pilot said he didn't like sardines and waited for the next dish until he finally realised that there was nothing more to come. He then complained bitterly, saying that serving such a poor meal showed a lack of respect for an official of the Egyptian government. Dick pointed out that we had just offered to share our meal with him and we'd had nothing more than what we'd given him. He sat sulking for a good while after that. Then, having probably figured out that we indeed must be poor and that he'd get nothing more from us, suddenly ordered anchor up and full speed ahead.

We arrived at Suez just before nightfall. Our pilot ordered us to slow down to two knots when a pilot boat came alongside. He jumped over to them without even saying goodbye. We were on our own in the Red Sea. We anchored for the night as we were all very tired from the transit of the canal and the nervous tension which had gone with it. But we were glad for having passed that milestone and were now well on our way toward Asia.

# 9

# The Red Sea

When we awoke the next morning, we found the anchorage rolly, disagreeable and crowded. Already we were being pestered by one bumboat after the other. Since we were also far behind schedule, there was no reason to delay departure—no reason except, that is, that this was Friday and any seaman knows that it's bad luck to leave a harbour on a Friday! Of course I know it's ridiculous to believe in such silly, old-fashioned superstitions, but then one never knows, so why take unnecessary risks?

In all my life, I don't think I've ever departed on a Friday, and I was loath to start now, but Lydia, being a fervent Christian, frowned on my belief in such "tales of the Devil," and insisted that was absolutely no reason to delay our departure and waste time in that dreary anchorage.

Even superstitious people will generally admit that, if we're willing to think about it coldly and logically, superstitious beliefs are not worthy of intelligent and civilised men. Yet, I've long been intrigued about how such superstitious laws and beliefs came about, and have wondered secretly if there weren't some truth to them. Little by little I've reached the conclusion that, in many cases, these silly beliefs were not so silly after all and we would be wise to take our warnings from them.

Surprisingly, the statistics do show that ships leaving on Fridays run into trouble more often than ships leaving on any other day of the week. How can such a fact jibe with superstition?

Simply because ships leaving on Friday all too often were not as well prepared as they should have been. The skipper rushed through her loading or her fitting out, or had disregarded the approach of bad weather, all in an effort to avoid laying over in port during the weekend, which would cost him money, time and perhaps a drunken crew. Logic, in this case, as in so many others, fits in with the superstitious rule which resulted from it.

Likewise there's an old belief that it's bad luck for a ship and its crew to have a woman onboard. In fact, many sailors would refuse to board a ship with a woman onboard. Silly? Yet statistically, such ships did run into trouble more often than ships without any women onboard. Why? I can easily imagine at least one example. Suppose the skipper brings his wife with him. Perhaps she comes along mainly to please him without really liking the sea, but hoping for a pleasant cruise. Then the weather becomes bad and soon the ship is hove to in a very heavy sea. Madame becomes seasick and frightened, and begs her husband to make for the safety of the closest port. The skipper knows the danger of trying to make some ports in gale conditions, but the moaning of his wife and her discomfort is more than he can stand, so he tries to make the port against his better judgment. Many ships have been lost trying to enter a port under unfavourable conditions rather than riding it out safely at sea. But how is he to explain that to his wife?

And how could it possibly bring bad luck to a ship to have a man whistle onboard? Ridiculous superstition? I would say no, for two reasons. Whistling can get fellow crew members' and officers' nerves so on edge that they can no longer work the ship properly and may get the ship in trouble. Or crew members who get irritated or upset by that whistling might find it tiring or difficult to ask or order the whistler to stop that annoying habit. It was much easier to spread the rumour that it brings bad luck and, thus, everybody had peace!

Others are more obvious, like the belief that it brings bad luck to walk under a ladder or scaffold. Indeed, chances of getting splashed with paint or having a tool fall on one's head must be far greater than if we take the trouble to walk around those obstacles.

As for the belief that it's bad luck to light more than two cigarettes with the same match—everybody knows that during World War I the flare-up of a match in the darkness of night would have burned long enough by the third cigarette to give the enemy time to aim and shoot.

Thus, I argued with Lydia, superstitious laws were not dictated by evil but by clear logic, and we should perhaps follow most of those rules, remembering that there's no smoke without fire. But I reluctantly admitted that my explanation for not leaving on a Friday didn't concern us in this case.

Yet I must have wanted to play it safe. Instead of writing in the log book "leaving today," I wrote, "continuing voyage" which had started on any other day but Friday—a bit childish, I suppose, and apparently not sufficient to fool fate. I can't help shivering when, rereading my log today, I see that Lydia's untimely and tragic death three years later happened on exactly the same date and at the same hour to the minute of our departure—both at 10 a.m. on February 20th—just a coincidence, of course. But there are stranger things under the sun than the mind can comprehend.

In any case, the long voyage ahead of us to the Asian part of the world started with a nice breeze from the north, giving us a good cruising speed under full sails of jib, staysail, mainsail, maintopsail and mizzen. Although I had no automatic steering device like most long distance yachts generally have today, we were fortunate to have a ship which could keep her course by herself once her sails, rudder and centreboard had been properly adjusted for the prevailing conditions. We were then relieved from the tyranny of sitting at the tiller day and night.

This did not mean we could expect a free ride to our destination in the crowded and dangerous waters of the Red Sea. The Red Sea is dangerous for several reasons. First, there are a great number of ships to look out for and stay clear of. Second, except for the main channel (which is crowded with ships), there are many reefs, some of them not properly marked on the charts and most with no navigational marks like buoys or lights. Third, as if this weren't enough, astronomical navigation is often unreliable due to the abnormal and irregular refraction in that part of the world.

However, we had one thing in our favour. The wind is practically always blowing from the north and would give us the wind from aft. Since the beginning of sailing, all sailors have loved following winds and have always disliked or even feared headwinds. With the wind aft, we get a fast, easy run with a minimum of strain, and can steer on a more direct course. On the other hand, having the wind against us necessitates making a series of zigzag courses, called tacking, to get to our destination. A sailboat can reach any destination she wants, but she can never sail directly against the wind. To sail a zigzag course among reefs, needless to say, makes for treacherous navigation.

With the wind aft, we could expect a faster and much easier sail going south. Djibouti was our next goal at the bottom of the Red Sea. Although we didn't need to sit at the tiller, we still had to watch out for traffic and verify that the ship did hold a true course. While working out the navigation problems, we also had to cook and leave ourselves enough time for rest and sleep. The difference between a pleasant cruise and an unpleasant one is often caused by trifling matters. Much of it is up to the skipper's and crew's state of mind and their ability to organise their life onboard properly.

During the night the wind freshened gradually. Suddenly I heard the sickening sound of breaking wood. As is my custom in following winds, I had let the boom out all the way until it was almost touching the shrouds, but had neglected to rig a vang at the gaff's extremity. While not necessary in light airs or on the wind, this becomes all-important in fresh breezes from aft unless you are willing to keep the boom half sheeted in and settle for slower speeds. The topsail pushing hard forward had put undue strain on the jaws and the gaff had broken. Although a good skipper should be able to repair almost everything onboard his boat, I had no great desire to repair it in the dark of night. So, after taking in the topsail, I just scandalised the main, dropping the peak of the gaff by slacking off on the peak halliard, and then lashed it straight up and down in the lee of the rest of the mainsail. This would relieve the strain, yet let the ship continue on her course at a slower speed until morning.

With the arrival of daylight, I started the repair. Because I had to take down the sail entirely, the balance of the boat was upset and it would no longer keep its course unguided, so Lydia had to steer during the entire time it took for the repair. It wouldn't have been so strenuous for Lydia except that her seasickness had come back and she was very ill. I half-regretted not listening to the doctor's advice and staying in Egypt, but we both hoped the seasickness would last only a day or two. Even some seasoned sailors have a day or two of seasickness after a long stay in port.

The repair itself was simple enough, but greatly complicated by the wind, which had become very fresh. The ship was rolling and I had to brace myself and hold my tools so they wouldn't slide all over the deck. I dismantled the jaw from the broken gaff, found a suitable piece of spare wood (any long distance boat should carry her stock of timber for possible repairs), then shaped it, taking the measures from the remaining jaw. I screwed and bolted it in place, then tacked on a new piece of leather and greased it well to serve as an anti-chafe pad. Otherwise, the gaff jaws would soon cut themselves into the mast and damage it. Finally, I hoisted the mainsail, remembering this time to put the rope vang at the end of the gaff. After a few minutes to adjust the sails, Lydia gladly returned to the quietness of the cabin to relax after the four hours it had taken me to complete the repairs.

A gaff rig is seldom seen today. Practically all yachts now use the "modern" Bermuda rig. This, admittedly, is faster to windward and looks simpler to those not familiar with the gaff rig, but there end its advantages, while its list of disadvantages is very long. As its mainsail lacks surface power, unless we can accept a unreasonably high mast, we have to compensate with large headsails called genoas and with huge balloon sails for wind from aft.

The genoas set up tremendous strains and tensions in the rigging which has to be very strong and set up with expensive fittings like rigging screws and even hydraulic tensioning screws, not to speak of numerous winches, to get enough force to sheet in and adjust the sails. For maximum efficiency, Bermudian rigs need a great number of sails adjusted to varying conditions because it's not practical to reef the headsails. In order to gain a little extra surface in the underpowered mainsail, it's customary to add a roach on the leach. To keep this from beating in the wind like a flag, it has to be held by battens sewn into the sails. This, together with the generally far too great friction of its slide holding the sail to the mast, will prevent a Bermuda sail from being lowered or hoisted with the wind aft—forcing the boat to face the wind until the sail is hoisted or lowered.

This alone would be sufficient reason for me not to have a Bermuda rig: I can hoist and lower my gaff sail at any point of sailing with no difficulties. All this tension and effort that use of the Bermuda imposes on both boat and crew has been overcome with modern technology and modern equipment, but only at tremendous cost, compared with the gaff rig's simple, unsophisticated equipment and no winches at all. Repairs are so much easier on a gaff rig than on the Bermudian, with its fancy, factory-made components that can be repaired only with factory replacement parts.

In my case, having broken the gaff, I did all the repairs with hand tools and odd pieces of material I had on board. And the repair was not makeshift, but permanent. In fact, I still have the same gaff and jaw today. Admittedly, on a Bermudian we could not possibly have broken any gaff jaws, as it doesn't have any. But countless other equivalent accidents could happen and in only a few cases could the crew even consider the possibility of repairing such sophisticated equipment. They would instead limp into the closest port and try to find either a replacement factory-made part or a specialised workshop, or they would have to order the faulty replacement part from the original factory and sit and wait—sometimes for months—until the air freight part would finally arrive and be cleared by customs.

For long-distance sailing, simplicity, economy and reliability, as well as sheer beauty, I feel the gaff rig is preferable to any of the modern rigs and thus will always be my choice.

Once the boat was repaired, we hoisted the full sails again. Going day and night at a good speed, we rapidly gained towards the south. The temperature changed day by day. While it had still been a bit cool by the Suez, especially at night, each day the temperature became milder. Each day we stripped more clothes off until, finally, we could live just in our bathing suits again.

As soon as we were out of the Gulf of Suez, our coal stove wasn't needed to heat the boat, so we lit it only for cooking our meals. In fact, it soon became bothersome and made the cabin uncomfortably hot during food preparation. Even though it would have been much easier for Lydia to open a tin of corned beef or whatever, she never failed to show her enthusiasm when I caught fish, even if it meant more work for her. She insisted that it was important for both of us to have "proper" meals, with fresh food as much as possible. We ate well on our cruise through the Red Sea—much better than we had in the Mediterranean Sea, which by then was nearly fished out.

In the Red Sea, I caught fish practically every day, though I'm generally a poor fisherman. I'm also a very poor cook, and never ceased to admire and be grateful to Lydia for all the delicious meals she always provided, regardless of how seasick she may have been. Seasickness is a miserable ailment, especially for pregnant women, because they can't take any of the modern motion sickness drugs. It made me unhappy to see her so ill, but I admired her willpower and her enthusiasm. She never failed to prepare three hot meals each day no matter how sick she felt. Often she even insisted on taking part of the night watch when she saw that I was getting tired from lack of sleep. Lydia was an excellent cook and we always had nice, healthy, good-tasting meals, something which greatly contributed to our pleasure and well-being at sea. Ignorance in culinary matters has led many crews to malnutrition, sickness or even death.

The days passed rapidly and soon we were in the southern part of the Red Sea where groups of islands restricted our passage. I was a bit worried. In that southern part of the Red Sea, the wind no longer blows from the north. On the contrary, the wind often blows from the south, frequently with gale force, which could render the last part of our voyage very difficult. If the wind should turn against us there, we would simply anchor under the lee of one of the islands and wait for the wind to again turn in our favour. I knew the islands belonged to Ethiopia, which had gained a reputation of being rather unfriendly to yachts, but I thought that if we didn't disembark, no one would object. Besides, the islands were uninhabited and it was unlikely that a patrol boat would pass by while we were anchored.

But we were lucky and the wind stayed in the north all the way until Djibouti, where we arrived only 10 days after leaving Suez. Our fast and beautiful passage proved, once again, how ridiculous it was to believe leaving on a Friday was bad luck. . . .

We didn't fully realise how lucky we had been until we anchored in the calm anchorage off Djibouti beside an Italian yacht called *El Terror del Mundo* and heard his story. His boat looked like a wreck with its broken bowsprit, torn-off chainplates and two huge, gaping holes in the planking, one on each side, through which the interior of the boat was clearly visible. When I went onboard to meet the skipper, he told us that they hadn't had our luck and lost the north wind through the lower part of the Red Sea. He had done exactly what I had intended, and taken refuge among one of the many islands there to wait for the proper wind to come back.

Once he had entered Ethiopian territorial waters, even before attempting to anchor, one of their patrol boats approached and hit them amidship, holing their one side.

I was horrified and demanded, "But how could they be such poor seamen?"

"Poor seamen?" he answered. "No, not poor seamen. Just very nasty soldiers—they did it on purpose."

"Are you kidding? Why should they do such a thing?"

"Because they don't want any foreign yachts in their waters and trust that the word will get around after a few examples like this and all yachts will stay away. If you still think it was an accident, take a look at my other side. How could you explain in any other way why, after having holed me on one side, they backed off, circled me and rammed me from the other side? Then they ran away, leaving us derelict with an injured crew member who suffered a compound fracture in the arm with bones breaking through his skin. Go and take a look at that sloop over there. She came in the day after me, about four days ago, with two sides holed by the same patrol boat. Go and take a look at her and see the captain."

I was horrified and soon realised that I had arrived in another part of the world where methods were more direct than what we were accustomed to in the western world.

We had wanted to escape the winter and had definitely done so here in Djibouti, one of the hottest places on earth. I doubt I have ever suffered from heat anywhere as I did there. I felt sorry for Lydia, who had become so big that she had only one dress she could fit into. It was elastic but, unfortunately, it was both black and down to her feet, neither of which would help to keep her cool under the tropical sun.

Before the trip, I had suggested buying her a maternity dress, but she refused, thinking it too great a luxury when we were so poor. She preferred to save the money to buy a pretty dress after the birth when she would be slim and beautiful again. In the meantime, she said, she would manage with what she had. It was true that she needed a dress only for the few days that we were in port. Onboard she was either in her bikini or completely nude, and I liked her big tummy.

Djibouti was still French, but the natives were very unfriendly, regarding us with hateful eyes and often not bothering even to answer us. The country itself didn't seduce us, either. In addition to the discomfort of its excessive heat, nothing would grow there, and its market was one of the poorest I have seen anywhere. Prices, however, were two to three times those in France, and for inferior products. It was a country in which we really felt like outsiders. Their way of dressing with long, colorful robes was entirely foreign, and their social customs were very different from ours.

We stayed in Djibouti for only seven days before hoisting sails for the long crossing of the Indian Ocean. The voyage promised to be long, not only because of the distance, but also because it was late in the season and we could no longer expect favourable winds. We would be due for variable winds coming from any direction, inter-mingled with calms and violent, short-lived squalls—just what a sailor hates most, as such conditions cause him constant concern and extra work, as well as slowing his progress. However, we had no choice, short of waiting six months for the next favourable season. We didn't even consider the possibility of lingering in that dreary place, so we had no time to lose. My salary would start only from the day I arrived for work in Taiwan.

The voyage was to be even slower than we had expected. We had persistent headwinds and head currents, forcing us to beat back and forth while gaining very little from day to day. The heat was nearly intolerable, even though we'd become acclimated to the Tropics. But the sea was calm and flat, which made it easier for Lydia to tolerate. Even so, she was sick every day and sometimes vomited blood. This worried me more than I dared admit, but Lydia pointed out that the blood was bright red and, consequently, must be caused by the bruising of the tissue close to the mouth from the repeated vomiting, not by a wound in the stomach, in which case it would have been darker red, or even brown if partially digested.

Poor Lydia. She never complained and still tried to eat to nourish the baby she carried. At least we had good, healthy food with a lot of milk, fresh fish almost every day and nice-smelling bread she baked every day from our large supply of wheat.

Unfortunately, all the vegetables and fruits we had bought in Djibouti at such high prices proved to be of even worse quality than we'd thought and soon spoiled. They had to be thrown overboard, making us regret even more having stopped there at all.

Lydia wrote in the log Sunday, March 21:

*Very slow progress. Persistent headwinds but changing both in strength and direction forcing the captain to constantly make new adjustments. We hope to get out of the Gulf tomorrow. That will make it 13 days! I'm still as sick and vomit every day. The captain is very tired from lack of sleep as I can no longer help him with watch keeping and there are so many ships we need to stay clear of. We're anxious to get out of this furnace. This is*

*supposed to be the cool season. Quarter past midnight: we are just avoiding
a small cargo ship passing very close.*

On the 24th she wrote:

*We at last came out of that Gulf with a light wind from the ESE. Very modest
averages from noon to noon. The day before yesterday, I started on my eight
month of pregnancy yet I'm still vomiting every day. Per is drawing a new
rig for the boat which will be faster in light airs yet easier to handle. Last
night caught two beautiful dolphins, which made us a delicious dinner
despite the heat. Crossed a tanker very close.*

It was now so hot that we couldn't stand to wear any clothes at all
and, in fact, avoided going outside the cabin as much as possible. On
the deck the sun was scorching while, inside the boat with all the
portholes open, we had a little draft and were protected from the sun.

Living in the nude with Lydia pregnant opened my eyes to a side
of life I had not properly known before. I had always thought that a
pregnant woman just carried a big fetus which was nothing but a sort
of huge egg growing bigger and bigger until it seriously distorted the
woman's figure—a fetus that was nothing but a lifeless egg until the
day of birth. But now, little by little, I began to consider that the fetus
was already a human being, and a live one at that. I could see the baby
kicking its legs inside Lydia's tummy, making big bumps appear here
and there, sometimes making her laugh at all the activity. Most
surprising of all was to realise that the new baby could hear through
Lydia's skin and would have nervous reactions like a real baby or a
grown-up. I became aware of that the day I dropped a tool on the
floor, making an awful noise. Instantly the baby jumped inside its
mother, just like a scared child might have done.

Sometimes the baby would hiccup so strongly that Lydia felt

uncomfortable and sat waiting impatiently for it to stop. I not only realised that it was already a human being, but also that we should not try to guess whether it was going to be a boy or a girl. I knew the baby already was a girl or boy—we just couldn't see what it was.

The solid fuel stove, which we had been so proud of while in the winter of the Mediterranean Sea, was now a source of irritation, heating up the cabin intolerably during the preparation of our meals. Then one day the wind blew its smoke right back into the already stuffy cabin, and I lost all patience. The thought of getting rid of its 260 pounds, as well as its nearly half ton of solid fuel, became irresistible when Lydia assured me that she would be able to cook for the rest of the trip on the primus cooker we carried as a spare.

The stove had been installed in the boat before the deck had been put on and was much bigger than the hatch opening, so I dismantled it in small enough pieces to pull through the hatch and throw overboard. When the last bit of the stove was well over the side, I shoveled the coal and firewood overboard with great relief. It took me the rest of the day to clean and wash out the fuel locker, which we could now use for storage. Finally, we would be able to clear some of the gear out of our cabins that we had not found room for in our other lockers and drawers.

Lydia was relieved to no longer have to suffer the additional heat of the big stove, and she was indeed able to keep on making as good meals with the little primus as she had done on the large stove. In fact, even without the oven, she continued baking bread, using a heavy cast iron pot over the little primus and turning the bread over when it was half done.

We'd been progressing very slowly over a flat sea when, on the 33rd day, we finally approached the Maldive Islands. We would have to find our way through this large archipelago of low lying islands to get to Sri Lanka, where we planned to stop and wait for the birth of the baby. Mostly unlit at night, the Maldives can be very dangerous to ships which are unsure of their position. Just as it became crucial for us to measure the sun or stars to calculate our position exactly, the weather spoiled, the sky covered over completely and the wind picked up to surprising force.

Lydia became very seasick in the heavy seas. In order to ease the motion for her, and not wanting to plow through the gale unsure of our position, I chose to heave to, that wonderful safety valve technique for sailing vessels throughout the ages.

Once the boat was stopped, I didn't have to worry about hitting any reefs or any islands even though I knew we weren't far from them. I rested and relaxed for the first time in more than a month. The gale lasted two days and was a turning point in the weather. The temperature dropped to the more moderate levels encountered in most places in the Tropics, which we both appreciated. It was no longer that scorching heat coming from the deserts of Africa.

Once the sky cleared, I made the necessary astronomical observations with my old sextant and soon knew exactly where we were and which course to steer. A few days later, under good speed, we finally reached to Sri Lanka and entered the port of Galle, where we saw only one other sailboat. It proved to be a native fishing boat from the Maldives which had been blown off course by the gale. The Sri Lanka government was going to ship the boat back to their country a few days later on the deck of a steamer. It was too late in the season for such a small craft to make it back safely on its own.

# 10

# Sri Lanka

*J*ust south of the southernmost point of India lies the island of Sri Lanka. It is another country where we felt completely foreign. The people have very dark skin, but no other Negroid features. Their noses are sharp and fine, and their hair is black but completely straight. Sri Lankans tend to be very short in stature. Lydia, who always had a complex about her height, felt very satisfied to be able to look down on some of the men. They were shorter than she, especially in her high heels, which she insisted on wearing despite her big tummy, though she would have been much more comfortable and secure in flat shoes.

Sri Lanka is a country where the women can't be considered "liberated." Far from it. A woman is completely tied to the house and seldom goes out. When she leaves the house, she must be accompanied by her husband, father or brother. As soon as a woman becomes pregnant, she doesn't leave the house at all until after the birth of the baby, except for the trip to the hospital, which she makes one month before her expected due date. She then stays in the hospital until the birth. Thus, no pregnant women are ever seen in the streets. In fact, men never see any pregnant women except for those in their own families and in their own homes.

Lydia was to cause quite some surprise, starting right from the moment we sailed into the harbour when they saw her running around on the deck, helping with the manoeuvering to get the sails down and anchor the vessel.

The authorities, who had arrived for the entry formalities, consisted of one man for each service, which included immigration, health, customs, the police and the harbourmaster. They were so surprised to see a pregnant woman as far along as Lydia, not in the hospital but exposing herself to the discomfort of a small boat, that they completely forgot their dignity and their red tape. In the following days, she continued to surprise onlookers as she jumped down into the dinghy and rowed ashore on her own several times to do shopping and other errands, while I remained onboard to work on the boat, which had started to look rather neglected after the long voyage from France.

Sri Lanka, formerly called Ceylon, is a very exotic country with palm trees, eternal summers, different religions, different customs and a different way of life. In the weeks we stayed there we were constantly reminded that we were from another world.

We had come to Sri Lanka primarily with the idea of having the baby there. Because our departure from France had been delayed, it was going to be impossible to reach China in time. But the days progressed and Lydia still hadn't been to a doctor. She came from a very old-fashioned family and she detested the thought of an internal examination. The only gynecologist she had ever seen was the one in Egypt, and that was only because she had been assured that Egyptian doctors don't routinely make internal examinations. She had no such assurance in Sri Lanka and hated the idea of making an appointment. But as her delivery time drew near, I decided I had to push the issue and made an appointment for her. It was set for the next day and she could hardly refuse to come with me. So we went together, but right from the start things went badly.

The waiting room was the filthiest Lydia and I had ever seen and I could feel her resentment. As we waited for the doctor, we sat on long benches with patients who cleared their throats and spit out big, yellow spittle right on the floor beside us. When the doctor finally came, he was wearing a coat which probably had been white at one time, but was now grey and covered with brown spots of blood. If he had come straight from the operating room without time to change and had red spots on his coat, that would have been forgivable, but the brown spots must have been several days old.

I could tell Lydia was on the verge of vomiting. She wrenched herself loose from my arm without a word and rushed out into the street, leaving me alone and somewhat embarrassed with the doctor.

The next day, I returned and apologised for my wife's behavior. I tried to explain that she feared hospitals and that, for sentimental reasons, we had decided to have the baby born onboard. Could he come to the boat when the moment arrived?

"Don't try to make excuses," he said in a rather stern tone. "I know perfectly well what the trouble is. You Americans have a complex about sterilization. And you can't stand the perfectly natural functions like a sick man spitting. I would like you to know that my hospital is clean enough for all practical reasons and that the floors are washed several times a month. I can also tell you that I've had countless successful births. But I expect the women to come to the hospital for the last month of pregnancy. You said you expect your baby in three weeks. That's already one week later than I like, but if your wife comes to the hospital immediately and takes a room here, I will accept her. If not, you're on your own. Don't count on me or anyone else to come to your boat where there are no facilities."

"Never mind that doctor and his filthy hospital," Lydia said when I told her about my visit to the doctor. "Let's get a midwife. That's all I need. She should be willing to come to the boat. Here everything is clean and peaceful. I just don't want to even consider going to that hospital. If we're not sick before we get there, we sure will be after staying in that awful place for a while."

I talked with the midwife, who readily agreed to come. She was probably already visualising all the money she was going to get out of us rich tourists. Everything seemed to be arranged and settled, but a few hours later one of her children came with a note. It said that she had talked with the doctor and he forbade her to have anything to do with us unless Lydia came to the hospital immediately.

Lydia stood firm. She was not going to that hospital regardless of what happened. She also didn't want to look at any other hospitals in the country because she couldn't see any reason why their standards should be any different.

She proposed instead that we leave Sri Lanka. "We both know that Malaysia is an entirely different country from Sri Lanka. They are reputed to have the highest standards of hygiene in all of Asia, second only to Hong Kong. They have doctors trained in England and the reputation of being friendly and honest. I know it's a bit late to start crossing a new ocean just three weeks before my expecteddelivery date, but you said yourself that with a good wind we should easily do it in 10 days. That should leave us a safe margin. If the baby should arrive before we reach shore, I still think we would be better off even all by ourselves with no help. At least we'll have fresh, unpolluted air and not be exposed to all the microbes in that hospital.

"Besides," she added, "it won't be harder for us than it was for my mother. I myself was born at sea in a small boat and all went well."

Lydia had indeed been born at sea, but that was no reason for us to do the same now! Her father at the time had been a missionary in the South Sea island of Lifu, not far from Noumea. When her mother thought the time for the birth was approaching, she and her husband embarked for Noumea on a small local schooner. They took along the local midwife as a safety measure in case they didn't arrive in time. This was indeed wise, as Lydia didn't wait for the boat to reach port to make her appearance. Lydia's full name recalls the event. In addition to Lydia, the name given to her, she was also called Esther, which was the name of her mother, Emma, the name of the midwife, and Henrietta, which was the name of the boat.

Even though everything had worked out well for her, I felt there was no reason for us to take the same risk. Besides, I doubted very much that we would be able to get a midwife to come with us. But Lydia was so determined that I gave in. Since the monsoon had arrived with fresh following winds, it would almost guarantee a fast crossing. I tried to make the preparations for sea but ran into difficulties with the authorities, who refused to give me clearance on the grounds that a woman as close to giving birth as Lydia was should be in a hospital, not headed for an ocean crossing.

Back on the boat, Lydia became almost hysterical when I gave her the news. She begged me to go back and try to convince them to allow us to leave or, failing that, she suggested we wait for darkness and leave without their clearance.

In the end, they did give us that all-important clearance, but not without a threat. Should the baby be born before we reached our next harbour and should we arrive there without the baby, they would prosecute us for manslaughter!

They probably meant well, so we didn't take it too much to heart and set sail, confident that this would be a fast, enjoyable trip.

# 11

# The Birth of Thomas

We hoisted sail gladly from Sri Lanka, which was not nearly as romantic and exotic as it had sounded from a distance. Lydia and I anticipated with great pleasure our return to the sea, where everything was so nice and clean and where we could breathe the fresh, pure, unpolluted air.

Propelled by the new monsoon, the boat forged its way towards Malaysia and our planned hospital stay at great speed. But our luck was soon to change.

On the third day, while the ship was steering itself, a collision with something stopped us solid, making us tumble down from our breakfast seats. Rushing up on deck, I expected to see the ship I had collided with but, to my surprise, there was nothing except a huge whirlpool in the sea all around us.

While I stood wondering what it could have been, a large whale surfaced just 30 or 40 yards from us, blew and dived again. We must have collided with it as it slept near the surface. I feared that such a brutal awakening might make the animal mad and that it might charge us, perhaps breaking our vessel to pieces. We waited rather apprehensively to see what was going to happen. I have several friends whose ships have been attacked and sunk by whales, their lives saved only by a miracle. We held our breath as minutes passed, but the whale had gone with no plans of retaliation against us.

This incident showed us once more that the oceans of the world are not as empty as all too many people believe. Even far from land in the "middle of nowhere" there is life—not just whales, but dolphins, turtles, sharks and jellyfish, like the beautiful Man-O-War with its "sail" sticking up above the surface, as well as a myriad of fishes. Indeed, even snakes, like the poisonous varieties of the Arafura Sea, can feel at home in the oceans.

In the air are many kinds of seabirds. Some never go too far out to sea and always return to land before nightfall, but others seem never to need land (except, perhaps, for laying their eggs), and settle on the water at night to sleep, no matter how rough the sea.

We were lucky to have escaped our collision with the whale with no damage (other than to our nerves!) but our luck didn't hold. The newly established monsoon failed us and was gradually replaced by the old monsoon. We had probably left too soon after all and, indeed, for the rest of our trip we had to keep fighting the headwinds, which never let up. We were forced to tack endlessly back and forth, progressing slowly towards our destination while we hoped in vain every day for the favourable monsoon to return.

A sailing vessel is a comfortable and fairly fast boat as long as the wind blows from aft or from the side, but when it turns against us, then the journey becomes slow, uncomfortable and tiring. Day after day passed with no letup until the expected day for the birth arrived. We were still far from the port and its hospital. We were just south of the Bay of Bengal, still outside the entrance of the Malacca Strait, when Lydia felt the first pains. Our chances of reaching the hospital seemed rather slim, but then the pains disappeared and we both felt we had a second chance after all. All that night I sat at the tiller, beating back and forth and trying to get the most out of the wind, but when I calculated our position from the sun the next day, I was disappointed to see we hadn't gained as much as I expected. Not only was the wind against us, but there must also have been a current against us, further reducing our chances of making it to the hospital.

That afternoon the pains resumed in earnest, and it was all too evident that we would have to be on our own. All afternoon Lydia suffered each time a new wave of contractions came over her. They would stop for a few minutes while she rested and then come back again. She asked me to reread a passage in one of our books which told how to relax and thus diminish the pains, and by evening she declared that although the pains were bad, she thought that women exaggerated when claiming that the pains of childbirth are intolerable. Poor Lydia, she didn't know that this was only the beginning.

We expected the baby to arrive that evening, but Lydia was to suffer another 24 hours before the baby finally came. The night proved to be a long one. Lydia was really suffering and began to accompany her yoga breathing exercises with deep sounds which were supposed to help reduce the pain. To me these exercises sounded more like common cries from someone intensely suffering. I was unhappy not to be able to help her. We had no painkilling medicine with us, but Lydia disapproved of all such drugs and wouldn't have taken any even if we had them onboard.

The sea was confused and the sky was filled with lightning. Having by now abandoned all hopes of reaching land in time, I reduced sails and hove to, allowing the ship to take care of itself and leaving me free to attend to my wife when she needed me. The night passed and then the whole next morning. Lydia suffered and was getting exhausted. She would fall asleep during the few minutes respite between waves of pain, only to awaken when the next pain came. She was lying nude on the wooden settee in the saloon completely soaking wet with perspiration. The heat was nearly intolerable. The lightning had stopped, but the weather remained menacing and the sea confused.

I was getting seriously worried. Why hadn't the baby arrived after all this time? Lydia was a very small woman and I was a fairly tall man at 6'1". What bothered me was that it's common for most Norwegians, and particularly so in my family, for babies to be born with very large skulls. This makes birth difficult even for large, Norwegian women. Was this small French woman going to be able to cope? If not, both she and the baby might die. I cursed the monsoon that had failed us. Had it stayed we would have arrived safely and been under medical care by this time.

Evening came and with it the frightful lightning which illuminated the whole sky as well as all the way into the cabin. Lydia was so worn out by now that she could hardly talk or react in any way. Then just before 10 o'clock, while I stood in the hatch watching the sea and the lightning, I heard a sudden strange noise inside the cabin and looked inside to see a very surprised Lydia.

"My water must have broken," she said. "But it didn't hurt—I didn't feel a thing."

Only minutes after that, I saw the top of the baby's head emerging. The head came out, but the shoulders apparently were still stuck inside and nothing more happened.

"I have no more strength," whispered Lydia. "Try to pull the baby out. I can't push anymore."

I tugged gently at the head with a slow, rotating motion, as our books had explained, so as to better disengage the shoulders from the mother's basin. The baby had a total lack of expression on its face and I feared it was dead. Then the shoulders came free and the baby shot out at such speed that I nearly dropped it. I had trouble holding it, as it was covered with a slippery substance, which made it difficult to grasp firmly. I held it up by the feet with one hand, ready to give it the usual slap on the behind to make it gasp for air, when the infant got ahead of me with one huge wail. Its face wrinkled up to an awful and wonderful grimace, its arms started to wave like a windmill and the whole little creature came to life in my hands.

That moment was the most extraordinary experience and the

most fantastic adventure I have ever known: life itself!

My son Thomas was alive and breathing, and I felt no more need to hurry with anything. I laid the baby on his mother's tummy, because the cord was too short to put him in her arms. When the cord stopped beating, I cut it off with some scissors I had boiled for that purpose. I bandaged the cord on the baby's stomach and then, now that he was a completely new, independent human being, no longer attached to his mother, I laid the baby in his mother's arms, perhaps the most wonderful moment any woman can experience.

The baby looked vigorous and healthy and Lydia was at peace, but the birth was not all finished. As the afterbirth came out, I noticed that Lydia had been pretty badly torn by the baby's passage. I looked all through our medicine locker but could find neither any curved needles and thread for sewing up the wound, nor any suitable tape to hold it together. I was at a loss until it occurred to me that, though my medicine locker was rather inadequate, my tool chest for the boat was well equipped. I had been able to build a boat and sew sails for it; I should be able to fix up a small tear in human flesh as well.

I found my needles and thread, but made the mistake of letting Lydia see the needles before I'd rubbed the rust off. Seeing those big rusty needles so scared her that she absolutely refused to let me sew her up at all.

"Why not just hold the wound closed and in place with a tape," she proposed. "If we don't have any tape in our pharmacy, couldn't you make one out of sailcloth and some of your glue? You've always claimed that the modern glues will glue anything. Surely they'll stick to my skin."

That's exactly what I did. I cut a piece of spare canvas to size and glued it in place, holding the wound closed and applying pressure long enough for it to set. It proved very successful and held the wound in place sufficiently until it healed. When it came time to take it off, about 10 days later, we both understood the reason why doctors want their patients to be shaved— a detail we had omitted, and one which Lydia was to bitterly regret!

During Lydia's pregnancy, I had rearranged the bedroom and made a small bed for the baby. After wiping the baby off and cleaning him, I laid him in the new bed where he immediately fell peacefully asleep, apparently not bothered at all by the ship's violent motion in the rough seas. But then, babies do like to be rocked. Next day, I brought the baby to Lydia for his first breast-feeding and we were both quite nervous about how it would work out. Suppose the baby didn't know how to suck and take nourishment. What would we do? We didn't have any baby bottles onboard. But we needn't have feared. The baby's mouth had hardly touched her breast when he started to suck energetically and methodically as if he'd had a great deal of experience doing it.

The marvel of that life will never cease to impress me, particularly because it began isolated and all by ourselves, far from civilization and all help. All was well, and we both felt it was the greatest adventure and the most beautiful experience any man and woman could ever have. In our case, it had been done under primitive and difficult conditions, in a small ship bouncing in a stormy sea.

While I agree that any birth would benefit from proper medical help, I think the fathers should always be allowed to be present during the birth to fully share the experience of parenthood with the mother. I feel sorry for fathers who have to content themselves with waiting on the other side of the door while the wife remains solely in the company of a strange man. After all, despite the fact that he's a doctor in a white coat, that's really what he is. Never have I felt as close to my wife as I did during the birth of our baby. The men and women who are deprived of these intense moments together because of unfair hospital regulations are being deprived of the most wonderful experience any human being can have.

Although we missed arriving at the hospital in time for the birth, we of course still steered for the hospital for a check-up and aftercare. Upon leaving the hospital, if all went well, we would continue our voyage directly to Singapore where we expected mail and money to be waiting for us. We also needed to get to Singapore to apply for a visa to enter China. Without the visa, we wouldn't be allowed to enter the country.

The typhoon season for the South China Sea had already started and would only get worse as the season advanced, so the sooner we could get through it, the better. We changed course and headed directly for Singapore.

The two weeks it took to get there was the most tiring trip I've ever made. Traffic was very crowded through the Malacca Strait, forcing us to keep a constant watch. Since Lydia was still unable to get out of bed, I had to do it alone. In addition to handling the boat, I also had to take care of both Lydia and the baby, as well as cook all the meals.

Navigating that strait, even under the best of conditions, is always difficult due to its frequent rain squalls and heavy winds, which cut visibility and make a collision a very real danger. I'll never forget the night when, sailing at top speed in a violent rain squall, I suddenly saw just in front of my bowsprit a huge wall, which should not have been there as far as I could remember from my charts. All I could do to avoid disaster was to throw the tiller over, gybing, all standing (the squall had reversed and pushed us full speed ahead), even though such manoeuvres are dangerous and could break the mast. Everything held and we did come clear.

While sliding past, I saw what it was—the great sides of a supertanker! When I got the chance to go down into the cabin and tell Lydia about our near escape, she confided that she had been scared. She thought we were capsizing when the boat heeled down during my violent gybe. She said she'd known we must have been on a collision course with some steamship. She'd heard its siren sounding alarm signals at a more and more frantic rhythm as we got closer and didn't understand why we hadn't changed course sooner. She didn't realise that I had been deafened by the drumming of the rain and the roar of the wind and couldn't hear the siren.

The steamship must have seen me on its radar, but had been unable to manoeuvre away from me—supertankers manoeuvre very poorly under the best conditions, but in narrow waters like the Strait of Malacca they may just barely get through, and only then if allowed to cruise through the deepest part of the straits.

Most of them carry the four red lights, signaling that they are under only limited control—admitting, in fact, that they are a public danger. It's strange that they can still obtain permission to operate under such conditions, but they represent tremendous amounts of money and power, and the power of money often can grant permits that common sense would deny.

Not all shipping was composed of those giants. I was excited to see "real" trading sailing vessels. By real, I mean pure sailing vessels without power. Most of them were junk-rigged with full length battens and controlled by sheets fastened to each of the battens. Others were sloop-rigged with only two sails, of which the main was hoisted on a short yard sticking up above the mast, thus allowing quite a big rig on a fairly short mast.

Most of these boats looked like derelicts, roughly built and poorly kept, but they sailed like witches. In fact, with my comparatively expensive and elegant yacht, I had difficulty keeping up with them. There are still many sailing vessels around the world and, invariably, they all look rough to yachtsmen. Yet, most of the time they'll surprise the self-contented yachtsmen with their speed and handiness under sail. Over the last 30 years, I have studied many of them and wondered why our expensive yachts aren't superior. But the main reason is simple—most of our yachts are influenced by racing rules, which tie a designer's hands, penalise features that give speed, and force many of the yachts to sail undercanvassed.

When I was interested in racing cars, we had a saying, "There is no substitute for horsepower." The equivalent for sailboats should be, "There is no substitute for sail surface." The various workboats working for money have long ago discovered that the cheapest part of a sailboat is its sails, even though sails are its driving power. Native working boats all over the globe invariably carry more sails than do yachtsmen, and they carry their power where it counts—in a large mainsail on a long boom overhanging the stern and in a jib on a long bowsprit overhanging the bow. Surface for surface, they may be inefficient, compared to the same surface hung on the tall and narrow-based sailplan of most yachts. But compared to the heeling forces inflicted on the hull, it is a very cost-efficient setup.

The days passed one after another with the same tiring conditions. The traffic prevented me from sleeping more than five or six minutes at a time, day or night. With the constant beating across the traffic due to the headwinds and the daily work onboard, as well as fighting those squalls with their shifting winds, I soon became exhausted. There's a limit to every man's endurance.

One night I felt I was nearing collapse and decided to anchor, no matter what, so I could sleep. I steered towards land, sounding the depth with my lead and sounding line, until gradually shoaling depths told me roughly from my chart how close I was to shore. I let go the anchor and dropped all sails to the deck. I must have fallen asleep the minute I hit my bunk. I had a wonderful and restful night's sleep, but next morning when I went on deck to see how the anchorage looked in daylight, I got a shock.

All around us were labyrinths of "Chinese barriers," those vast, much-feared fishing traps made of heavy tree trunks planted in shallow water and interlaced into long barriers which lead the fish into a final chamber from which they can't escape. These aren't generally marked on the charts, because they may be moved to different locations when needed, but they are mentioned in the "pilots," those books describing all coasts to seamen. The books claim they always show a light at night so sailors can see them, yet I had been surrounded by these barriers and hadn't seen a single light. That I'd been able to arrive where I'd anchored without hitting a single one was a miracle.

To find my way out of that labyrinth, I had to climb to the top of the mast to see which route would lead me clear and then try to remember the way! We did get clear but, needless to say, from then on I either kept sailing through the nights at a safe distance from shore, even if I had to tackle all the traffic, or else looked for an anchorage close to shore while there was still daylight and I could avoid those dangerous barriers.

Even the slowest passage eventually comes to an end. We finally sailed into Singapore Harbour, the most crowded port I've ever seen. Nobody there seemed to know that a sailing ship has the right of way. Certainly none of those cutting right in front of us seemed aware of the fact that a sailboat has no reverse gear to stop. With a sigh of relief we finally dropped the hook right in front of the immigrations and customs building. I had scarcely had time to furl the sails when the authorities' launch came alongside and half a dozen uniformed men swarmed onboard.

Everywhere in the world there are officials we must meet and security regulations we must satisfy before we're permitted to go ashore in their country. Onboard were customs and immigrations officers, the quarantine doctor, police, harbourmaster, health inspector and possibly some others I have forgotten by now.

The health inspector wanted me to pay for a deratification certificate "good for six months." Would that mean that no rats could get onboard for a period of six months? The police wanted to know if I had any guns onboard, which I quickly denied, knowing if I admitted to having the shotgun, they would confiscate it for the duration of our stay in port and then charge us $75 for its storage.

While the immigrations officer examined our passports, the baby began to cry and startled him.

"What's that?" he asked.

"That's our baby, born at sea two weeks ago," we said proudly, expecting them to be amused and tickled to be the first to greet the new citizen. We were wrong; they were not at all amused. On the contrary, they acted highly alarmed.

"What? Born at sea? With just the two of you? You mean to say you have a baby onboard with no papers at all? Not even a birth certificate, since there wasn't a doctor onboard?"

I smiled and thought the situation rather amusing, but I wasn't smiling for long. The immigrations official had me running from office to office, to our consulates as well as to the courthouse and the police station. But no one wanted to sign any documents as this was a highly unusual case, they all said. A very serious matter . . .

In fact, it was to take six full years before I was able to get "proper" papers for my son. During that time various authorities threatened to take my child away from me. After all, they said, he could be a stolen child for all they knew. The fact that Thomas looks like a younger carbon copy of me never impressed any official.

Papers are what count!

# 12

# The South China Sea

Singapore is a big, modern city run by the Chinese. It's also an independent "country," even though it's smaller than a good many cities. They try to compete with Hong Kong as a powerful commercial free port and are trying to become westernised in all respects. They've succeeded in making it the cleanest country in the east, perhaps even the cleanest in the world—but at a price.

It will cost you $500 to throw an empty cigarette pack, or any other piece of paper, for that matter, into the street. It will also cost a stiff fine if you cross the road outside a pedestrian crossing. If you cross on the wrong light, even if there's not a single car in sight, you'll pay a fine as well.

If you're found in possession of 15 grams of heroin, it will cost you your life, and you'll suffer the additional humiliation of being hung in front of television cameras, so your execution can serve as a warning to anyone else interested in drugs. If you're found with less than 15 grams of heroin, the penalty is much less—only 25 years in jail! Granted, crimes are few in Singapore and the town is clean, but to obtain that result, the country is nothing but a police state, with a law officer standing on practically every corner. Every time I face one of their policemen, I wonder, "Now what have I done wrong?"

Had I known in the beginning about the strict discipline of that country, I would have been more careful about not declaring the gun I had onboard. In fact, the very first night at anchor we were suddenly awakened at 2 a.m. by a boat boarding us brutally and a dozen or so men swarming onboard in full battle dress uniforms. They were armed with either sidearms or submachine guns and all carried powerful torches. They immediately proceeded to search our vessel from one end to the other, turning things upside-down, while I sat in the saloon being interrogated by their officer.

Had I known more about the police and politics of Singapore, I would have been worried, but thinking about their tiny country—hardly noticeable on the world map—and seeing these individuals taking themselves so seriously just amused me. I felt like I was at a child's theatre and forced myself not to smile at their ridiculous conduct. But when they pulled the baby from his bed to search under the mattress and shined their powerful lights right in his face making him scream, I shook my head at the officer to let him know what a sorry lot I considered them.

I wasn't worried about my hidden gun, because I didn't realise what a crime they would consider it. I just thought that if they found the gun, I'd tell them they could keep it if they wanted to make a fuss about it. But Lydia was more realistic and worried that they would give us serious troubles if they found it where it was stored under our double bed. When one of them pulled at the sheet where she was still lying completely nude, she pretended to have a hysterical fit and screamed as only a woman can scream. The officer sitting in front of me was beginning to feel uneasy with a screaming baby and, now, with a screaming hysterical woman, and my almost making fun of the situation. He took out his whistle and blew a short blast which put an almost instantaneous halt to the search. All the men scrambled back into their boat and sped quickly away.

The next day I told the story at the embassy in a rather amused tone, but none of their personnel were at all amused. On the contrary, they looked quite alarmed and said, "You don't seem to realise how close you came to serious trouble. Just now, as we sit here talking, one of our countrymen is sitting in jail for three years for doing exactly what you did. He was found in the possession of an undeclared weapon. Had they found your gun, they would have handcuffed you right on the spot and taken you away immediately, letting your wife and child manage on their own for the few days it would take to deport them. Your boat would have been confiscated, and there would have been absolutely nothing we could have done to help you."

"But I never disembarked with the gun, and my ship is flying a foreign flag and is foreign territory to them," I protested.

"Your boat may be foreign, but you were in their port in their territory and asked admittance under false declaration, saying that you had no weapons. As far as they're concerned, you were smuggling in a firearm, and for that they have severe penalties."

I was so scared that when I returned onboard, I very nearly considered slipping the gun over the side, even though the danger, for the time being, was over. Coming from America and Europe, where the laws are much less strict and the police and courts are much more lenient, it takes time to realise the lack of freedom present in most countries in Asia.

Singapore proved disappointing in other ways, too. The money we expected from Monsieur S. had not arrived as promised and the visa to China seemed to be taking forever to be granted. After two weeks of running from office to office and spending more money than I could afford in telexes, I got tired of it all and hoisted sail for Hong Kong. I thought it would be safer to wait for both the money and the visa there, where we would have most of the South China Sea and its typhoons behind us. From Hong Kong, it was only a few days' sail across the strait to reach our goal—Taiwan, Republic of China.

We sailed out at noon, dodging the hundreds of boats and ships in that very crowded harbour. With great relief we passed the last one and got back into the open sea which, for all its dangers, seemed a friendlier and safer place to me and my family than the unfriendly city of Singapore. We now had the mysterious and exotic South China Sea to cross before reaching Hong Kong.

There are three routes for crossing the South China Sea from south to north: either along the mainland of Asia, which may have been the most interesting, but which now was impossible due to the political situation and local wars; the route going along Borneo and the westernmost part of the Philippines, which is called the Palawan Passage and is patrolled by the U.S. Navy, and therefore is the recommended route for protection from the many pirates who still infest the waters of Southeast Asia even today; and the route going right in the middle of the sea between the reefs lying on either side. This third route is not recommended because it's completely unprotected from both the pirates and the typhoons.

I chose to take this latter route between the reefs because it was the quickest; I had a hard time believing there could be pirates in the 20th century, and just hoped no typhoon would get too close to us.

During the first days of our voyage we had beautiful weather with a flat sea but enough wind to give us a good daily average of around 140 miles, which was all we could ask for. The ship is capable of taking us more than 200 miles in one 24-hour period, which may sound exhilarating, but we don't usually strive for such speed. In order to get that much speed, the sea invariably has to be quite rough, and the ride becomes uncomfortable and wet. At 140 miles we can still expect very comfortable conditions without water splashing on the deck. The ship slices her way through the water effortlessly, leaving us time to enjoy the sail, to fish, to prepare nice meals and to relax. That is sailing at its best and the way we prefer it, rather than trying to establish speed records.

While we'd had little luck with our fishing in the Atlantic and even less in the Mediterranean, since entering the Red Sea our fishing luck had changed completely. It was rare that we didn't get our daily fish for our dinner, which not only saved us money because we didn't have to use our canned food, but also was much better for our health. In addition we had the great pleasure of eating good food.

Our happiness was troubled only by our baby's developing a rapidly worsening infection in one eye which caused pus to run out of it. We were now far from hospitals or doctors and had no suitable medicine in our ship's pharmacy. In desperation we finally decided to try some old wives' tale remedies we remembered from childhood. I had heard that some drops from a lemon or lime would be a good disinfectant. Lydia had had experience with a clay and water poultice which, when laid directly on an infected sore, would heal it rapidly. We discussed the respective advantages of each method and finally decided to use them both. We first poured a few drops of lemon juice into the baby's eye, something he didn't at all appreciate, judging by his horrible wails. But the clay poultice we applied seemed to soothe him. We changed the clay every two hours, day and night, to prevent it from sticking to his skin and, much to my surprise, within 36 hours the eye was completely healed.

The weather started to deteriorate. Unfortunately for the sailor, good weather never lasts forever. The wind increased gradually while the sky clouded over so that I could no longer measure the sun with my sextant to find and correct our position. This was very unfortunate because we were approaching the Courcelles, those unlit low islets stretching far into the South China Sea. I would have to sail through them, trusting solely my deadreckoning, finding my way just by keeping track of my compass course and the miles covered.

Deadreckoning is an age-old system, but not a very accurate one, because it doesn't take into consideration the currents, drift of the boat, or compass errors other than those we think we know. Worst of all, one day's errors will compound the next day's, so if we have to content ourselves with using only deadreckoning over a long period, we can soon feel very insecure about our exact position.

It was just my bad luck that the sun and stars should be covered by clouds when I needed them most. My spirits sank even lower when I heard over the Hong Kong radio that they had alerted the population to take cover from Typhoon Ruby, which was coming their way down from the South China Sea, not far from where we were! Indeed, even without the radio announcement, it soon became obvious that we were going to suffer a tropical typhoon. The barometer was falling rapidly, menacing heavy clouds darkened the sky and the wind increased alarmingly. We were worried about all those reefs and islets, which would spell complete destruction and death should we be unable to avoid them.

Typhoons are tropical revolving storms, which travel along a fairly predictable path, yet are not always easy to avoid despite modern radio weather forecasts. Sailors try to minimise their danger by avoiding getting caught in the regions of strongest winds. Admittedly we can't outrun a tropical storm in our small vessels, which generally never go faster than six or seven knots: the storms can travel two or three times as fast. But we can try to steer as far as possible from its centre and from its "dangerous semi-circle."

We consider any tropical storm as having two distinct halves— one half blowing in the same direction as the path of the storm, the other half blowing against it. Thus, if we have a storm blowing at 65 knots around its centre and that centre itself travels at 20 knots along its path, a vessel in the one semi-circle will have winds of 65 knots plus 20 knots, or 85 knots. In the other half of the semi-circle, winds will be 65 knots, less 20 knots, or only 45 knots. This is the reason for naming the one semi-circle the "dangerous" semi-circle and the other the "safe" semi-circle. Of course, if the storm is a severe one, even the so-called "safe" semi-circle may be dangerous, but in all cases it will be less dangerous than the other one.

To determine where the centre of the typhoon was and in which direction it was headed, I stopped the boat for several hours so that my bearings and observations of the wind and its progress would be more accurate. To my great relief, I found we were not in the direct path of the storm. We could expect strong winds but not dangerous ones and, best of all, we could expect following winds for the greater part of the storm's passage. So instead of staying hove to, which would probably be the safest in any gale, I preferred to keep going, despite the proximity of the dangerous Courcelle reefs, or, perhaps, *because* of their proximity, in case the winds should later change for the worse. I still knew fairly accurately where I was from my last sun observation, and I could now use the present strong but favourable winds to make a quick passage through and get past them.

To be sure I steered a straight course safely away from the reefs on either side of the passage, I stood watch at the tiller all night while we boiled through the darkness, despite my reefed-down sails. The excitement of the fast sail prevented me from feeling tired until far into the following day. By that time, I knew that we were through all the reefs, which now lay safely behind us.

I balanced the sails and the tiller against the centreboard to keep us on a reasonably straight course further on towards Hong Kong, and fell asleep with a clear conscience while the ship maintained her wild speed on her own.

A few days later we knew we were approaching a big city by the steadily increasing number of planes, all headed for the same point in the still distant horizon. We knew it could only be Hong Kong, as there were no other big cities in that part of the world. We received further proof of approaching land when the beautiful blue of the ocean changed to the dirty brown colour so typical along coasts where a lot of heavy rains wash mud out to sea through their rivers. During the following night we were greeted by the powerful flashes of a lighthouse and many more lights as we got closer.

Normally these lights should be enough to safely guide anyone into the protection of a harbour but, unfortunately for us, we had not been able to get the proper charts because we had originally intended to sail directly to Taiwan from Singapore. We didn't even have the "pilot" book for that part of the world—the universal bible of the seaman. In fact, the only thing we had to guide us even this far was my old school atlas which showed Hong Kong as a tiny dot, but it had been enough to give us the approximate longitude and latitude.

With proper charts, all the blinking lighthouses we saw would be marked off and it would be an easy matter to find our way by following them. With no charts, the problem was entirely different. I saw the flashes, but then what? Should I steer to the right or the left? Between a pair, or on the outside of them? We had no choice but to wait for daylight when, aided by my binoculars, I would be better able to guess the proper channel to follow. I was very tired, so I hove to the vessel and we all went to sleep.

Feeling satisfied to be so close to our goal and relieved that the wind, although still blowing hard, had moderated considerably, we slept peacefully. In fact, we overslept. The next morning when I got on the deck, I was disappointed to see that we were no longer just in front of Hong Kong's lighthouses, but had drifted so far along the coast that I could barely see them through my glasses. Not only would we be delayed in entering port but, worst of all, we were now out of the territorial waters of friendly Hong Kong and into the forbidden waters of Red China!

Just as I realised the situation, I noticed two large junks in the distance, changing their course to steer straight towards us. I was a bit worried, as I had been warned not to enter those waters and that, if I did, I would be seized by their patrol boats and towed into port to be interrogated and probably held for weeks.

As they came closer, we were relieved to see that they were old fishing boats, crowded with grandmothers and children, so we presumed we had nothing to fear despite their very unfriendly faces. Suddenly, however, I was filled with apprehension when I saw Lydia about to come on deck with her camera. I firmly told her to leave the camera below, which rather angered her, thinking that my chronic pessimism would make her miss an exciting picture, but she left the camera below. As they came closer, I started to worry again. One of them was on either side so I could do nothing to get away.

They were sailing junks, decorated with beautiful if unintelligible Chinese scripts, but they had cut-down rigs and were really motor-sailors with huge diesel engines which were both noisy and poorly adjusted, judging by the black clouds coming out of their large exhaust pipes. On each boat a man stood, swinging a grapnel, which made me wonder what kind of fishing they did. They kept on coming closer until I was very upset about their poor seamanship and lack of manners in wanting to scrutinise us so closely. They then made frantic signs for me to lower my sails. I could hardly believe my eyes. Through their own poor judgment they had come dangerously close to us in a heavy swell and now wanted me to remedy it so *they* could get more searoom!

Even though I had gotten a full night's sleep the night before, I was still tired from several days of tricky navigation. Suddenly I lost all patience and blew into a fit of temper. I screamed back at them, telling them what I thought of them and their seamanship while waving them furiously away. They probably didn't understand one word of what I was saying in English, but the tone of my voice coupled with my arm waving left no doubt as to what I meant. In any case, it brought immediate response. As each boat sheared away from us, I noticed that the two men who had been swinging grapnels now laid them aside to handle the ropes adjusting their sails. They followed us for a short distance and then suddenly changed course for their mainland while we again entered Hong Kong waters.

We remained a bit puzzled by the incident until the next day, when we got a full explanation. Those two junks were indeed fishing boats, but they were also coast guard patrol vessels. The thrifty Chinese consider it a waste to let a patrol boat idle back and forth while they could be paying for themselves by fishing and watching their coast at the same time. When they handled their grapnels and ordered me to lower my sails, they had intended to hook into our rigging and moor themselves tightly to us, one on each side, and escort us into port for interrogation since we had illegally entered their waters.

Needless to say, in that heavy swell left over from the passage of the typhoon, they would have, in all probability, damaged and crushed our fragile yacht beyond hopes of repair. We had no way of knowing how long we could have been held in their jails before being released. In fact, a year later, I went to see and survey one such yacht which had about 75 percent of its frame cracked or broken in Red Chinese waters before being allowed to sail on in a nearly sinking condition. We were also told about others held for weeks and even months before being released.

So how did we get away so easily? Perhaps the typical all-obedient Chinese who is so respectful toward authorities could only have seen my outburst of anger and lack of respect towards them as justified if I had a special permit of which they were not aware. They probably never suspected that I didn't realise they were law-enforcement patrol vessels.

Thinking back, I was scared, but for now, as we sailed into the beautiful waters of Hong Kong, we just felt happy at the thoughts of soon arriving successfully and safely to anchor in a new and exciting part of the world. As we came closer, a sailboat approached us and, to our surprise, we recognised our good friend Guillaume. He shouted to us in delight, having recognised our boat from a distance.

"How glad we are to see you, Peter. We expected you, but we were worried about Ruby. Come and follow us. We'll show you the way to a good mooring inside the yacht club basin." As he said so, he turned around and guided us in.

To his close friends, Guillaume was just "Guillaume," but in business and in his official life he was the Lord of Montravel, an important businessman who had to content himself with sailing his sailboat on short weekend trips, dreaming and envying sailors like me who, although poor, had the freedom to sail away to distant horizons. As soon as he had us securely moored to the buoys which he'd already arranged for us, he said he hoped that we didn't object to having him come to dinner on our boat, quickly adding that he, of course, would provide the dinner. He wanted to enjoy the atmosphere of a real long-distance seagoing boat. Naturally we were only too glad to have him onboard, especially seeing the wonderful dinner and all the extra food he brought after a quick trip ashore.

It was exciting to meet him again and to talk about the good old days in France. It was late night before he went home to his fancy apartment where he lived close to his shipping business. In addition to being a good friend, he proved invaluable, giving us the use of his office telex for free, which saved me a lot of money communicating with the authorities, as well as with my future employers in the Republic of China. I needed to obtain permission to enter their territorial waters, which were normally closed to all pleasure boats as well as to all sailing vessels.

To obtain a simple 30-day tourist visa to land by plane would have been easy enough, but to obtain a more permanent visa to be permitted to work was an entirely more complex matter. To enter with my boat further complicated things. They even wanted, among many other documents, photographs of my boat under sail "so as to avoid a regrettable error," which we were to realise the significance of later on.

Hong Kong is a sharp contrast to Singapore, which tries to be its equal. But Hong Kong is still a British colony and, apparently, proud to be so, yet it is indisputably China—a mixture of Asia and the western world, which was very pleasant. Here the over-disciplined Chinese spirit was softened by the more easy-going and courteous British, letting us feel relaxed and free—quite a different spirit and atmosphere from the police state of Singapore, where I had felt so ill at ease. For example, the next day after the euphoria of arriving safely and finding my old friend Guilluame again, I suddenly realised that I had forgotten all about the entry formalities, that all-important procedure. They gently reproached me at the yacht club, saying that I should have waited for the authorities to clear me in the reserved quarantine anchorage before even coming to there. But when I explained that I didn't have the sailing instructions and didn't know, the secretary courteously offered to drive me to the administration building himself to try and straighten out matters. This was all done in a few minutes with both a smile and a simple admonishment "not to forget the next time to do it the prescribed way and wait at the quarantine anchorage."

I know of a good many countries that not only would have fined me heavily but also would have confiscated my ship and thrown me and my crew in jail for the "crime" of ignoring their laws. This shows the importance of knowing the laws of each country before searching to profit from the "freedom of the sea," a freedom which is getting more and more elusive as all too many countries are tightening up on their laws and regulations.

Hong Kong, everybody knows, is a shopper's paradise with everything available at much lower prices than almost anywhere else.

Sometimes the prices are even lower than in the product's country of origin, which sounds impossible but is easy to explain. For example, how could we buy a Japanese camera cheaper in Hong Kong than in Japan? What about the cost of transport and duty? Hong Kong is a free port and a real one. Not one cent is charged by the government in duty or taxes. As for the transport expenses, compared with the cost of the camera it's a negligible amount. But Hong Kong merchants have become so competitive because they can content themselves with a smaller margin of profit, due partly to lower wages, but mainly to the greater volume advantage they have over their competitors. They can make good profits despite the low prices charged to their customers, amply demonstrated by the large number of Rolls Royces being driven in the streets of that little country.

In fact, Hong Kong has more Rolls Royces per square mile than any other country in the world. Here if a hotel guest asks a porter to bring his car from the parking lot, he can't just describe it as the Rolls Royce or as the black or white one or whatever colour it may be: he would have to give the porter the license plate number if he wants to make sure to get the right one!

While we waited for our visas, as well as the money from Monsieur S., we fully enjoyed this exciting little country made up of a very successful mixture of east and west.

When our promised money finally did arrive, we couldn't resist the temptation to buy some extra photo equipment, partly for our own pleasure and partly for my work for Monsieur S., who required regular photos with close-ups and details of the building of the boats so he could control their progress. I bought a complete darkroom setup to develop and enlarge my black and white pictures. I also bought a macro lens for taking closeups and the bellows and necessary equipment to make duplicates of my colour slides, all at prices far below those in either Europe or the States.

At Any Cost

When our visas had been granted and what shopping we could afford was done, we had no further excuse to linger in this pleasant little country. Once again we tackled the South China Sea, but this time just for the short crossing to Taiwan, a crossing we hoped to do in just a few days. We left with a good weather report, but already the next morning, the weather had deteriorated and, again, the Hong Kong radio warned the population to take cover from a new typhoon which had been given the name "Violet." I was rather angered at the weather forecaster, who only 24 hours previously had promised good weather and now was alerting the population. Indeed the wind was increasing at an alarming rate.

Why hadn't they foreseen the typhoon a bit earlier? Only later, after I had seen conditions in Southeast Asia, did I understand the reason. Tropical storms in Southeast Asia are far more numerous than in any other region of the globe. They are so numerous that, if the radio warned against every one of them, the population would be under constant alert most of the year! (Only two months of the year are considered free from typhoon danger and even then it's not 100-percent safe.) So what the authorities have to do is wait, hoping the typhoon will go somewhere else. They give the official alert only when it becomes obvious that the typhoon is going to hit.

So here I was in a new typhoon in rapidly increasing winds, too far from the coast to seek refuge. I would just have to battle it out again. At least we had searoom and were in no danger of being blown ashore on a reef. The centre was to pass fairly close to us this time, but we were fortunately in the "safe" semi-circle again. Maximum winds were 50 knots, which is bad enough, but not overly dangerous for a good boat properly manned and with sufficient searoom.

# 13

# Taiwan, Republic of China

*I*t took us much longer to reach the waters of Taiwan than we had expected. The typhoon had forced us to heave-to and stop the boat for a good while, yet it seemed that we were expected. As soon as we reached the outer limits of the territorial waters, we were awed by the sinister sight of a submarine emerging less than 50 yards from us. At that moment we remembered how the consulate had insisted we give them a photo of our boat under sail before issuing us a visa giving us permission to enter their territorial waters. We now understood what they'd meant when they said the photo was necessary to "avoid the risk of a regrettable incident!"

The submarine circled us slowly, pitching and rolling in the huge swell left in the wake of Typhoon Violet. I'd never realised that a big submarine would suffer such violent motion when cruising at the surface. While I didn't welcome the sight of the sub itself, I felt sorry for the men inside her. Our sailboat had a much sweeter motion, although no boat could really be comfortable in such a huge swell. They kept circling us until two small navy craft came towards us and took position, one on each quarter, to escort us to port. The submarine then submerged and disappeared from sight. Had it been waiting for us or had it just happened to cross our path while on routine surveillance? I'll probably never know.

The two escort vessels were to cause us a lot of inconvenience. We had to beat against the wind, which was blowing straight from our destination, forcing us to steer a zigzag course. This seemed incomprehensible to the power boat crews, who stayed too close to us and hindered our manoeuvres. My shouting and arm waving was to no avail. Little by little we approached the harbour entrance where we were met by a strong, nauseating odour.

Inside the port, we found the cause of that smell—the harbour served as the town's sewer system! In addition to the awful stench, the air pollution was so bad that we felt we were choking. Most of all we just wanted to turn around and steer back to sea, but we were absolutely broke, having spent the last of our money in Hong Kong. We had no choice but to stay. Our contract called for a six-month stay but we thought, under these circumstances, we would have a good excuse to stay only a couple of months—just long enough to get some money and leave. Little did we know then that 21 long months were to elapse before we would be free to sail again.

Taiwan is a police state where practically everything that doesn't contribute to the country's benefit is forbidden. At least that's the feeling we got. All pleasure sailing is forbidden, due partly to the fact the government considers it a waste of money and energy which could be better spent strengthening the country's industry, and partly so that the authorities can more easily control the borders against illegal emigration.

But the general outlawing of yachts didn't prevent the Taiwanese from building thousands of yachts for export—even though they didn't have the slightest understanding of what's expected of a yacht, since none of them sail. They were building yachts for the simple reason that they could bring valuable foreign currency to the country. Had it been more advantageous to build bathtubs, pianos or office chairs, they would immediately have converted their factories to do just that.

All these factories depend on foreign technicians to show them how to produce the products. Customers should protect themselves by hiring their own inspectors to insure against bad workmanship, such as, for example, having screws knocked in with a hammer instead of driven in by a screwdriver!

In Taiwan, or the Republic of China, as the natives call it, everything is very different from what we are used to. When I was hired in France to watch the construction of these boats, I assumed that I would be free during the weekends, or at least, free on Sundays. But even if my employers were on the other side of the world and couldn't control my working hours, I was soon to be a slave to Chinese custom. How could I expect to be free on Sundays when the yards worked full-time? I had to watch for so many mistakes which could easily be controlled if I were on the spot, but which would be nearly impossible to detect later on.

It was easy to ensure that screws would be driven in properly with a screwdriver if I watched the workers, but how was I to prove that the job had been improperly done with a hammer once they were in place? It was easy to ensure that they put the proper amount of hardener in the fiberglass if I watched them, but if they had added extra hardener to the mixture to save time when I wasn't there, I wouldn't be able to tell the difference—although the yacht's owners would know after a few years when it started cracking.

Whenever a critical phase of the construction was going on, I had to be there whether it was Sunday or not. For example, when they were hand-laying the fiberglass over the mold, I could make sure they didn't leave any air bubbles, no matter how much time it took to smooth them out. If I wasn't there, they could save a lot of time by leaving the air bubbles in and going on to the next layer, knowing they'd be impossible to spot once the job was finished. They always gave a "free" first coat of white gelcoat, which effectively hid all defects.

Of course, by tapping carefully over the whole hull, inch by inch, I could still detect any voids, but I'd then get into an endless argument with the yard about whether or not those hidden air bubbles warranted all the extra work to break them up and refill the voids. Being on the spot and making sure the work was done right the first time forced me to have to work much longer hours than I had anticipated. I often worked seven days a week and sometimes late at night, because they had two shifts working.

Fortunately for me, the Chinese don't work day and night seven days a week. They are Buddhists and don't follow our holidays, but they have their own. I would take a day off when they did, but I had to make sure they let me know in advance, since their calendar works on a different system from ours. Each 1st and 14th of their month coincides with the new and full moon, which means that some years have 13 months to catch up to the shorter months. This explains why the Chinese New Year doesn't often coincide with ours.

In any case, I was feeling lost.

Despite the very low prices the yards in Taiwan were charging, compared to what those same boats would have cost in Europe or the States, both Claude G. and the two owners expected perfect work-manship. Our first difficulties began when we discovered many faults and discrepancies in Claude's drawings. This probably could have been anticipated since he worked alone and had no one to double-check his drawings, as would have been the case in any large drawing office. For me, it became an additional headache.

Many times I was able to spot the error and get the various plans to coincide, but all too often, unsure of what Claude's intentions were, I had to telex him and wait for an answer. Work had to either stop or be switched to something else until we got the answer. After a while, the yard complained about the lost time and I had to make the decisions myself, trying to read the designer's mind. Generally it all worked out, but one time Claude's view was not the same as mine and I had to suffer endless reproaches until I got mad and stood up to him. An inspector's job is an ungrateful one. No one will ever see all the mistakes he avoided, while the one fault that slips by will stand out like a sore thumb forever for everyone to see.

I said that if they wanted a Rolls Royce, they should have gone to England, not Taiwan—and then pay the price! I told them it was impossible for me or any inspector to get perfect work from workers who had never aimed at perfection. I could only claim that, without me, the work would have been worse. But not everyone was as critical as my employers were. Monsieur S. took the boat that cost him less than $100,000 U.S. and resold it two years later on the French Riviera as a second-hand boat for $200,000 U.S.!

Both 50-footers were shipped over to France on a freighter. One sailed the Mediterranean Sea before being sold; the other sailed to the West Indies where it was used as a charter boat for several years that I know of. Then I lost trace of it.

As for the 80-footer, Monsieur S. hired a professional crew who sailed the boat to the West Indies via Japan and the Panama Canal. But the boat didn't prove successful as a charter boat. The local French authorities inflicted so many regulations and taxes that arguments between them and the ship's owner finally led to the ship's seizure. I then lost trace of the ship until last week, as I write this, when I happened to spot her in Key West, Florida, tied to a dock and converted to a floating bar! As for her nine sister ships, they have never been built—and probably never will.

My job as an inspector made me feel like some kind of policeman and I didn't like it. But in less than six months I became the technical consultant for one of the Chinese yards, doubling my salary and making our stay in Taiwan more worthwhile. At the same time, I didn't violate my contract with my French employers, since they were the first ones to propose that I take an extra job and thus make their tight wages more justified.

In fact, we now had not just two salaries, but three. Thanks to Lydia's extraordinary ability to learn foreign languages, the Chinese yard officials noticed that she was speaking their language better than any of them spoke English, so she was hired as our interpreter and my secretary. When the first six months had elapsed, I had honoured my original contract and was free to leave, but we decided to stay on. The boats were far from ready and, because of the money we were making, we were willing to stay for many more months.

Yet even those first six months should have been more than enough, considering the unhealthy living conditions in that country. Water had to be boiled a minimum of 20 minutes to be fit to drink, and the air was so polluted we could hardly breathe without constantly clearing our throats. The stink of the town's sewer was everywhere. We were in Kaohsiung, which, though it was a big, rich town, had no proper sewers. All the water from the houses just ran down into the trench between the street and sidewalk. The ditches were more or less covered by flat stones to prevent people from falling into them, but in no case were they airtight. The foul odors invaded the streets and, in fact, the whole town. And these horrible trenches drained into the harbour!

I once talked with a doctor about the unsanitary conditions and he admitted it was a health hazard. But he concluded by saying that it was a problem which would have to be dealt with after their economy became strong enough and "stabilised."

We had never intended to move out of the boat, which was our real home, but were forced to move ashore because of the unbearable stench in the harbour. We rented an apartment on the top floor in one of the better districts, where the sea breeze reduced the stink.

Our experience in Taiwan was not all negative. For example, the food was absolutely first class, whether we bought it at the market or dined in a restaurant. And there were plenty of restaurants—from the fanciest, capable of rivaling the most luxurious ones in New York, London or Paris—to the most modest ones, the tricycles carrying their own traveling kitchens in a box between the two front wheels. At the slightest sign of a potential customer, the rider would stop, unfold a wooden leaf along one side of the box to make a narrow table, and put out a few stools.

These makeshift restaurants were often operated by just one tiny Chinese woman. She would pedal that heavy contraption with apparent ease, while at the same time tending her fire and making sure everything was cooking right and keeping an eye out for traffic and possible customers. She would serve, take the money in, wash up and get back in the saddle to look for new customers. We often made use of these traveling restaurants which were not only ridiculously cheap (about 30 cents U.S. for a full meal) but also excellent.

Surprisingly enough to us, the meals served by either class of Chinese restaurant were nothing like those which have become so common in the western world. They must have been invented by immigrating Chinese to please westerners' tastes at a minimum of expense and labour for them. In fact, in the Republic of China, chop suey and chow mein were completely unheard of, despite the fact that most of us would imagine those dishes to be the most typical Chinese food. But we didn't lose out in China. All the dishes were delicious, although most of them required long preparation and a lot of work by the cook. The western versions of these dishes are simpler and easier to make and the "white devils" didn't know any better.

The food was first class, the people were friendly and always polite, our salaries were good and life was very cheap, so why did we dislike the place so much? It wasn't just the poor hygiene, especially after we moved to the top floor. Perhaps one reason was that we felt too much like foreigners and got tired of being stared at wherever we went. It was nice, of course, that they admired Lydia's long, blonde hair, but less so when they openly laughed at my big feet, which were enormous by their standards. Also my height never failed to raise roars of laughter when I banged my head in their buses, which had been built for people their size. Their laughter was good natured, but nevertheless tiring after a while.

Lydia learned Mandarin, their language, in just a few months, and could speak it even over the telephone, something I still marvel at, as I was never able to learn a single word of that strange and weird language. So, while she had no language barrier, I suffered from it greatly, even having her as my private interpreter. In addition, I was starting to feel guilty about having subjected our little boy to such unhealthy conditions as those of Kaohsiung, where the child mortality rate was high.

In addition, I was beginning to worry about the boat as we were approaching a new typhoon season. I hadn't forgotten the previous year's Saorama, a typhoon of force 16 on the Beaufort scale, which ran through town and uprooted a metallic hangar, tearing it from its foundation. The metal piece catapulted through the air and landed on top of my boat, inflicting damage which took months to repair.

As March approached, bringing with it the threat of a new typhoon season, I made up my mind and gave my notice. They offered me even higher wages and, as a bonus, offered to finish the work on my boat free of charge. They even offered to build a new mast for my schooner rig. (I was rigging the boat over, now that one of my yawl's masts had been broken during that typhoon.)

But enough is enough. Nothing could tempt me to stay any longer than the minimum length of time it would take to get the contracted boats sufficiently finished so that the other yard workers could manage to complete them without my help.

My own boat was put back in the water, where I completed the bare minimum to make her seaworthy. Not wanting to take the time to make that new mast, I contented myself with a jury rig set on the one mast I still had from the yawl rig. On the 10th of April, 1978, we at long last set sail out of that port. On the way we were boarded no less than three times by patrol boats wanting to make sure we weren't leaving illegally—first by a military boat, then by the Chinese customs, and finally by the harbour police. They each searched the boat from one end to the other, carefully checking all our papers. Afterwards they escorted us to a narrow exit channel, where they instructed the crew in the armed towers on either side of the channel to let us pass.

Finally we cruised into the open sea, the sewer-brown waters little by little changing to the clear blue I like so much. At the same time, we gradually sailed free of the brown smog in which we had lived for nearly two years. I felt then that this was the happiest day of my life, as we sailed back to freedom and away from a country where no stranger can ever feel at home.

But my happiness was mixed with guilt when I saw how Thomas, not two years old, marveled at the simple sight of seagulls flying around us. I realised that it was the first time in his life that he was seeing any type of birds; no birds of any kind were able to survive in Kaohsiung! Thomas had never known a blue sky, but only the smog of that big town, which was often so dense we were able to see only a few hundred yards, if that. Lydia and I vowed never again to expose ourselves or our child to such unhealthy and depressing conditions. Life is too precious to be valued in money.

# 14

# Towards the Philippines

We hoisted sail from Taiwan with only one thing in mind—to get away from China and get back to sea and to freedom. As unbelievable as it may sound, we hadn't decided where to sail exactly. Before it had seemed unimportant, but now we had to make up our minds about where to set course.

We were tempted by Hong Kong, which we'd both liked, and which we'd be able to really enjoy now with our saved-up money. We could also sail north towards Japan and visit a country which many claim is fascinating. But we felt that both countries were too Asian and we wanted a change from China. Besides, the northern winter would soon make itself felt if we headed north, so our choice seemed obvious—we steered south towards the tropics and towards the Philippines.

As we looked at the charts, we became more and more enthusiastic at the thought of sailing to the Philippines, with its hundreds of anchorages among the myriads of islands all lying within the tropical belt which comprised the Philippines.

I also rejoiced at the thought of no longer having to suffer from a language barrier. English is the universal language of the Philippines, which serves as an aid not only for the English-speaking foreigner but also for the inhabitants to understand one another. They come from different islands and regions in the Philippines and all have their own dialects. Lydia had been able to learn Mandarin and she'd been an invaluable help to me, but nevertheless, it would feel wonderful to be able to understand and talk directly to people again.

Early the next morning we were safely clear from land and Chinese territorial waters. We turned left and set the course towards Manila. Note that I say "towards" and never "to," following the practice of the old sailing ship skippers, who never wanted to risk annoying the weather gods by being too presumptuous and taking for granted that they'd arrive regardless of what the gods had in mind. They felt safer in being humble, indicating "towards" and hoping that the gods wouldn't put any hindrance in their way. Also, to a certain extent, a skipper would not lose face should he not arrive at his goal on the first try! A sailing ship today, just as then, doesn't run on rails, and, although some claim that the sea is safer than the road, I know that a sailor's life is still a very chancy one.

The trip started well enough with light airs and a fairly good response from the boat despite its jury rig. In fact, even though I had no type of self-steering device, I still got it to self-steer and keep a course well enough by adjusting the sails and the centreboard. So, despite the boat's lack of a main mast, we didn't have to sit and steer, which is always tiring when you're short-handed.

Climate is a capricious phenomenon and one very subject to location. In some regions you can travel for miles and miles without noticing much difference in temperature. In other places, traveling just a short distance may mean a change to a radically different climate. That's the way it was between China and the Philippines. Just a few days' sail or a few hundred miles changed the climate from the temperate climate of Taiwan to real tropical weather. As we came closer to the Philippines, we noted the change with delight, gradually stripping more and more until we were practically in the nude again.

One night we were nearly becalmed under a bright moon, but were nevertheless rolling and pitching miserably in a heavy sea, which was still running high after several days of strong winds. We heard the distant roar of a powerful engine gradually getting closer to us, but could see no lights. The roar came closer and closer until finally we could discern the contour of a vessel in the moonlight. To my dismay it kept on coming towards us, then slowed down to adjust to our very slow speed. It stayed just a few feet away, a man onboard shouting something over to us which we couldn't understand. We felt ill at ease in such heavy seas. If our two bouncing ships were to hit each other, they could be very seriously damaged—ours certainly much more than theirs. A delicately built yacht is no match for most of the heavily built commercial steel ships.

What did they want, anyway? Were they the Coast Guard wanting to check our papers? Were they fishermen or some small commercial vessel wanting to do some trading or begging? Were they pirates or just some idle boat wanting company? And why were they navigating with no lights—which is forbidden by international law and extremely dangerous?

Our questions were answered once they got closer to us and handed over a net attached to a long pole. I made out the shape of a fish in the net and, through a powerful loudspeaker, we could finally make out the words "cigarettes" and "whiskey." So that was it. They were fishermen wanting to trade a fish for either cigarettes or whiskey or both! It just infuriates me that people can become so dependent on cigarettes and alcohol that they don't hesitate to endanger property and even lives in order to replenish their supply! In any case they were out of luck, since we neither drank nor smoked, never carried cigarettes or alcohol onboard and had no difficulty catching our own fish. I lost no time in getting rid of our dangerous neighbour as quickly as possible by shouting back negatively. They instantly responded with a full throttle and their wheel hard over. Although this made them shear away from us, their unnecessarily brutal manoeuvre swung their stern within inches of my boat. And I mean it literally—the sharp corner of their square stern swept within inches of our topsides, pushed by hundreds of horsepower in a turmoil of churning water. Had they hit us they would have, in all probability, broken a huge hole in our thin, one-inch wooden planking and sunk us. And this was all so unnecessary, caused by the frustration of not getting any cigarettes or alcohol from us!

No actual harm had been done, however, so our nerves soon calmed down and we concentrated on our navigation, expecting to arrive in Manila the next day. But by then the sky had covered up with ugly, dark clouds, which should have forewarned us of the possibility of a tropical storm. But the barometer remained steady and the radio didn't announce any storms in the region. Besides, the typhoon season hadn't started yet, so we weren't too worried, especially since we expected to be safely in port soon. But we underestimated the possibilities of troubles in these waters. Indeed, reading about it later, we were to learn that although most typhoons develop during July, August, September and October, only February and March are entirely safe. It was now the latter part of April.

As we approached Manila Bay, we saw in the distance an obnoxious and thick black cloud, forming above the bay and coming rapidly toward us. At the same time the barometer suddenly dropped in spectacular fashion. Only then did the radio make an announcement about the storm. It fact, it had already been given a name and was called "Atang." The name began with an A, the first letter of the alphabet, signifying that it was the first typhoon of the year.

The wind hit us as we became engulfed in the cloud. It had turned and was blowing straight against us, disintegrating all hopes of reaching the peace of the harbour. I had to douse everything in the very fierce wind but, in order to have a chance to manoeuvre the ship, I rehoisted my storm trysail. It was a very sturdy sail made of oversize flax and able to stand nearly any force wind. I could have opted for bare poles, but that would mean I would have been left drifting to the caprices of the the wind. If the storm should turn again, we could be thrown upon the shore and wrecked. By keeping some canvas, I had a good chance of remaining in control of my boat enough to be able to steer clear of the coast.

As it was, under short sail we were able to let the ship drift parallel to the coast but, unfortunately, only in a northerly direction—which was back to where we'd come from. This would normally be rather discouraging, but under the conditions we were thankful for staying in control of the situation while remaining relatively safe in hurricane force winds. To say we were happy or even comfortable would have been a great overstatement. We were scared and very uncomfortable as we were bounced violently by the waves which had become enormous in a surprisingly short period of time. When we feared we'd reached the ultimate conditions any seaman could stand, our conditions stabilised. Fortunately the wind direction remained steady, so the boat continued to  drift at a safe distance from shore.

The three of us had lain in our bunks under closed hatches and waited for the storm to abate. It had taken about 12 hours for the storm to reach its full strength from the moment that first black cloud hit us. We were in hurricane strength winds for another 12 hours when, to our relief, the wind started to soften little by little until, about 36 hours after it started, it was nearly back to its normal strength.

But the seas continued to be very high, so life onboard remained rather uncomfortable. At least we could put our normal sails up again and gain full control over our ship and lay the course in a direction that suited us, not one dictated by a storm.

We could steer our course, but, due to the storm, had drifted so far north that we were now much closer to the little town of San Fernando (which we'd passed several days before on our way to Manila) than we were to Manila. We were very tired. After discussing our options we decided that, after all, we had no urgent business in Manila and we were just searching for a nice, peaceful and pleasant place. For all we knew, San Fernando might be just as nice as Manila, and in fact even nicer, so why not go there? Who knows, perhaps it would be a good place for building the new mast. Thus we arrived at the little town of San Fernando though we'd had no intention of ever sailing there at all.

# 15

# San Fernando, Manila & Iloilo

The town and harbour of San Fernando were in the bottom of a long, fjord-like bay and were very beautiful. But as I waited for immigrations officials to see our yellow quarantine flag asking permission to enter their country, I noticed that the bay was completely open to the north. We would have no protection should a gale spring up from that direction. Of course, as Lydia pointed out, why let the possibility of future troubles spoil the present? And the present was pleasant enough. We were in beautiful surroundings in a new and exciting country.

The authorities soon arrived in the harbour launch and were courteous and efficient, but insisted we tie up against the pier, something I always dislike doing because it doesn't feel safe. Should the wind start blowing, I feared being bashed against the pier. Tying up to a public pier also creates a lack of privacy, especially in poor countries where a good part of the population seems to be idle with nothing better to do than sit on the dock, if not on our rail, and watch every move we make with unashamed, staring eyes. Further, the lines tying us to shore could allow cockroaches and rats a means to get aboard. In this case, with the harbour open towards the north, I doubly disliked the idea of not swinging free to my own anchor or to a mooring buoy which should be strong and reliable enough.

The harbourmaster laughed off my fears, saying that in the 20 years he had been stationed in the harbour the wind had *never* blown from that quarter. To settle the issue he told two of his sailors to lift up my anchor and pull me over to the dock, disregarding my weak protests. I was tired, and figured he must know his part of the world better than I, but I still wanted to know about the typhoon.

"What about Typhoon Atang? Couldn't that still send a north wind in here?"

"Don't worry about that," he said. "The radio has just announced that it has passed us well towards the northwest and is going to die soon in the South China Sea. So don't worry about anything now. Just enjoy your stay here and have a good night's sleep."

There were two other yachts on that same dock, and on the other side they were loading a tramp steamer with cement bags. It all looked peaceful enough, but while preparing dinner, I thought the ground swell, which had been there since our arrival, seemed to be increasing gradually, pulling alternately on our stern and on our bow warps. We'd intended to go to bed early after dinner, but I worried in earnest as the swell was getting stronger and sometimes made the boat jerk on its lines. Suddenly one of the steamer's heavy wire ropes broke with a sound like a gunshot, and I made up my mind. Regardless of the harbourmaster's assurances, I wasn't going to spend the night tied to that dock. If the radio said Atang was dying out far from us, I wouldn't disbelieve them, but I felt sure there was something wrong and I wasn't going to wait until it was too late to find a safer place.

I rushed over to the harbourmaster's office and was told he'd gone home because it was after office hours. I went to his home and told him that I wasn't going to stay along his dock. He could give me a secure mooring to swing to at whatever place he liked, as long as I found it safe, or else I would choose an anchor spot myself and swing to my own anchors.

"But I told you you're safe at my dock," he insisted.

"Famous last words," I replied, trying to joke it off, and then carried on. "I'm not trying to say that you're wrong. I just know that

I'll worry so much about it that I won't be able to sleep. So, for the sake of giving me a good night's sleep, I hope you can give me one of those moorings for the night," I said, pointing at a huge steamship mooring buoy. I felt it would easily hold my boat no matter what might come, even taking into account that its chain was probably quite rusty.

"You're being difficult, but if it makes you happy, you may use that buoy tonight, and even for another 24 hours," he conceded. "I don't expect any ships until then."

Greatly relieved, I lost no time in warping myself over to that big buoy and made fast to it with a double nylon line, 1-1/4 inches in diameter. Then I went to bed and immediately fell asleep.

But I didn't sleep for long. Far from dying out in the South China Sea as the radio had predicted, Atang changed its course nearly 180 degrees and came charging back towards land, where it hit the north coast where we were. The wind then blew straight into the harbour, precisely from the north, where we were completely unprotected. The fierce wind soon blew the sea into a turmoil with such incredible force that I knew I would have no control over our boat should the mooring fail us. I had to trust the buoy. It was laid out for steamships weighing many, many times our weight, but I knew the nylon lines were being subjected to enormous force and were very susceptible to chafe. Should they part, we'd be thrown onto land in a matter of seconds, our yacht broken to pieces.

In the fury of the wind, it was entirely impossible to walk forward to check my lines, but I managed to get there by crawling flat on deck and finding solid points to hold onto so I wouldn't be blown overboard. Once there, I was glad to see that the chafing gear I had put on as a precautionary measure seemed to be up to the task. But I wondered how the two yachts along the pier were faring and felt glad to be on that big buoy where my ship was free to swing unhindered in the wind and the waves.

In the dark and the blinding rain I could see nothing, but next morning when the wind stopped, I was surprised to see the pier was empty. Only later when I was able to go ashore again did I learn the story. The yachts hadn't left, they'd just been bashed against the pier until they both sank and now lay at the bottom, twisted, hopeless wrecks. The steamship, after breaking eight more of its steel hawsers, had been ordered to leave at 2 a.m. by the harbourmaster, before it would demolish his pier.

On shore, Atang had left a trail of desolation and destruction in its path. It had been the worst typhoon in years.

Once again I congratulated myself for being what many people might call a hopeless pessimist. I feel that my pessimism saved me yet again and it's the only reason I'm still here and still have my boat, while so many of my more optimistic friends have lost their boats, if not also their lives.

On the morning I prepared to leave the buoy as promised to the harbourmaster, he happened to be on the pier watching me as he stood over the spot where the two wrecks lay. Their masts stuck up above the water and he looked embarrassed. Another man might have felt justified in making some sarcastic remark, but seeing him so unhappy made me feel genuinely sorry for him, even though normally I never cared much for officials and their restrictive world. I just told him with a friendly smile that I was leaving the steamship buoy to give him room for the expected ship as promised and asked him where I could have permission to anchor.

With a rather sad smile he replied, "I trust you'll be able to find the best place without my help, so just suit yourself and anchor anywhere you think best."

I was glad to have saved my boat, but I wish I could have done it without having him lose face, as I knew how awful he must have felt about the two wrecked boats, especially when my boat proved that the accident could easily have been avoided.

Later, after we anchored, we went ashore. Our first visit was to the harbourmaster's home to pay him a friendly visit. We wanted to show him that we held no grudge, but rather sympathised with him. I said that a seaman's job wasn't easy and the radio couldn't be trusted because it sometimes gave completely inaccurate weather information. It felt good to see his face light up. He asked us to sit down and served us soft drinks. Each day thereafter we went ashore and paid a visit to either his office or his home and he became a good friend. We took great pleasure in listening to him tell us about his country, which we were able to better understand thanks to him.

San Fernando was pleasant, but it soon became apparent that it wouldn't be a handy place to build our new mast. Everybody recommended that we go to Manila for that purpose. We said goodbye to the harbourmaster, who seemed genuinely sorry to see us leave and spontaneously offered us a basket full of fruit he'd picked from his own garden. He made it clear that this was a present and he wanted nothing in exchange. We hoisted sail and were on our way towards Manila, hoping we would have more luck this time in reaching that fabulous-sounding city.

We arrived there a few days later and had the agreeable surprise of being hailed from a small but beautiful cutter. The owners, Lin and Larry Pardey, were completely unknown to us at that time, although we soon realised that they were quite well known in the States by readers of the yachting press.

"Hello, Peter," they hailed me. "Glad to see you in this part of the world."

"Do we know each other?" I asked, hesitantly and a bit embarrassed, as I always am when I don't recognise someone I should.

"No," they answered with a smile. "You don't know us, but we know you through your book, *Sea Gypsy*. In fact, it's because of you that we didn't install an engine in our boat. We thought that if you were able to sail around the world in your old *Dorothea* with no motor, we should be able to do the same."

"I'm very flattered and also a bit awed that my book should have influenced you so strongly, but how come you recognised me in an entirely different boat?" I asked.

"Because we still don't know of anyone but you or us who would come in under sail alone in a crowded place like this."

We had a good laugh at that one. It was to be the beginning of a long friendship. They even dedicated one of their books, "To Peter Tangvald, a Self-Sufficient Sailor," which would have flattered even the best of sailors.

Years later we were to get into a heated argument about the question of guns. I was to tell them they'd had more luck, perhaps, than they'd deserved, going through notoriously dangerous areas without any mishaps. They felt sure that people were all good everywhere if we just keep on smiling. By that time, having suffered two terrifying experiences, I knew better and strongly felt that sailing unarmed leaves one a sitting duck for the first criminals that cross one's path, and shows a total lack of responsibility towards ourselves and those who put their trust in us onboard.

But in Manila, the question did not arise as until then, I, too, had sailed unscathed for years.

It was nice to make friends in Manila but, except for that pleasure, the town proved a disappointment to us. It was dirty and noisy, even if not quite as bad as Kohsiung had been. But it was still far too dirty to seduce us with its tropical charms. It was a big city and we had to resort to taxis, a means of transportation I hate, especially in a city like Manila, where we got cheated by everyone. Although we took taxis on several consecutive days to the same place, we were never charged the same amount twice. When we questioned the charges, each of the taxi drivers claimed to be new to the city and "perhaps didn't know the shortest route," so we paid, but we resented the whole city more and more. It seemed no matter where we went, whether to the market, a restaurant or the dentist, the general attitude seemed to be to empty strangers' pockets as quickly as possible.

The local newspaper ran an article about our cruising in Asia with a small boy who'd spent the first two years of his life in the Republic of China, and reported we were now having a holiday in their country. The Norwegian ambassador, himself a sailing fan, read the article, noted that I was born in Norway, and kindly invited us to the upcoming 17th of May celebration at the Embassy—the equivalent of the U.S. 4th of July. I hadn't forgotten how to speak Norwegian, so it was a very pleasant evening. The three of us enjoyed the excellent table, although some of the more patriotic Norwegians thought it a shame that my little blond boy (who looked so Norwegian) spoke only French and not a single word of Norwegian.

None of this prevented Thomas from spotting the waiter who dished out the ice cream and letting him know that it was excellent and that he would like several extra helpings, which he was given. Observing the whole operation from a distance, I was amused and, at the same time, quite proud of that little boy who, though not yet two-and-a-half years old, was able to manage so well on his own. I concluded that, when he reached a suitable age to look for a bride and to find a livelihood later on, he would succeed in getting the best on his own initiative. However, later in the evening I became a bit less amused by his sense of initiative.

We were all seated in a large room, listening to the Ambassador's solemn speech reminding everybody of the reasons for the day's celebration. Like most speeches, it seemed to drag out longer than the ability of most of the audience to look interested. In fact, I discerned a few discreet yawns, when suddenly the loudspeakers went dead.

L'Artemis de Pytheas *as she was rigged in 1976 with Peter and Lydia Tangvald at the helm.*

*Building L'Artemis de Pytheas in French Guiana. Peter pulled the boat out of the shed and turned her right side up, using only block and tackle and a small truck.*

Peter and Lydia crossing the Mediterranean, bundled up against the cold in
November of 1976. This marked the
beginning of their voyage to Taiwan
from Port Grimaud, France.

Peter taking a sun sight with his
sextant.

*Lydia, pregnant with Thomas, on the way towards Malaysia after leaving Sri Lanka.*

*Lydia, Peter and Thomas in Taiwan
and Iloilo, Philippines.*

*The Orientals were fascinated by
the beautiful blonde woman and her
chubby, fair-skinned baby boy.*

L'Artemis de Pytheas, *anchored in a peaceful river in the Philippines. Note the palm-thatched Bimini top!*

*This is the photograph taken by the police after the shooting of Lydia, as they reconstructed the view the pirates had of Thomas clinging to Peter's leg.*

*Ann Tangvald*

*Ann with Carmen on her back, scrubbing the bottom of the boat.*

Peter, Thomas and Carmen
after the death of Ann.

Peter, Thomas and Carmen
in Puerto Rico, shortly
before their tragic journey
to Bonaire. These are the
last photographs of Peter
and Carmen.

This gave the Ambassador the appearance of a person miming, because he kept on talking, though no one could hear what he was saying. He stopped his speech; everyone looked uneasy seeing his embarrassment. An electrician was called who, after what seemed an eternity, finally appeared and was quickly admitted to the side room where, apparently, the installation was wired. The loudspeakers came on again after a few minutes but, to my dismay, I saw the electrician coming out of the side room carrying a little boy under his arm. Ours! Having finished his ice cream, Thomas had gone into the side room and apparently played electrician, or at least had pulled out some of the wires, preventing the system from functioning. The electrician found it very funny and laughed heartily while returning Thomas to us. He reminded us to hold on to him, at least until the end of the speech, which we did, observing that the ambassador's laugh hadn't sounded nearly as good-natured as the electrician's.

As soon as the speech was over, I released him from my grip, whereupon this time he rushed to the swimming pool, stripped unashamedly and jumped right in without hesitation. It was the first time he had seen a swimming pool (not counting the sewers of Kaohsiung) and I was stunned to see him jump in with such confidence, considering he didn't know how to swim. I went over for a better look when, to my dismay, I realised he'd jumped, not into the shallow part, but into the deep part of the pool. Rushing to the edge, ready to jump in to save him from his foolishness, I saw two muscular swimmers pulling him to the surface. Far from exhibiting the small, scared face I had expected, Thomas was laughing and as happy as he could be.

I was just thanking his saviours when I heard another splash. It was Thomas again, still in the deep part of the pool. I have heard many people claim that a small child falling into the sea will float up on his own account. Perhaps a chubby kid may, especially if wearing a lot of clothes for buoyancy, but that wasn't the case with Thomas. I could see him sitting in the bottom of the pool, apparently just waiting for someone to fish him out! Such trust in mankind baffles me, although it was quite justified this time.

Except for the embarrassment of my son's choosing the wrong moment to play electrician and the scare he gave us in the swimming pool, the party had been pleasant enough and would serve a double advantage. One of the guests told us in glowing terms about the ideal harbour, Puerto Galera, which the old galleons had used as their headquarters. There they had stockpiled their gold in one of the safest and prettiest harbours in Asia.

We lost no time in getting there, hoisting our sails the morning after the party since we neither liked Manila nor felt safe there. Not only did the town rank high in crime, but our mooring at the yacht club didn't feel safe. The moorings were far too close together, so that the yachts kept bumping into each other, and of far too light construction for a boat our size in any but the mildest of breezes. This was just the beginning of the typhoon season and no true sailor can enjoy a harbour that he doesn't feel is safe for his ship.

With the very light winds it took us three days to reach our destination. In fact, the wind even died completely as we came close to the port, so we had to enter the narrow, fjord-like entrance with Lydia towing the ship from the dinghy while I sculled it from the stern. It may sound prehistoric to move a yacht in that fashion now, in the age of modern motors, but it works as well as it has done for thousands of years with a minimum of fuss, maintenance and expenses. It might be considered hard work, but the exercise doesn't seem to harm us. In fact, some people go jogging every day for no reason at all except to get some exercise while, for us, the number of times the wind really fails us are rare and certainly wouldn't justify the great inconvenience of having a motor onboard.

Nevertheless, the occupants of the three other yachts at anchor in the tiny and beautiful harbour looked amazed to see us enter in that manner and teased us about it for the duration of our stay. We stayed over a month in that beautiful, palm-fringed harbour and life was easy enough. The other yachtsmen there seemed to want just one long easy vacation, doing little more than partying from boat to boat with songs, guitars and drinking. Alcohol was exceedingly cheap in the Philippines, but since neither Lydia nor I drank, we soon tired of the atmosphere, especially since I couldn't get much work done on the boat. While the harbour was beautiful, there was nothing there— no timber merchant, no foundry, no ship chandlers, all of which I needed to make my new main mast, the bulwarks, the cleats and all the fittings required to make the boat the way we wanted it.

The closest big town to Manila was Iloilo, where we decided to sail on the 25th of June, despite the fact that we were now very much into typhoon season. We would lose the safety of Puerto Galera where the other yachts had decided to stay for the whole critical season. It may sound like they were the only sensible ones, but the typhoon season lasts for most of the year. Six months of the year are highly critical and only two months are considered completely safe.

I felt, and still feel, that living on a boat is a wonderful thing, but only if we can take advantage of the freedom that goes with it. If we have to hole up for ten months a year for the privilege of sailing the remaining two, then we have less freedom than most people living ashore. For that reason I always sail when it suits me, even if I have to take what comes.

As if to contradict this philosophy, the very day after we left the harbour, the gods must have wanted to teach us a lesson. The sky became black and the barometer plunged downward. This time we were much worse off than in Typhoon Atang, when I had land on only one side. Now we had islands all around us and could be thrown against the land and broken to pieces. Of course, some may think that islands in all directions would also mean harbours in any direction the wind might push us. Unfortunately for the sailor, it doesn't necessarily work that way.

In a real gale, when we most desire a safe and peaceful harbour, it's generally quite impossible to get to one. In a blinding rain, it can be nearly impossible to find the entrance to the harbour. Granted, today, with all the sophisticated navigational aids, one might be able to enter a harbour without even looking outside, just by following the instruments and the chart table. But even those who would not be loath to blindly trust instruments and mechanical aids must admit that, in a real blow, handling a yacht through most narrow harbour entrances or through the breakers would be highly risky. The number of shipwrecked boats close to the entrances of harbours around the world testifies that the risks are great for those who can't resist trying for the peace of a harbour during a storm.

The typhoon started to blow on the 26th of June and increased so rapidly that we had to give up all hopes of reaching any port while the weather was still manageable. We tried to keep track of our position as accurately as possible, but had none of the modern instruments and so were dependent upon only our old sextant and timepiece which, of course, were useless in a typhoon with a completely overcast sky. All we could do was try for as accurate a deadreckoning as possible.

To deadreckon, we draw a line on a chart from the last known position in the compass direction we estimate the ship is sailing or drifting, and tick off the number of miles we estimate the ship has gone. Most boats have an instrument called a log, which measures the distance sailed between checks. Some have more modern instruments which also measure the vessel's speed.

We had neither, and had made no effort to acquire either. I

consider them unreliable and know from experience that we can simply guess our speed and distance covered, at least as accurately as those instruments and at far less cost.

We were down to storm canvas as night fell, and having dead-reckoned our position, I announced to Lydia that we were going to see a lighthouse which would give us better visibility as soon as the rain let up. But time passed, and even when the rain let up some, we never saw the light. I started to worry and lost confidence in my deadreckoning just as the wind increased to such a fury that I had to take the storm trysail down lest it pull everything to pieces.

To fight the sail down and lash it was no small feat. I had to hold on for dear life to avoid being blown over the side. When it was finally done, I noticed that just the windage of the fierce wind on the bare mast was enough to give us a frightening speed downwind, despite the fact that the rudder had been lashed all the way down to lee. The force of the wind completely overrode the rudder's control.

Since I was unsure of our position now that I hadn't seen the expected lighthouse, I could not afford to keep the boat moving at full speed in a direction which could mean land or rocks and potential destruction. What I did know is that we had deep enough water right where we were, so I wanted at all costs to stop the boat as much as possible. Of course, the rigging had been finished, the situation would have been different—the boat would have been balanced. But now, without the mainmast and only the foremast far forward, I was out of control. The only thing I could figure out to do was to lower one anchor with as long a line as I dared, in hopes that, even though the anchor would be left dangling in the deep water, it would give enough resistance to brake the speed of the boat. Indeed, it worked beautifully—the resistance inflicted by the 600 feet of heavy line held down by my 64-pound stock anchor was enough to hold the bow towards the wind at an angle of about 45 degrees, and the ship just drifted slowly downwind at less than one knot speed.

I continued to watch for the lighthouse with no success. Not seeing it where I expected it to be meant that I didn't know where we were. All I could do was hope that we still had enough room down to our lee so as not to go aground until the wind moderated and I could regain control of my ship, rather than leaving her to drift wherever the gale might blow us.

All of a sudden, after a few hours of the most frightful wind I could ever recall experiencing, the wind died completely, but the waves stayed as high as ever. So the ship, instead of getting an easier motion and having mercy on its crew, shook us even more, making us very uncomfortable. We didn't get seasick, though, and for Lydia this was a great change from the time she was pregnant and so miserably sick most of the time.

But the calm didn't last long. Only about 10 minutes later the wind returned with a vengeance, screaming down on us, but this time from the opposite direction. I realised then that we had been in the exact centre of the typhoon. The wind was just as strong as ever, but I rejoiced to see that we were drifting back exactly from whence we had come, where I knew we had enough water and would be in no danger of hitting land. I also knew that the worst was over and the wind would gradually moderate.

I explained all this to Lydia, and we went to bed and tried to relax as best we could despite the rough motion in that mountainous sea. We tried to sleep like our little Thomas, who had been doing so quite peacefully all along. We had been worrying, but he certainly hadn't, judging by his happy, relaxed face. All this bouncing around had provided the best possible rocking. What little child doesn't like to have his cradle rocked? And what baby could wish for a better rocking than the one given him that night by a tropical typhoon?

During the night the boat drifted slowly back to where we had been the evening before, where I had expected to see the lighthouse. As daybreak approached, I could see the shoreline and there, through my binoculars, was the lighthouse! Not its flash, but the lighthouse itself with its tower and attendant lightkeeper's house. Thus my deadreckoning had been right after all, and the lighthouse had been where I expected it to be—it just hadn't been lit. When we arrived in port, we complained to the harbourmaster about the unlit light. I thought it scandalous that a light which could spell the difference between life and death and could avert endless tragedies should be subject to such gross negligence. But to our astonishment, the harbourmaster, completely unconcerned, answered, "Oh, that light. Well, perhaps it is the lightkeeper's vacation at this time of year," Then, apparently searching his memory, he added, "Yes, I'm sure this is his vacation time."

Despite my revolted astonishment, his aloofness persisted. "Well, lightkeepers need yearly vacations too, you know," and that closed the issue as far as he was concerned.

I didn't insist, feeling it would be of no use, but thought that different places sure have different customs. Ever since that time, I never put my trust in any lighthouses anymore.

Iloilo is the main harbour on the island of Panay, one of the central islands of the Philippines, and one that is entirely different from those we had known further north. We were to realise that the Philippines, which are reputed to consist of 10,000 islands and to have 750 different languages, really are composed of entirely different peoples of different origins and customs.

While the inhabitants further north had been friendly, we found the people here outright unpleasant. The harbour consisted of a winding river with crowded, dirty docks and many wrecks sunk along the riversides. We searched about for a reasonably pleasant place to tack in as the wind was blowing dead against us. Finally we came to a low bridge spanning the river and blocking the way, preventing us from prospecting any further. I regretted having made my mast so it couldn't be lowered, which would have allowed us to reach anchorages that were free from crowds. As it was, we had to anchor there, thinking ourselves reasonably safe close to the bridge and away from the main traffic.

We had barely anchored and were still furling the sails and coiling up the ropes when we saw a crowd gathering on the bridge not far from us. They started jumping up and down and scratching themselves, screaming like monkeys in a zoo while watching and pointing to us. We couldn't figure out what it was all about and so tried to disregard them, though they kept shouting at us. Perhaps they were speaking English with a very strong and strange accent.

Only later did we learn from some American friends there that they had been simulating monkeys while pointing at my hairy chest. Asians are almost completely devoid of hair on their bodies except for their heads and sometimes a bit on their chins. Perhaps what disturbed me most, thinking of that episode, was that their mimicking had not been done as a poor joke, but with cruelty in their attitude. I soon discovered that white men were not welcome in Iloilo. We were also to discover that crime was even more prevalent here than in the big city of Manila. Yet we stayed for a while, because it was a convenient harbour for getting work done on the boat.

On the second day there, I found a nice foundry run by a Chinese man, who gave me as much confidence as I could expect in that part of the world. He quoted me a price which was very reasonable for casting my stanchion fittings out of "propeller bronze," provided that I made the patterns myself, which he wanted painted and with the proper depth on the required surfaces. He sounded like he really knew his business, so I went right back onboard to draw and make the pattern. He had promised to have 50 of them ready for me two days later. He surprised me by not asking for even a deposit, considering that I was a stranger and that it represented a sizable amount of money. I admired his trustfulness, though Lydia claimed it just proved that he was able to judge an honest man. I smiled at her for the compliment and, indeed, two days later all 50 fittings were waiting for me and the bill was exactly the amount agreed on. The job was beautifully done, and I paid with no complaint. The man even insisted on showing me his supply of scrap bronze propellers to prove to me that he was really going to cast my fitting out of real bronze and not out of ordinary brass, as all too many less conscientious foundries might do.

I was so pleased with my castings that I also ordered a new fancy boom gooseneck, as well as a few other fittings, from my patterns. He gave me the same good service as for the first order, and a deep smile to show he was pleased to see me become a repeat customer.

Another Chinese man in Iliolo owned a lumberyard, which looked like a good one. I would have liked to order the wood for building my mast, but couldn't think of a place where I could build it. While I considered the problem, I started buying wood for my new mast's mainstep, which would keep me busy cutting and fitting it. There would be time later to decide what to do with the mast itself.

The Chinese manager went out of his way to find me a perfect piece of lumber—a beautiful tropical hardwood—and we became such good friends during the search that he invited my family and me to dinner in his home with his wife. He picked us up in his elegant, air-conditioned car. To display such signs of wealth is contrary to Chinese custom, and he seemed a bit embarrassed about it.

"Don't think it's my habit to throw my money away. But air conditioning is not a luxury, it's a necessity for us Chinese. You see, we're not liked in the Philippines, because most of the money is in our hands."

"Probably because you are the ones to work the hardest," I interrupted, "but what does that have to do with air conditioning?"

"We do work hard, but they still don't like the fact that we have most of the money. You may be surprised to hear this, but several Chinese people have been killed, for no other reason than that we are Chinese—and the most common way of killing us is to shoot through an open window. So I always drive with my windows up, and that's why, here in the tropics, I have air conditioning."

"But the windows will not stop a bullet unless it's a special armoured glass," I said, thinking that they looked quite normal.

"Oh, by shooting, I don't mean shooting with a gun. Firearms are very strictly forbidden in this country and very few people are able to get one, even if they are willing to take the chance of being caught with one in their possession. No, they shoot and kill with homemade slingshots, which work with rubber bands,"

Seeing my disbelief, he added, "Yes, just slingshots. But deadly slingshots which have the advantage, for the killer, of being perfectly silent. They do kill, but they don't go through a car's security glass. They make the slingshots just like children's toys of many countries, but these are heavy duty ones with a powerful string, used by grown men who train themselves for maximum power and accuracy. They are deadly because they don't use stones or even steel balls, but they use six-inch nails or the biggest nails they can get. They cut a groove close to the point in the shape of a hook, and the hook lies over the wire which forms the centre of the slingshot with a rubber string on either side of it. In other words, instead of the usual leather pad made to hold a stone or a steel ball, they have a wire which hooks on a filed groove of the nail close to the tip, which they file to a sharp point. Then they tie feathers to the head of the nail to give it stability, just like an arrow shot from a bow. This makes such a dangerous weapon, the nail can pierce a man's skull when shot at close range."

I asked my host why he remained in such a country where he was unliked and unsafe. His answer—that we have to accept certain drawbacks when making good money—made me think that it all boils down to that we are all more or less prostitutes, selling ourselves for money. He was risking his life and that of his family so as not to abandon a business which brought him money. In the same way, I had exposed myself and my family for two years to unhealthy and unpleasant conditions because I had been tempted by money paid to me for fulfilling another man's benefit and convenience.

In the harbour, in addition to the gang on the bridge leering at us, we had also been pestered by a group of swimmers climbing on our boat and in our dinghy, which they considered a public toy. They would rock it until it swamped, causing them to laugh hilariously, but creating a long and tedious bailing job for me after they left. We tried to explain to them that the boat was our home and they were not to climb onboard uninvited, but it was useless to try to explain it in a friendly way. They would just stand on the deck, looking insolently at us, while shouting words in their own language, which I suspected were probably obscene by the way they looked at Lydia. She was getting more and more exasperated by our lack of privacy. We could get them to dive off the boat by walking toward them, but while we were getting rid of some, others were laughing and shouting and boarding from the other end of the vessel.

When a police squad happened to pass by, we shouted to them and pointed at our unwanted guests. They immediately blew their whistles, which seemed to work like magic. Those onboard dove in the water and disappeared in all directions.

The police wanted to talk to us, so we bailed our dinghy as fast as we could to row over to them, but when we got in the dinghy we discovered one of the rowlocks was missing, so we had to scull over. We complained to the police and said that we'd never had any peace due to those swimmers who bothered us constantly, played with our dinghy, swamped it and lost one of our rowlocks in the process. The rowlocks were made of bronze and were very beautiful and quite impossible to replace, except by having them specially cast, which was a costly proposition.

The police listened and said. "We're very sorry these teenagers are such a nuisance to you, but there is very little we can do, and I fear that, as soon as we leave, they'll be back pestering you. We're not so sure your rowlock was lost by accident—it's more likely that it's been stolen. They can sell it to any junkyard if it's bronze.

"But that will bring them only a very small amount of money as junk," I protested.

"Well, I fear this is the way they live. They roam the streets and steal enough here and there to buy some food or wine."

"In that case, why don't you put them in jail?" I objected.

"We can't put half of our population in jail, and besides, our jails are already overfilled," he replied with some bitterness. "But let us have your other rowlock until tomorrow, and we'll try to find the missing one that matches it."

I thanked them for wanting to help me and handed them the missing rowlock without thinking, but back on the boat we wondered if we'd been taken a second time—perhaps, in such a crooked country, the police were also crooked and this was just a trick to get the second rowlock from us. We didn't worry too much about it, though, because we knew we'd found a good foundry and I could easily make a new pattern for rowlocks as nice as the ones that were missing, and at a cost that wouldn't break the bank.

But the next morning we were hailed by a very big policeman who handed us both our rowlocks with a big smile. He didn't want to tell us where he'd found the lost one, but did say, "We did get your rowlock, but we can't answer for the future. Please don't remain where you are now, where we have no control. Please go further down the river next to those ships," he said, pointing to the berth he had in mind. "There you'll be close to one of our armed guards and no one will bother you."

While he had asked politely, it was really an order, though one to our advantage even if we didn't want to moor next to those rusty hulks. Due to the fairly strong current in the river, and the ever-present possibility of bad weather springing up, especially now at the height of typhoon season, I moored very securely along the steel wall of the sunken steamer that we'd been directed to, using one line fore and one line aft, as well as two breast lines and two spring lines, a total of six altogether. We felt safe there and were finally rid of the swimmers who, apparently, didn't like to swim that far in the current.

Our troubles were not yet over. That afternoon Lydia came back from the market in tears, looking scared and furious. "Do you know what happened?" she sobbed to me as soon as she came onboard. "I was attacked by a man in front of the market. He came close to me, took out a long knife from a bag he was carrying and held it against my stomach. He told me to give him my purse or he would help himself to it after he stuck the knife through me! Then, after I gave him my purse, he ran down the street and I yelled for help, telling people he'd robbed me and to stop him. But everybody just laughed! One of them who spoke good English even said to me, 'Let him run, he's poor and needs the money. You're rich and have much more.'"

She was still indignant at the thought that such a thing could happen in broad daylight, and disgusted at the witnesses' indifference, but I was scared, thinking how easily she could have been hurt. I was beginning to dislike the island even more, yet I told myself that criminals are found everywhere and we shouldn't hold that against the country. I suggested that she should never go to the market alone again, that from then on I'd go with her. But the next day we were to disregard that rule as new troubles crept upon us.

I saw a rusty old fishing boat the size of a small freighter casting off his lines and making ready for sea. He hadn't started his motor and was just letting the current carry him. Many large motor ships can't disengage their propeller from their engines. When the engine is running the propeller is also turning, and putting the engine in reverse simply makes it run backwards. It sounds like a difficult way to handle a ship, but being able to start either forward or backward is so reliable that it is a generally adopted system for many ships. It's simple, trouble-free and cheap.

As she drifted closer and closer in my direction, I began to wonder why they were waiting so long to start the engine. My usual pessimism took over and I could already visualise that big, heavy ship smashing into my delicately built yacht and squashing it into a wreck. It came closer and closer before I realised that they were having trouble getting the motor started. I took out my loudspeaker and called over to them.

"Ahoy, *Bofideco*," I shouted, as I could see the name of their ship. "If you can't start your motor, please anchor immediately before you crush me."

The crew looked at me with apparent indifference, doing nothing as their ship drifted still closer. If I hadn't had all those lines tying me so securely to my berth, I could have cast them loose and tried to kedge myself clear of their path. But removing six lines would have taken far too much time and they were still coming towards me. Finally, just as I was diving into the cabin to get our little boy out so he wouldn't be trapped as the boat was squashed, their engines finally started. But, despite going full blast ahead, it was too late. He hit us and pulled the boat over until the bowsprit hit the steel wall with the sickening sound of broken wood. From the noise I thought the whole bow of my boat had been broken, but as the ship powered away, I examined the boat carefully and, to my relief, found no other damage than the broken bowsprit.

It was annoying to have to make a new bowsprit but, considering that the damage wasn't permanent and how close we had come to losing the whole boat and everything in it, I was greatly relieved. Nevertheless, it was disturbing that the fishing boat hadn't bothered to make the slightest excuse and just powered out to sea.

The boat returned the next day and, although we waited for the captain to come and check with us about the damage, hours went by with no sign of him. Urged by Lydia, I went over to see him and was not too surprised to get a very poor reception by the rough-looking skipper. He regarded me very insolently from his deep chair, never offering me even a place to sit down. To my request for him to pay for the repair, he just barked back at me.

"This is a commercial harbour made for us. You yachtsmen are just nuisances to us here. I've been going in and out of this harbour for years with no troubles. The trouble now is only because you were there, so it's your fault, not mine. I'm not paying anything!"

"You're in the majority, but that doesn't mean that the harbour belongs to you. It was your authorities that insisted we moor at the berth where you hit us," I retorted.

"I'm not going to discuss it any further," he bellowed, glaring menacingly at me. "Now get lost before I lose my patience and order my men to throw you out."

Not having the spirit of a fighter, I have always preferred to retreat and accept my losses when a battle seems to be in my disfavour. But back in the boat, Lydia didn't see it that way. "We're in the right and shouldn't give up. Let's get a lawyer and bring that skipper to court. Let him learn that he is not making the law around here," she insisted.

"Listen," I said, "don't think that I'm a coward if I don't want to fight this out. I'm just trying to be practical. We're strangers here and we'll be at a disadvantage with everyone, including the court. In any case, even if we do win a court case, it will cost us more money than it's worth, and take us more time and worry than to simply go ahead and make our new bowsprit."

Lydia, a much more energetic person than I, completely disagreed. After thinking about it a while she said, "Let's share the work on this matter like we always share everything. You go ahead with the repair and make the new bowsprit and I'll take care of the legal matter and will do what's necessary to get that rascal to pay for it."

"That is no place for a woman to go," I pointed out in alarm.

"Don't worry," she smiled. "I know what to do and, of course, I won't go to that ship alone. I'll see the harbourmaster. He's a nice guy and I know that he likes me. I'll get him to help me."

I didn't like her approach much, but for fear of being accused of being a silly, jealous husband, I let her do what she wanted and indeed she got her way. The harbourmaster immediately froze the fishing vessel in port; it would not be permitted to move until the matter was settled. Naturally the skipper had no choice but to pay us for the new piece of timber, but not much for my labour. When he paid Lydia, however, who was accompanied by the harbourmaster, he literally threw the money in her face and snarled at her that if our boat remained in port after the next day at noon, we would live to regret it. Both the harbourmaster and Lydia ignored the threat and returned to shore, leaving the skipper free to proceed to sea.

Lydia was triumphant when she came back onboard and showed me the money, but she was a bit embarrassed to have to admit that shaking off the harbourmaster on the way back was no easy matter. Apparently my lack of enthusiasm for her to enlist the harbourmaster's help was justified.

During our stay we'd met a British yacht enthusiast who lived in town permanently. I've forgotten his name, but he was the manager of the British bank there. He often came aboard to enjoy the atmosphere of a yacht. He no longer owned one since being transferred to this branch, but it was something he was always dreaming about. We also were invited to his home often and had become very good friends. To us, he was a living dictionary and could always answer our questions about the Philippines.

On the evening after Lydia's confrontation with the skipper, he hailed us from shore and I went to fetch him in the dinghy for a chat and a cup of tea onboard. We told him about the accident, and he was very surprised to hear that we'd been able to get money for the repair. When Lydia told him with no hidden pride that it was due to her initiative, he began to look quite worried. When she ended her story by telling him about the skipper's "silly" threat, he was aghast.

Emphasizing every word, he said, "Listen, and please believe me. You don't know the conditions here, but I do. Some of the Philippine Islands are safe and have friendly inhabitants. But others are unsafe for everyone, especially strangers. As much as I like your company and hate to think about your leaving, I implore you, don't take this threat lightly. You must leave before the deadline he gave you. Don't sail any later than tomorrow morning and make sure you are out of these waters by tomorrow noon as he told you."

Lydia laughed and calmly said we weren't going to be bullied by a fishing boat skipper, no matter how big a bully he may be. We'd go and tell the police about the threat and they would protect us. But I was getting tired of living under such conditions. I said I wanted to sail away and try to find some friendlier place to live. I thanked our friend sincerely for his warning, which I felt in all probability was justified. Early the next morning we sailed down the river and out to sea in search of a better place.

We wondered where to sail next, as we were getting tired of these insecure conditions and longed for a more "civilised" country. We finally decided to sail as directly as possible to Australia and make our main mast there. In any case, we felt sure that Australia would be the perfect country to finish the boat and to make friends among the many yachtsmen there.

To reach the open sea and sail to Australia, we figured the easiest route would be to sail north of Negros, Cebu and Leyte Islands, then through the San Juanico Strait to the Gulf of Leyte. We'd make a last stop in the Philippines in Tacloban (the birthplace of the president's wife), which we'd heard a lot of good things about. It would also be a good place to stock up for the long voyage to Australia.

The trip as far as the entrance strait was easy enough in good weather, but had we had the proper pilot books, we'd have chosen a different route to reach the ocean. The currents in the straits were nerve-wracking. Huge whirlpools threw the boat hither and thither with surprising violence. We were later to hear that yachts never ventured through the straits and could readily see why. We were doubly handicapped under our jury rig without full normal control of the ship. Gradually our progress improved through the strait, especially after a few hours when the tide pushed us with a three-knot current. We were learning to counteract the whirlpools by climbing part way up the mast to spot them in advance.

We were just congratulating each other on nearing the end of the strait when we rounded a point and saw a great suspended bridge straddling the whole strait from the island of Leyte on our right to the island of Samar on our left. There were no bridges on the charts, which were several years old, and apparently a bridge had been built since they had been printed! Now the big problem was to determine if there was room for us to sail under the bridge.

From the deck of our low boat it was very difficult to estimate the height of a bridge and determine whether or not our mast would clear it. We had to make up our minds fast. With a three-knot current, we could be pushed into the bridge with disastrous results. I readied my biggest anchor in a panic, hoping there would be enough time to assess the height of the bridge.

Lydia was thinking about the big job it would be to get the anchor up again in a place with such a strong current. She was also thinking about the good progress we were making and the probability that we'd make Tacloban before nightfall if we could keep going. She figured out a very clever way to quickly measure the clearance.

"Look at that bus crossing the bridge," she shouted to me on the foredeck. "How many buses do you think we could put on top of each other from the water's edge to the underside of the bridge?"

Seeing what she was getting at, I quickly tried to visualise how many buses there was room for. We decided how tall we thought a bus probably was and multiplied the height by the number of buses to get the clearance of the bridge.

I blew a kiss to Lydia, grateful to have avoided that awkward anchoring manoeuvre and proud to have such a clever wife. We passed beneath the bridge with several feet to spare and before sundown found ourselves securely anchored in front of Tacloban.

# 16

# Tacloban, Cebu & Consolation

*F*ortunately we weren't going to leave the Philippines with only our negative impression of Iloilo. Tacloban was to prove itself to be a nice little town with friendly people—entirely different from the island we'd just left. As we went ashore the next day, we immediately began making friends. At the first building, a medical training school for nurses, we asked permission to fill a jerry can from their garden hose. The headmistress, Narcissa Araneta, offered us all the water we needed and invited us in to tell her all about our travels, which seemed to fascinate her.

She was later to be very helpful to us in organizing a jumbo sale of all the unwanted things we had collected onboard. The never-ending accumulation of all kinds of gear and goods is a common problem for all live-aboarders. These things not only make the boat cluttered, but also add weight, causing it to float deeper in the water and become slower and less seaworthy. Some yachtsmen try to hide the problem by raising the painted waterline, but the only real remedy is to get rid of all nonessential gear.

We tried not to think about what we had once paid for the unwanted items and kept only what we really needed. The damaged and worn out gear had to be discarded, but much could be sold. This wasn't often easy to do when traveling, because we generally didn't know where to find buyers, so when Narcissa offered to organise the sale, we were overjoyed and grateful. She offered us her big reception hall, fully equipped with long rows of chairs and a powerful loudspeaker, and also printed up notices which we could put up on bulletin boards around the town to advertise our sale.

Narcissa made it clear that she wanted nothing from us and just waved away our thanks saying that we were really giving the town a break by offering to sell so many things that they were short of, such as our electric portable saw, for instance, which we'd told her about. With no electricity onboard, the saw merely took up room and would eventually be ruined by the damp, salty conditions.

We hung up notices all over town on telegraph poles, in the post office, the market and most everywhere. Indeed, the day of the sale there must have been several hundred people there, all curious to see what would come ashore from a yacht. I get quite frightened in front of such a crowd, especially if I get a microphone thrust in front of my face, so I was glad to see that Lydia, quite on the contrary, enjoyed the situation. I hid in the background, trembling for fear my dear little wife might not be up to the situation and the task would fall to me, but it soon became obvious that she was completely at ease and her enthusiasm seemed to spread to the audience.

Very soon the atmosphere was very relaxed and happy with bids coming in faster—and quite a bit higher for most items—than we had dreamed possible. Our sewing machine was the favoured item and brought in just about as much as we had paid for it several years earlier when it was new. We also sold a small transistor at a very good price, and many other items such as extra dishes, toys which Thomas didn't play with anymore, blankets, hand-painted silk scarves that Lydia had made long ago, clothes of all kinds, curtains that we'd bought while in our apartment in China, lots of books, cassettes for tape recorders, spare jars and other miscellaneous items.

Back on the boat after the successful sale, I kissed my dear little wife for having managed so well, and we congratulated each other for taking in more money than we'd ever thought possible and clearing the boat of all that unnecessary weight. Life onboard would be much easier, now that we didn't have to dig down to the bottom of our lockers to find what we were looking for. When a boat is no longer overcrowded, it's much easier to get hold of our daily things.

Another advantage was that now everybody seemed to know us. Few tourists came to town, so we were made to feel more like welcome guests. Often people would greet us on the street with a friendly smile, welcoming us to their town. After a few words they would be on their way, but sometimes the conversations lingered on and they would invite us to their homes, sometimes just for a chat, sometimes for a full dinner.

We enjoyed the place, but the harbour was really just an open anchorage and not at all safe should the wind pipe up, which it was bound to do sooner or later. We were once again just about at the height of typhoon season and, for our own safety, the sooner we left the better. With much regret we stocked up with food and left again, headed for Australia, where we expected to find both friendly people and a safe harbour with all the timber and materials we would need for finally finishing our yacht. It would mean that we would no longer have to content ourselves with a jury-rig.

We had hoped to get into the Pacific Ocean with its open waters and gain enough towards the south to get out of the typhoon belt before the next one would strike. Ordinarily, we consider that tropical storms don't form between 10 degrees north and 10 degrees south. Since Tacloban is 11 degrees north, it would seem that we'd only have to get one degree, or 60 miles, further south to be out of danger. Unfortunately, that part of the world is an exception to the general rule and tropical storms can go quite a bit further south. Nevertheless, it would be only a few days before we would be out of the danger zone.

So with complete optimism we bade our friends farewell and set course southeast. We planned to get out into the open ocean between the south port of Samar and Homonhon Island, north of Mindanao.

The weather, which had been pleasant at our departure, soon deteriorated with a falling barometer. Progress was painful as the wind had changed and blew straight against us. Should we turn back? With the southeasterly winds blowing straight into the anchorage, we would have no protection at all. We would probably find a safe anchorage by returning into San Juanico Strait, but I hated to go that far in exactly the opposite direction of where we were headed. And after all, why fear the worst? It could just as likely be a local minor depression which would soon clear up, and not a typhoon. We kept on going, hoping for the best, though the wind increased more and more, forcing us to reef down despite our lack of mainsail.

By the time we reached the strait between Samar and Homonhon, we could fool ourselves no longer—this was, in fact, another typhoon. We could still carry enough canvas to retain control of our ship, but we weren't capable of beating against the wind. Or at least we weren't gaining anything anymore. But where to go? There were no safe harbours anywhere in the region.

While we discussed our options over the roar of the wind, we heard another unfamiliar sound for just a few seconds and then felt a big draft through our cabin. The hatch over the chainlocker had not been securely tied down and was now lost, having been carried away by the wind. That settled the matter. In order to prevent the seas from filling the locker and possibly sinking us, we had to ease the motion of the ship and prevent any more water from coming on deck until we could rig up a makeshift hatch and plug up the opening.

We hove-to the ship, which instantly made it feel as if the gale had quieted down to half its force. A ship rides so much more easily when hove-to, compared with being forced on its way. The wind was strong, but not as strong as it had been the last time, so we were able to figure out that the centre of the storm was passing not directly over us, but quite a bit to the north. But coping with any tropical storm is always worrisome and tiring.

To make matters worse, a tooth which I'd had fixed by an expensive and reputedly good dentist in Manila chose that occasion to flare up with such pains that all thoughts of continuing the long way to Australia vanished. I needed a dentist now! Our medicine chest had some painkilling medicine which I tried, but the pain remained almost as strong as without the medicine and the pills had the side effect of making me sleepy, something I could not afford. The safety of the ship largely depended on me. Lydia was a very small woman and didn't have the strength required to handle the boat. I stopped taking the medication, and Lydia and I discussed where we should sail as soon as the weather would permit.

Tacloban, where we'd just come from, in addition to not having a safe harbour, also lacked a properly equipped dentist. In fact, while we were there, I'd learned that the dentists in all of Leyte were only equipped with old-fashioned drills, powered by a leather string working through a collection of wheels along a great articulated arm. These were similar to the ones I had seen in my childhood, which had left me with countless nightmares for years afterward.

We had heard very little about Mindanao, the next island to the south, except that it was an island of fanatic Moslems. Most Moslems are not fanatical and live their religion peacefully, but these people, we had been told, were really fanatics. The island wasn't safe, due partly to a lot of piracy and partly to a general hatred of white men. I disliked the thought of even getting close to that island. I wouldn't be able to avoid it should I decide to go further through the Surigao Strait, whose southern edge was Mindanao. If I hugged Leyte, the northern side, I might be sufficiently safe from any of their ships to take that chance, perhaps going through at night with no lights on.

Recalling what we'd been told about Cebu and reading about the island with its main town of the same name, we thought it was our only choice. It was a big city with good medical services. The people, as on Leyte, had a good reputation and the port was supposed to be excellent.

When the wind moderated the next day, my tooth was hurting more and more, so we lost no time in reaching Cebu as soon as possible. We passed the critical strait and Mindanao during the darkness of night with no problems, and arrived the next evening at the harbour of Cebu. We'd had a strong wind the whole way, but not so bad as to endanger us. We were glad to have been able to get there before dark, but were disappointed to find the port was not nearly as safe as we'd read. We were soon to realise that it was meant to be safe for big ships, but not necessarily for small, fragile yachts.

To our joy, we spotted another yacht there and hoped its captain could give us information about the place. It was the American yacht, *Ingrid*, a very beautiful Atkin double-ender, riding very uncomfortably up and down in the waves which formed against big wooden piles at that part of the dock. We passed her under sail and, hoping that there were better anchorages, I shouted over to the skipper, "Yacht, ahoy! Where can I find the best and safest anchorage?

"Right here," was the discouraging answer.

I really didn't want to bash against the dock and couldn't understand why the *Ingrid* wanted to take that chance. Should the winds increase, surely the boat would be damaged. Instead I anchored right in the middle of the port, though I knew I wouldn't be allowed to stay there since I would hinder the manoeuvering of steamships to and from the docks. I took a chance there wouldn't be any traffic until I had the time to inquire about a more suitable place.

I put the dinghy in the water and rushed ashore to see the harbourmaster but found only the coast guard station. I told them of my troubles—that I had to get to a dentist, but first I had to find a safe spot to anchor or to moor my yacht. The officers were nice enough, but at first couldn't think of any better place than next to *Ingrid*, until one of them proposed the local sailboat harbour, which lay behind a small breakwater a short distance away from the big ship docks.

Later I understood why they hadn't proposed that harbour to begin with. They must have presumed that I would never want to anchor there, as the whole district was a horrible slum. Only native sailboats whose owners could not afford motors were anchored there. But they didn't judge me right, for to me a motor is not a sign of standing. On the contrary, a motorless sailboat to me is a sign that the boat must really be able to sail well and, thus, always interests me.

Nevertheless, there were some motorboats there that caught my interest. Among the native sailboats, I spotted a couple of slim, very low motorboats equipped with double outriggers for stability. On each outrigger were two huge outboard motors on each side, in addition to a small, central diesel engine driving a small propeller. Even before someone told me about them, I had guessed they were smugglers. They would normally travel just under the economical diesel engine unless they were pursued—then down would go the four big outboards, which must have made them practically fly. In addition to the fantastic speeds they could reach, their shallow draft would allow them to take shortcuts over shoals which would stop the heavier, deep-drafted patrol boats.

There we were in a slum district, amid smugglers and perhaps worse, but we entered their domain on equal footing. We were as simply equipped as most of them, and they treated us as peers, rather than as rich tourists and possible prey. In any case, we felt safe under the circumstances, even if some of them may have been criminals.

Next day, I lost no time in getting to the dentist, where I was agreeably surprised to find a super modern dentist office with soft lighting, soft music and, more importantly, equipped with the most modern equipment. My tooth was repaired swiftly and inexpensively. The trouble, the dentist explained, was that the previous dentist had failed to isolate the tooth's nerve, which had become irritated by the plastic filling. Strange how the human body functions so well, yet just a little bit of malfunctioning and the whole body goes to pieces.

The town was very beautiful and seemed to have everything I needed for finishing the boat. I still had to look for a proper place to put my boat. Despite all the romance and exoticness of our present anchoring place, I had my doubts about its suitability for a longer stay. Indeed, that very night I found a good reason for not staying there too long when a breeze sprang up, making two of the neighbouring boats drag down on me.

It's a sad fact that safety is not assured by having good anchor gear on our own boat. We must also depend on the anchor gear of our neighbour for our own safety. If they drag on top of us, we can be in as bad a position, or even worse, than if our own anchors don't hold. As it was, my own anchor did hold despite having to also hold those two native crafts as their owners had apparently gone ashore. Lydia and I were unable to push them clear as their huge outriggers had become hopelessly entangled on top of us. We stayed up most of the night tending our fenders and trying to avoid the outriggers damaging our boat. Even when the owners finally showed up, we had great difficulty getting untangled. The fact that they were a bit drunk didn't help the matter. In any case, I should have known that yachts and native crafts don't make a good marriage, as invariably the native yachts (as well as their owners) are rough and don't mind a few scratches here and there.

Lydia and I discussed our situation again. We still had several months of typhoon season and would be gambling with death if we continued to try to reach Australia. Yet we couldn't stay here in the harbour. Neither was it a good idea to continue to sail under jury-rig with only partial control of the boat. In short, we had to find a safe harbour and finish the repair of the boat during the rest of typhoon season. The closest place I could think of was a nearby lagoon which had been marked on my chart as too shallow, but perhaps I could find a small corner of it where the water would be deep enough for us to find peace and safely.

Leaving Lydia and Thomas onboard, I took the dinghy and went for a long row to the lagoon to investigate it. Once by the entrance, I penetrated into the lagoon itself, which consisted of a multitude of narrow arms, making a perfect labyrinth. I was careful to try and remember as many landmarks as possible so as to find my way out again. I penetrated deeper into the wilderness, sounding the depth the whole time, and soon became convinced that, despite the chart's pessimistic soundings, it should be possible to get the yacht in there when the tide was high. It didn't matter if we touched bottom when the tide went out, provided I could find spots where there were no rocks or other hazards.

As I came around the bend, still watching for a place that would also give me access to a road for our future supplies, I suddenly spotted a mast. I thought I was dreaming and curiously rowed over for a closer look. As I rounded the next bend, I saw it clearly—a modern trimaran with a woman on deck. She hurried down below when she spotted me. I presumed she was going down below to get her binoculars to better see who was coming, or perhaps just to get some more decent clothes on, but she didn't come up on deck again.

A bit surprised, I came alongside. She still hadn't reappeared, so I called, "Yacht, ahoy! Yacht, ahoy!" but no one answered. Presuming that she and the other occupants, if there were any, wanted to have peace, I was starting to row away when I noticed the French flag. My good manners weren't going to deprive me of a talk with a fellow countryman. Since I was raised in France and speak without an accent, I can pretend to be a real Frenchman when I wish.

So I called out, "Allo du bateau, ne faites pas les timides; venez parler a un vieux compatriot!"

Still no signs of life onboard. By now I was really curious and insisted, still in French, "I saw you up on deck. I can wait right here until you'll be willing to talk to me."

It helped. I heard some hesitating steps, and then a pretty, but rather sour face emerged through the hatch.

"Hello," I said with the biggest smile I could manage. "Never have I seen anyone so keen for her privacy. I would have thought that you'd have been glad for some company, living in such a wilderness so far from people."

"This place is not as isolated as you think," she retorted. "In fact, we're in shouting distance of that house over there."

She was right. Following the direction in which she pointed, I could clearly see a house not too far away through the bush.

"Fine," I said. "If there's a house, there must also be a road, so this may be just the place I'm looking for. Perhaps we will be neighbours. I also have a yacht and I'd be safe here from the typhoons."

"I don't think you can come here," warned the lady, with no enthusiasm at the prospect of my being there. "First of all, no boats come as far as I am except for very shallow boats like ours. But in no case can you come here. This is private property. This part of the lagoon belongs to the owners of that house. They are Chinese and don't like visitors. We're here only because we're special friends."

I wasn't going to let myself be brushed off that easily. "So they're Chinese. That's really good news. We've come from China and my wife speaks fluent Mandarin. I'm sure we'll become good enough friends to be allowed to stay here," I said, and hurried back to Lydia to announce the good news.

Early next morning we hoisted sail in a fresh breeze and soon boldly entered the lagoon under full sails, disregarding the warning shouts of the crew on a small freighter anchored outside it.

As we got further in, the water shoaled gradually, and little by little I raised the centreboard. I had sounded carefully the day before for depth or possible rocks and felt confident. When at last the board was all the way up, I had to lower the sails because, without the board, I'd lose control of the boat. She is a true centreboard vessel, relying on her board, unlike a so-called keel-centreboarder, where the board just improves a boat's performance to windward.

We continued on our way, poling ourselves with long bamboo poles. When we finally hit bottom, as the tide was running out, I jumped over the side and walked around the boat in hip-deep water to check for possible rocks or other hazards which could damage the delicate planking of the yacht. Finding an even, soft bottom, we just let the boat heel over as it wished as the tide kept on going out. Finally all the water ran out and we were lying over the side at an alarming degree until the next tide came in. The boat gradually straightened out when the tide came in, finally floating as before.

By then it was the middle of the night, but the moon was so bright I felt sure we could find our way, despite the intricacy of the channels. With Lydia on the bow and me on the stern, we poled our ship further into the lagoon in the moonlight, accompanied by all the strange sounds of the various animals of the tropics. I felt I was the happiest man on earth. I didn't have to fear any more typhoons as long as we stayed here, for we had full protection.

We ran aground again long before daybreak before we reached the anchorage where the trimaran had been. But we were close enough to it that, as soon as daylight came back, I chose to row the rest of the way in the dinghy to see the owner of the house and introduce ourselves before we arrived with the yacht itself.

Mr. and Mrs. Go turned out to be charming and were very

surprised to hear my blonde wife addressing them in their own language. They opened their house to us, telling us to consider it our own and suggested we moor the boat right in front of their veranda. They explained that they were owners of a chicken food-processing factory in town, but they were now also starting a new business harvesting fish. Their house was brand new and they had just moved into it to be better able to watch their fish ponds. They also had to watch for neighbouring fishermen who would come and fish in their ponds, a much easier way to catch fish than going to sea.

The Gos were second-generation Chinese in the Philippines, but they hadn't forgotten their Chinese hospitality and spontaneously invited us to dinner that same day. In the meantime we could bring our boat when the tide got high again and have time to get organised and rested in our new anchorage.

The dinner proved both excellent and very friendly. Our hosts assured us that we had come to the right place if we were looking for peace and safety, as well as a convenient place to finish my boat.

When I asked if they would object if I used their road to have a truck deliver the timber I would need, they assured me it was perfectly all right and offered to let me store the wood in their four-car garage. They also invited me to work in the garage to make the mast, so I'd be protected from the broiling sun and the tropical downpours. We could hardly believe our good luck, especially compared to the unfriendly and unhappy conditions we had found in Iloilo.

Next day, Mrs. Go offered me a ride to town where I ordered all the wood I needed, not just for the mast, but also for making my bulwarks and its stanchions. The lumberyard owner promised delivery in two to three weeks, so I used the delay to install the bronze stanchions broken during the last typhoon. This time after patching up the fiberglass with epoxy resin, I sealed the edge with the bronze rail that I'd purchased in Taiwan but hadn't yet had time to install.

By the time the work was finished, the truck arrived with a load of nicely cut and planed-down timber to my specifications. I started first with the bulwarks, carefully adjusting the stanchions individually and screwing one to each of their bronze legs, which was tricky work. I had to adjust each stanchion so that we could get a pleasing and sweeping curve from bow to stern with no kinks or unfairness. I cut the bulwark sides and spliced them together, as they don't make timber long enough in one piece to go from stern to stern of a 50-foot boat. It was very satisfying to see the progress day after day, and I was pleased to hear the compliments of our hosts, who told us our ship was getting more and more beautiful as time passed.

Part of Lydia's work as a housewife consisted of doing errands and buying food for everyday needs. The closest store was in a small village called Consolation, and Mr. and Mrs. Go often gave Lydia a ride there on their way to work. In addition to their new business, they still put in a lot of time running their factory in Mandaue City, a small town on the way to Cebu City.

As time went by, Lydia made friends in the village. One especially good friend, Vasia Abucat, was a teacher and spoke very good English for one living in a lost little village in the Philippines. Thanks to Lydia's willingness to do all the errands on her own, I was able to work full-time on the boat, which progressed rapidly. Having finished the bulwarks, I could then start on the mast which I made this time as a thick-walled, hollow square box. I glued one plank at a time, then waited 24 hours before undoing the clamps and gluing the next one. The mast was nearly 50 feet long and had to be made of three staves on each side to make up the length, which meant 12 planks altogether, not counting the end plugs as well as the two plugs by the partners and by the shrouds. After finishing the mast as a square box, it needed to be cut down to a round pole. Since it was a gaff rig, I couldn't use the rectangular section fairly common in

Marconi rigs where the sail runs on a track. I had to have the round section for the gaff jaws to swing on.

By then, I had worked for several weeks on the Gos' property. I thought about all the wood chips which would result from adzing down the square box to make a round shape, and tried to keep the mess cleaned up as the work progressed. Lydia, who liked it more and more in the village where Vasia lived, announced that she had discovered a small river leading all the way to her friend's village and that perhaps we would be able to get the boat up to the village and finish it there. It would make life so much easier for Lydia to be next door to the grocery store and nearer her friends without having the long road to travel in the heat. She worried that I would not want to move, knowing that I was very happy where we were.

But she saved the strongest reason for the last, saying with a teasing smile, "And you know, Per, they are just now installing electricity in the village. Vasia has already arranged it so that if we come to her village we can lay to next to the small dock and they'll hook up the electricity so we'll have it right onboard. Then you could use your electric tools and thus save so much pain. They said electricity won't come to this part of the lagoon and the Gos' house for several more months, so you'd have to keep working with your hand tools here."

Lydia was so enthusiastic about the thought of going to the village that I wouldn't have disappointed her for anything by insisting that we remain where we were. I proposed we first explore the passage by dinghy to see if it would be possible to navigate up that tiny river as far as the village. She looked so happy as we all embarked in the dinghy that I really hoped it would be feasible to get there. I knew that one reason she was keen on changing was to get away from our neighbours in the trimaran, whom she thoroughly disliked.

Both the dour woman and her husband, who had been away

when I came upon their trimaran the first day, were French, like Lydia. I would have thought countrymen meeting each other so far away from home would sympathise, but it didn't work out that way. Perhaps they resented us for breaking into their territory and becoming such friends with the Gos, but perhaps their main reason to keep us at a distance was their fear that we could harm their "business" of exporting and selling antique religious statuettes, which they managed to send to France where an agent sold them at tremendous profit. Lydia, a fervent Christian, frowned upon such practices and even suspected their holy statues might have been stolen from churches.

It was a long row to the entrance of the creek, but it would be easy enough for us to get that far with the yacht. As we entered the tiny river, I was getting more and more discouraged, seeing how very shallow it was and also seeing how the trees had grown, leaning over the water so that many of the branches from one shore were entangled overhead with branches from the other shore. When we finally arrived in the village in the dinghy, I was fascinated by the peace and beauty of our potential anchorage.

When Vasia came down to greet us, I expressed my doubts about the possibility of getting there, due to the shallow water and the overhead jungle. Vasia was not a woman easily discouraged and assured us in her slow, calm English, "You've come all this way from the other side of the world without any trouble, and now you're going to let yourself be stopped by minor difficulties in our river? I have many friends in the village. They've all got sharp machetes and they know how to climb trees. They'll cut an opening to clear room for your mast. That's no problem at all. As for the shallow waters, you told me that you need only three and a half feet of water. Go back to your boat and sail it over to the entrance of the river and anchor there. At nightfall, I'll come with a pirogue and many friends with long bamboo poles and a machete. We'll make it to my village in the moonlight and you'll be happy here."

Thus it was that we went back to Mr. and Mrs. Go's house to load my yet unfinished mast on the boat. We cleaned up, thanked our hosts very much for their hospitality and hoisted sails for the entrance to the river. Everything was to work out exactly as Vasia had said. As our crew of volunteers cleared the way overhead for our mast, we poled ourselves to the village in the moonlight.

The native pirogues had been going up and down that creek for centuries, but I well believed the villagers when they declared after our successful arrival that this was the first time in history that any yacht had been there. And what an anchorage it was. No fairy tale setting could have been prettier with palm trees all around, calm water, a picturesque village of small houses built on stilts, and very friendly villagers who all spoke English.

The very next day, we had the electricity hooked up as Vasia had promised. No yachtsman could ever dream about anything more. Here protection was at a maximum and I could laugh at the typhoons. In fact, I even stopped keeping up to date with them.

Perhaps the only drawback to the anchorage was the excessive heat. Good protection from gales automatically means a lack of breeze in light weather. We would have greatly appreciated a cooling air stream, but here, once again, Vasia came to our aid. She decided to build a thatched roof over our boat, which was much more efficient than the usual awning yachtsmen use. She came early in the morning with a half dozen of her friends, and by noon the roof was finished. It gave us cooling shade for the entire duration of our stay, which was to be for several months.

Life in the village couldn't have been much different from what life was like several hundred years ago. True, they now had electricity and two cars which came nearly every day—one was a van bringing supplies and mail to the little grocery store and the other was a jitney, taking passengers to and from Cebu and Big City, the capital of the island.

The houses were all built on high stilts—the only sensible way to live in the tropics—high above the dampness and insects. Most of the houses had floors made out of slats which, although uncomfortable to walk on, allowed a breeze to blow through the house from the ground up through the roof. The people were poor and contented themselves with small houses. Each house invariably had a kitchen just inside the entrance at the top of the long wooden staircase. On the other side was the door to the main room where the family would gather and have their meals. From there a door led to the only other room, the bedroom. The toilets were outdoor affairs, but properly made and nicely arranged so that no offending odours came from them, as always seemed to happen in China. The river was their source of water. It was slightly brackish when the tide came in, but the rest of the time perfectly sweet and clean as there were neither industries nor any other people for miles.

Even our little Thomas was happy. There were few dangers for him and we let him run free in the village where, of course, everyone knew the beautiful, blond boy who became everyone's friend.

I began to notice that Thomas went ashore each day with a great deal of determination. It was as if he were headed to a particular destination, rather than strolling along, as I would expect a small boy not yet 3 to do. Out of curiosity I decided to follow him at a distance one day and see what he was up to. He went straight through the whole village as fast as his short legs could carry him, then turned left at a small side road without hesitation. He kept on going to the grocery store, where he climbed up on a stool and called over the counter to the storekeeper. To my surprise the storekeeper dished him up a piece of cake and a glass of Coca-Cola. Thomas sat a bit and enjoyed his snack, returned the empty soda bottle to the storekeeper and made his way back to the boat, never telling me about his escapade nor his free extra snack!

I told Lydia about what our young son had been doing every morning and we both felt a bit embarrassed to think of his having begged food and drinks. But we were also a bit proud of his sense of enterprise and concluded once more that he would certainly be able to manage for himself later on in life.

Now that we were right in the middle of the village and Thomas had a safe place to run and play, Lydia had a lot more free time and could help with the boat, which made the work go really quickly.

Soon the mast was ready to be stepped, a day we had both looked forward to. With the help of a half dozen friends we rigged the main boom on the foremast to act as a big crane, and pulled ropes through a series of tackles to get more purchase. We hoisted the mast up over the partners on deck and carefully lowered it down through the hole until the foot of the mast rested securely in its maststep, which I'd made in Iloilo.

We couldn't find the proper wire for staying our mast, so we contented ourselves with some local heavy diameter rope that we'd bought very cheaply. Once in place and tightened down, the lines seemed to hold our mast securely enough, and our boat was finally the schooner I'd wanted so much. Of all rigs, the gaff-schooner rig is without a doubt the most beautiful, as well as the most romantic. I was also confident it would be fast and efficient. We'd know for sure only after putting to sea again.

Its mast and bulwarks completed, the ship was a beauty to behold. Even though we still had a lot of work to do to finish everything, we felt the main work was done and we could take life a bit easier. From then on we only worked a few hours each day, generally from sunup until about 11 o'clock. Then we'd break for lunch and a siesta during the hottest time of the day. In the afternoon, we'd go swimming in that peaceful little river or visit some of our friends in the village. They were always glad to see us and would tell us about their lives and their customs. We bought fresh produce directly from the farmers at the same prices they sold to each other— far below the prices at the marketplace in Cebu, not to mention the prices tourists were asked to pay. We lived not only very cheaply but healthily, eating wonderful, fresh produce.

The farmers used buffalos for drawing their plows, and I'd been warned to be careful about getting too close to them. They were dangerous and I was told especially to teach Thomas to stay well away from them. In fact, one day as we passed a field where an elderly woman was using a buffalo to plow her field, I was told that very buffalo had killed her husband the year before. The buffalo had a fit of temper when the farmer had been careless, and ripped his stomach open with one of his horns.

"How come they didn't kill the animal?" I burst out, horrified.

"Why should they?" a villager replied, a bit surprised at my reaction. "It was just an accident and the widow needed the buffalo to plow her fields. How would she be able to survive and nourish herself if she no longer had her buffalo? Who would plow her fields?"

I looked more carefully at the woman and asked permission to take pictures of her plowing. She said yes, but wanted to go back to her house to put on a nice dress. I had a hard time persuading her that I thought her very beautiful just the way she was, in her masculine work clothes. I was sincere. Today when I look at that picture, I see her working hard behind her buffalo, walking with long strides to keep pace, slim without a gram of extra fat, her face as stony as though cut out of rock. She had a determined look in her eyes as she guided the animal to drag the plow where she wanted it. I marvel at the energy radiating from that woman. I was fascinated by her personality and I did find her strikingly beautiful despite her deep wrinkles and gray hair. There are many forms of beauty—not only the kind found in a young and pretty face.

Beside being hard workers, the people in the village also had hobbies and were expert kite flyers. Their kites were much bigger than those I remembered from my childhood—at least five or six feet long. They were light, but strongly built of bamboo framing covered with thin fabric and painted the brightest of colours. I have always thought kite flying a wonderful pastime—cheap, pollution-free, silent, yet requiring know-how to obtain the best results. Here they managed to spoil it by adding a "motor," which, of course, isn't needed on a kite. It had neither the looks nor the function of a motor, but was there just to make noise!. Fastened under the kite, the motor was made of specially slitted bamboo which, when exposed to the wind, made a very penetrating noise resembling a motor running without a muffler.

Both Lydia and I, watching the kite flyers preparing their kites, expressed our disappointment at spoiling such a beautiful art with unnecessary noise, but to no avail. The kite flyers couldn't comprehend our criticism and explained that it was very difficult to obtain a powerful sound with the lightest possible "motor," and it took a great deal of experience to make a powerful one.

Looking at the enormous length of line they carried on each kite's spool, we took heart and figured if they flew the kites anywhere near as high as the long lines seemed to indicate, the noise shouldn't bother us much. Indeed, the kites climbed and climbed, much higher than I would ever have dreamed possible. They flew so high they became just points in the sky. I wondered if they could become dangerous to airplanes, as many private planes and helicopters in the Philippines often flew very low to the ground.

I was very surprised to see that, when each kite had reached the height the kite flyer wanted, he climbed a tree and tied the string there. They were going to fly day and night until either a storm came or the tradewinds stopped and the kite fell.

The power of the kites was impressive, but we were to discover that even the long strings couldn't keep the noise away completely. As it happened, the wind placed the kites almost directly over our boat where the noise seemed to be even further amplified by an unfortunate resonance, like an echo, coming from between the hills on either side of the river.

Kept awake by the noise, Lydia and I tossed and turned in our bed most of the night. We were irritated to think of our beautiful and peaceful spot being spoiled by such an unnecessary thing. The owners of the kites slept close to where the strings were tied, so they didn't have to suffer from the noise as we did.

The next morning, Lydia complained to Vasia. As a school teacher in the village, she carried a lot of weight and arranged a special meeting with Lydia and the mayor. The mayor admitted this was a serious matter and after some deliberation made a new law on the spot, saying that these noisy kites were unworthy of civilised people. The kites were to be pulled in and returned to flight only when the motors had been removed.

I wasn't present when the two kite owners were called and the new law read to them, but Lydia told me that if a look from eyes full of anger and hate could kill, she would have dropped dead. That night, the kites were perfectly silent and we should have been able to sleep well, but we thought about those angry eyes and knew we had enemies in the village now. In fact, we regretted trying to make our own laws in a small village where we were the intruders amongst people who had been so kind to us. We'd lived with noise most everywhere and no doubt, after a few days, we would have grown accustomed to the noise of the kites.

Next day, to our surprise, the kites were taken down again briefly, then returned to flight, their motors roaring as before. We didn't dare go into the village, suspecting that either they had sent them up fully equipped again out of spite, or they'd succeeded in having the new law revoked. Soon a very embarrassed Vasia came and asked us to excuse her village. Some of the villagers had been so outraged at having their age-old kite flying spoiled just to please some foreigners that they threatened to elect a new mayor at the very next election. The poor mayor beat a hasty retreat, saying that he'd acted without sufficiently thinking over the problems involved and hereby abolished the unjust law.

That was the end of the affair. Nevertheless we never felt as welcome as we had before the incident. We were foreigners after all, and still had to suffer those darned kites for the rest of our stay.

Besides the villagers, we also enjoyed the company of some European and American friends. First there was a German named Wolfgang who had heard of us and came to visit with his girlfriend Gesti. He drove one of those very nice local cars which were rebuilt entirely from the thousands of wartime Jeeps abandoned by the American army after the war. He was building a new 55-foot catamaran, and explained that he'd lost his previous one on a reef a couple of years ago and was washed ashore without a penny. Because he'd lost everything, I was surprised that he'd been able to get back on his feet so quickly. He looked quite affluent with a nice car and told us that they were living in a large rental house and had three carpenters building the catamaran for him.

"You're wondering how I find the money?" he said. "Well, I'll tell you, even though I risk making a competitor out of you. I get my money from shells. There are plenty of shells in the water here and I send them to an agent in Germany who mails me back regular checks. I find it much less trouble to do that and hire carpenters than to do the actual boat building myself."

"But did you know about shells before? Doesn't it take a lot of time to learn about it before you can make money?" I asked.

"Yes, so I don't fear your competition now," he smiled. "I had a tough time in the beginning. I just had a book to go by and then dived for shells that looked promising according to the pictures and the descriptions in the book. I sent some of them to my friend in Germany and got some cash by return mail. Naturally that encouraged me, but diving is tiring work and I don't like it all that much. After I got some more money from Germany, I hired a diver and then several of them to do the diving for me. I'm bringing in enough money to rent a nice house and hire those carpenters. I think my new boat, which will be called *Taboo III*, should be finished in about six months. We plan on sailing to the Indian Ocean and either picking shells or doing some charter work."

Other friends didn't manage as well. An Australian who had arrived in Cebu shortly after we did preferred to anchor next to the shipyard outside of the lagoon's entrance. He was to become too fond of the liquor and spirits which are exceedingly cheap in the Philippines. We often went to see him in the beginning as he was a most charming friend, but as the weeks passed we found him drunk more and more often until we finally realised that he had become an alcoholic and was, in fact, becoming a human wreck.

We hear so much about the terrible results of drug abuse, yet many people seem to think that drinking a bit too much alcohol is forgivable. I honestly can't see much difference. Both are just as habit-forming and both have similar degrading effects.

"I can't afford *not* to be an alcoholic in a country where alcohol is as cheap as it is here," said the Australian when we reproached him for drinking too much. Lydia and I had gradually lost all desire to see him under the circumstances and never went back. We felt a bit guilty for abandoning him to his fate, but I knew it was of no use to try and get him off the bottle.

Our own life in the lagoon and in the little village could not have been happier. Sometimes I wonder why we didn't stay there forever, but a sailor always strives for new horizons. So the time came when we thought we would move on. The work on the boat was finished and hurricane season was over. It was the beginning of February and the only two really safe months of the year were ahead of us. We had no excuse to stay any longer. If we did stay, we'd need to stay until the following February for favourable conditions again. We hadn't forgotten the danger and misery of sailing through typhoons, which seemed to come in a never-ending stream, and so decided not to waste the good weather we had in front of us.

"I think we should go now," said Lydia, "but somehow I've lost my zest for Australia."

"Because of that drunkard of an Australian yachtsman?" I asked teasingly.

"Of course I know that one drunkard doesn't mean his country-men are all drunkards," Lydia said.

But we both had to admit that we were getting impatient to go to the States again, and Australia seemed like a detour that would only make us lose time. I was getting homesick for the States after all the years of vagabonding, and I'd talked so often to Lydia about America that she wanted to see the country where I had citizenship. We decided to sail straight there, but didn't know which route to take. After considering many possibilities, we finally decided to take the same route we'd come, as we were familiar with the route, we could escape all cold weather and we liked the idea of revisiting Europe on the way.

However, we didn't want to sail directly towards the Red Sea. We thought it would be a pity to miss Hong Kong and all the good shopping there, now that we had some money. From there we could steer for the Red Sea and perhaps take a break at Brunei along the way. Brunei was a stable and safe place, still under British control.

As soon as we made up our minds, we broke the news to Vasia and all our other friends that we were going to leave. We were very touched by how sad many of them looked at the thought of our departure. Vasia cried openly while hugging Lydia.

Our friends once again helped clear an overhead passage for us to get the boat down the river. Our new main mast was taller than the foremast and they had to cut more of the overhead branches. When we were safely out of the tiny river, they turned their pirogue about and bade us a fond farewell.

Night was falling as we arrived at the outer anchorage outside the lagoon. There we saw a boat we hadn't seen before, a sleek trimaran called *Allegra*. Rowan Talliaferro was onboard, a man with whom we would become good friends during the two days we laid for anchor there. He knew Asia better than most foreigners, having sailed there for many years. I gained such respect for his knowledge that I didn't hesitate to follow his advice when he warned us not to sail directly to Hong Kong as we'd planned.

"I well understand your desire to see Hong Kong again," he said, "but this is not the right time of the year. For one thing, it's still winter there and it's cold. The worst part is that you'll have to fight strong headwinds the whole way. It would be much better for you to wait here two or three months until the monsoon turns and gives you an easy, comfortable ride. Winter will also be over by then. If you're too impatient to get out to sea, you could kill time by sailing to Brunei, which is a pleasant little country. When the monsoon turns you can sail up to Hong Kong."

His advice made good sense, so we followed it. But tragedy was to befall us in the Sulu Sea. Later, after receiving a letter from him expressing his regrets for having advised us to take that fateful route, I was to ponder how fickle life could be, often hanging by just a thread. Had Rowan been enthusiastic about the idea of our sailing towards Hong Kong—had he said, "How I envy you, going to Hong Kong, that fascinating place. Never mind that it's up-hill to get there and that it'll be cold. You have a good boat and warm clothes and you'll make it. Send me a postcard when you get there," we would not have changed our plans for the seemingly easier Sulu Sea passage and Lydia would still be alive.

In his letter, Rowan wrote that he couldn't forgive himself for having recommended the route across the Sulu Sea, even if it was the best one, because he knew that the sea had a bad reputation for pirate activities. But so did I. I should have been the first one to know to stay away from that sea.

But who could seriously believe in pirate stories in the 20th century, an age of civilization—an age of radios and coast guards most everywhere. Pirates couldn't possibly get away. The radio officer on any attacked ship would simply send an S.O.S. distress signal and the coast guards, as well as the navies of the world, would arrive with high speed crafts, airplanes and helicopters.

I paid no mind to the "silly" tales, confident that we were choosing the best route any sailor could wish for. We hoisted sail at 12:30 p.m. Wednesday, the 14th of February, and waved goodbye to our friends.

# 17

# The Pirate Attack

*P*erhaps the best way to give an accurate picture of that fatal crossing would be to present our log book or ship's diary which, according to age-old law, is compulsory for any ship at sea. I have added some explanatory notes here and there, but am presenting the log itself exactly as it was written without any corrections whatsoever, grammatical or otherwise.

*Wednesday 14th of February.*
  *Leaving today at 12:30 from Cebu Harbour. Came here the day before yesterday.*

*Thursday, 15th Feb.*
  *In the morning sailing out of Bohol Strait under very light NE wind and beautiful weather. Rig very makeshift and speed slow. Pilot does not work. Expect to stop at either Jesselton or Brunei for proper refit before tackling South China Sea to Hong Kong.*

The pilot I'm writing about was a very makeshift affair which I'd made in less than a day while in the river. I wanted to experiment before investing the money and time necessary to make a proper one and had used a system of a large horizontal vane actuating the tiller itself. This setup gave tremendous power, but the way I'd made it meant only two orders possible—either full right or full left, with the result that the boat steered in a miserable zigzag course. Realising that I'd need a more sophisticated system, I scrapped the old setup, tossing it overboard. As for the makeshift rig, which may sound surprising after all the months of hard work rigging the boat, I was mainly referring to the lack of a mainsail which I'd not yet had time to sew for the new rig. I'd just recut my old yawl mainsail to fit as a foresail for my new schooner rig, while one old staysail was used as a makeshift "mainsail" on the schooner's main mast. In strong winds it probably would have been adequate, but in the very light winds predominating in this part of the world (when a typhoon wasn't blowing) it left us very under-canvassed, giving us very slow speeds.

*Friday 16th of February*
    *Very tired both of us as autopilot did not work and we are steering day and night. We try to compensate by good food and Lydia is cooking three excellent meals a day with eggs, fruits and fresh vegetables.*

*Samedi 17 Fevrier 1979.*
    *Sommes maintenant au centre de la Mer de Sulu. Encalmines toute la nuit. Position at noon 8 degrees 33 N – 121 degrees 18 E. Rain squalls this morning.*

Half of the preceding entry, which is in French, was written by Lydia. It was to be her last entry in the log.

*Sunday 18th Feb. 79.*
    *A small cargo crossed our bow, southbound, about two miles off at 11:30. Good weather. Light Northerly wind."*

*Monday 19th of Feb. 79.*
    *Passing about seven miles north of Maender Reef. A boat looking like a fishing boat was either at anchor there or circling very slowly back and forth. Good weather. Light northerly wind.*

Perhaps we should have worried about that boat. I often wondered later on if this was the boat which was going attack us. On that fateful day, still stunned by what happened, I wrote:

*Tuesday 20 Feb. 79*

*This morning was boarded by wooden motorboat and they shot Lydia and killed her. I still can't understand it has happened. Thomas is OK, but cries for his mother and I don't know what to make him eat.*

It was just a short entry, which I wrote out of an old habit and in obedience of the age-old maritime law which demands that all happenings at sea be immediately written down for possible reference later on. But the next day I was able to write in more detail what actually happened.

*Wednesday 21 Feb. 79.*

*I am very tired having hardly slept or eaten since it happened but I will try to describe everything while it is fresh in my mind.*

*We just passed the Bancoran Island around 10 o'clock yesterday morning. Both of us were sitting inside to protect ourselves from the sun and only going out to correct the course when needed. Suddenly we heard a motor. Going on deck, we were surprised to see a boat very close by, following us and steering towards us. Because the Sulu Sea had a bad reputation, we were a bit apprehensive and Lydia suggested we take our gun and fire a warning shot to tell them to get away.*

*I told her it was too late. They would be alongside by the time we got the gun out. If they were just curious fishermen, there was no need for the gun anyway. If they were pirates, firing at them would be a declaration of war. There were at least a dozen men and it would be easy for them to outshoot us.*

*Lydia didn't argue and went down below leaving me at the tiller. Shortly afterwards to my dismay, I saw her come out of the forehatch with the gun. She fired a shot from forward of the mast over the boat which was alongside us a couple feet away. The reaction was immediate—a shot was fired at her from inside the deckhouse just abreast of her and only about three yards away. Lydia fell into the sea immediately tainting the water red with her blood.*

*The man came out and sighted me with his gun. I looked into his gun which had a very big bore and expected to meet the same fate as Lydia. I wasn't scared—I just didn't care anymore and was resigned. But the shot I expected didn't come. Instead he lowered the cross of the gun from his shoulder keeping the gun pointed above my head. Only then was I aware of Thomas who was clinging to my legs looking at the strange boat. At sea we normally kept him locked up in his cabin for fear that he would fall in the water. But in her haste to get on deck through the forehatch, Lydia must have forgotten to lock the door behind her. Thomas went through the main saloon up to me. It must have been the sight of that beautiful little boy with blond hair clinging to his father which softened the man so that he could no longer shoot. Besides, I was not armed.*

*Two men jumped onboard and went below through the forehatch away from me, while the man with the gun kept watching me. From the saloon, two of the men showed me some money and by signs made me understand that's what they wanted. I pointed through the hatch to the drawer where we kept our money. One of the men emptied the drawer taking all the money, about 100 U.S. dollars but didn't search the ship for any additional money. They both came on deck through the forehatch again and picked up the gun which had fallen on the foredeck. They also carried two boxes of ammunition, about 40 shells of caliber 12, which they must have seen when they went through the bedroom.*

*As soon as they jumped back to their boat, they sheared off and soon disappeared towards the south. The boat was about 50 feet long wooden and fairly low and narrow. It looked old and dirty, but had a very smooth and silent engine. There were about 12 men onboard between the ages of*

*25 and 40. They were small and dark and didn't appear to speak English. Weather was clear sky, smooth sea, light N.E. wind.*

Later, as night approached, I added a new entry:

*18:00*

*A new night is coming. I am so tired and feel so depressed. The ship is so empty without her. Getting closer to Balabac Strait leading out of the Sulu Sea but am afraid to tackle it without Lydia. If I can get safely to port I will sell the boat.*

I passed a horrible night alone with my thoughts and fell deeper and deeper into despair. As the entries in the log will show, in the following days, far from adjusting to the situation, I was wearing myself out with my thoughts. I had regrets for not having managed better, guilt feelings for having been the cause of my wife's death, even if indirectly, because of my way of life. I regretted ever having come to the east in the first place, where a white man is no longer welcome.

*Thursday 22 Fevrier 1979*

*A new day has come. Awakening this morning at 4:00 after having taken down all the sails, letting the ship drift. I was too tired to take care of the navigation. This ship is so desperately empty without Lydia that I can't help crying all the time. In addition, I feel sick, something in my throat hurts me. I wish I could get in a hospital and do nothing but sleep and not think about anything, while somebody else takes care of Thomas and sells the ship with everything inside it. It's unbearable to look at all Lydia's things which she was so fond of and know that she is dead drifting around in the sea.*

*Yet it all could have been avoided. I never saw any of the other men with a gun, so Lydia was probably right to try chasing them away with a warning shot. But in our case, it was just too late. Had we been on deck and not below when the boat approached, we'd have been able to scare them off before they got close enough to engage in a fight. Had their motor not been so silent, we'd have heard them in time. Or at least if we'd had the gun ready and not packed away, we might also have had a chance. And of course if Lydia had been as passive as I am, she probably wouldn't have been killed either. They didn't looked like hardened murderers. In fact, they all looked a little scared and anxious to get away. Life and death depends on so little. I miss her so desperately. I relied on her completely. Thomas had diarrhea yesterday and I didn't know what to do. It's now 9 o'clock and he hasn't awakened yet. I'm worried because he generally wakes up at dawn, just as the sun comes up. With Lydia, everything was so simple and she took care of everything. Will have to try and cook something, but don't even know how to work the stove. I've never done it on this boat.*

Here I was wrong. I'd forgotten that I'd operated the stove while in the Malacca Strait after Thomas was born. The log continues:

*What about the future of Thomas? Had it not been for him I would have preferred to die also for what future is there for me now. I can't stand the memories in this boat and want to sell it. It represents five or six years of my life in hard work and three of four years of Lydia's and a small fortune in materials. Always nothing but the best. But, I'll get only a fraction of its worth because people don't appreciate wooden boats any longer, not the gaff rig. They are also sceptical about homemade boats. Then at 54 what will I do to assure a living for Thomas and me? Must I live until I'm 74 years old if I want to take care of him until he's 20. With Lydia and her great energy and optimism, I never worried. Now with her gone I feel my life is coming apart.*

*10:30 Thomas awake but sick with swollen red eyes and does not want to eat or drink. Hope it's nothing serious.*

*Sailing out of Balabac Strait.*

Here I'd written only "sailing out of Balabac Strait" with no further comments, showing how run down I must have been. Nothing interested me anymore, not even getting through the dreaded strait. Today I wonder how I got through that reef-studded strait with its strong, irregular currents. I was singlehanded and worn down by sorrow and by the shock of seeing my wife killed right before my eyes. Perhaps I made it through the strait thanks to the seaman's instinct we acquire little by little after long experience, but maybe it was just plain luck. After all, I'd had more than my share of bad luck, so perhaps I was just due for some good luck. In any case, I would follow the west coast of Borneo until I reached port. Unfortunately, that part of the South China Sea is far from free of danger and full of reefs with uncertain currents. Nevertheless, the hardest part was behind me.

*14:00. Thomas has fever. Just lays in bunk and wants nothing. East wind. Good speed southward. Worried about tonight. Without Lydia I don't have the force to keep sailing all night. I will try to anchor before sundown if possible.*

*18:00. No suitable place to anchor. Cooked corn and fried bananas but Thomas didn't want any. He has eaten nothing all day. I remember now that I cooked before when Lydia had just given birth and didn't leave her bunk for a week, but then I cooked under her instructions.*

*Friday, 23 February 79*

*Hove-to and stopped ship last night as too tired to continue. Started again now at 4:30.*

*Thomas very hot with fever. Only wants water. Very worried. 150 miles left to Brunei. If he doesn't get better when we get abreast Jesseltown,*

*I'll have to stop there to see a doctor despite the port being unsafe. He keeps calling his mother and it breaks my heart. Three days have passed and I still can't quite understand I don't have Lydia anymore. Nothing onboard has been touched. Just the cash in my wallet, the gun and the cartridges. Nothing else was taken. I can't quite remember the colour of the boat, so yesterday I leaned over the side to see if there were any scratch marks from the boarding, but I saw none. I don't think we ever touched, both boats just keep a steady course a couple of feet apart. Yet the boat is empty for Lydia. How I regret ever building this boat. For all the work and money we've put into it we could have had a nice house in the south of France and lived happily there for many more years.*

*Saturday 24 February 79*
  *6:00. Becalmed. Thomas is better this morning has no more fever. He asked me for a baby bottle of Cerelac and brought me both the bottle and the can so I could prepare it for him.*
  *10:00. Still becalmed. Forgot to wind the chronometer and now no longer have the exact time for my navigation.*

This last entry I wrote in French in the log, but have translated here into English. My sudden switch over to French could only be explained by my state of exhaustion; I no longer realised what language I was using.

Forgetting to wind the chronometer was a serious omission, as our little receiver radio was not working anymore. With no way to get the precise time, I could no longer calculate my longitude other than deadreckoning or transferring and adding the estimated run of each day to the previous day's position. This is a very inaccurate system, as it makes no account for the errors caused by currents, compass or distance covered. Furthermore, each day's errors are added to the previous ones until we become very unsure of our exact position—a situation very undesirable in places such as this, where there were many reefs and underwater dangers. The voyage continued and next day I again entered the log in English as I normally did.

*Sunday 25th of February 79.*

*Light baffling winds all night. Very slow progress. Now becalmed. Tried to clean up ship to get my mind occupied. Feeling very depressed. Wish I could get to port and talk with some people. Thomas has no fever anymore, but still has diarrhea. I don't know what to do about it. Very little appetite, just half an egg and half a baby bottle. He cries all the time. I don't know why.*

*Although sailing far from the coast, this part of the ocean is so shallow that it's often possible to anchor in what may seem like mid-ocean. Although if it's blowing even moderately, it's far preferable to anchor in the lee of some of the reefs. Of course, we have to know where we are on the chart and make sure to locate the right reef, otherwise we would soon go aground and in all probability wreck the ship which would most likely mean our death. Yet there is a limit to how long a man can deprive himself of sleep. At some point he either has to anchor, let the boat sail on her own, or just hove-to and try to get the ship to stop.*

*In the middle of the ocean where there are no reefs, the most usual solution is to try to get the ship to steer herself either with the help of an automatic pilot, or by carefully trimming the sails and adjusting the tiller—a feat some ships will do, but most not.*

*We can also stop the ship by either taking down all the sails or by adjusting them in such a way that some of the sails will work against the others and stop progress, a method called heaving-to the ship. Heaving-to is an excellent way to give the crew a rest, for example when in a gale. But no ship can be certain to stop 100 percent. All ships will drift, some more than others, so the system is only good where we have room enough and can be sure that we are not going to hit shore or hit a reef while we sleep.*

In this case, there were a lot of reefs most everywhere along this route. It would be safest to anchor if I could find a suitable place. Anchoring, if done properly, is most restful for the sailor as the ship stays securely in place until he is ready to continue his voyage.

*Monday, 26 Feb., 1979*
*Too tired last night to try to navigate with all these reefs everywhere. Anchored in 18 fathoms, 5 miles offshore Tg Nosong despite favourable north wind. Slept all night. Feeling a little better today. Started at 6:00 but at 7:00 almost becalmed. the breeze came about 10:00. Sat at the tiller all day until 20:00 and anchored outside inlet to Brunei.*

*Tuesday, 27 Feb.*
*Anchored at Brunei Harbour 9:30.*

That was the last entry I was to make in the log until the day I left Brunei. I thought that finding a safe port would mean that I would find rest and peace. I was sadly mistaken.

# 18

# The Police Investigation

When I try to remember my arrival at Brunei, it's as though I'm looking through a haze. Today it seems a miracle to me that I was able to bring my ship in to port at all in the condition I was in. I was completely run-down and in despair, yet I'd been able to safely pass all the reefs of the Balabac Strait, avoid all the reefs along the coast and then manage the long, tricky entrance channel known for its strong cross currents.

I hardly remember all that today, except for what I'd marked in the log. I do remember letting go the anchor in the middle of the harbour, not far from some official looking building I guessed would be the authorities' offices. I was in doubt about what to do. I didn't have the pilot book about Brunei, which would have explained the quarantine formalities.

While I stood there, wondering what to do, a small motor launch passed very close. I hailed them, asking if I was supposed to go ashore to look for the authorities or wait for them to come onboard. Suddenly, hearing a human voice, I no longer felt all alone. I lost control of myself and screamed in what must have sounded like incoherent talk from a sick man, "My child is sick and I don't know what to do with him. They killed my wife. They shot her."

Hysterical as I must have looked, they didn't react, or answer me. I screamed again, "I'm telling you, they killed her right in front of me. Please get the authorities. Please get a doctor for my son."

"All right, we'll call them, " they answered. I still remember their calm voices which sounded indifferent to me, as if they heard of such happenings everyday. More likely they must have thought I was drunk or drugged, or just had a screw loose.

It seemed like only minutes had passed before a boat carrying a man in a spotless white uniform came alongside. He introduced himself as the official doctor and jumped onboard while the launch's crew fended off and secured alongside. He took just one quick look at Thomas and me before declaring that he was taking us both to the hospital immediately.

I protested, saying I couldn't leave my ship until the harbour authorities had cleared me, but the doctor waved my objections aside. "Nonsense, I'll take responsibility for this. Health comes before paperwork. You both need immediate medical attention. I'll drive you to the hospital myself and see that you get treated."

At the hospital, doctors soon determined that Thomas was suffering from an acute intestinal infection and began treating him with antibiotics. As for me, they never told me what was wrong. They just gave me a shot which made me feel quite relaxed and sleepy. I was told I should try to sleep as much as possible and to come back for several days for additional shots.

Our uniformed doctor drove us back and personally took me to the harbour authorities office, where he explained the situation to them. True to his word, he declared that it was upon his order that I'd left the ship before they'd cleared me. They accepted the explanation, and said they would now come on the ship to do the clearance, which they did in an efficient and courteous manner.

I had hoped to be able to get some sleep, but I was disappointed. A police boat came towards us and about eight or 10 uniformed men came onboard. They wanted a full report, asking question after question about what had happened in the Sulu Sea with my wife. It all seemed to take forever as they wrote down everything I said. Despite the fact that I was near collapse from exhaustion, it seemed

At Any Cost

to me that they couldn't pay attention. They kept repeating the same questions. I also didn't think they had very good manners when they asked me if I had a picture of my wife to show them. I picked a picture I considered appropriate from our photo album to show the policemen, but they grabbed the whole album out of my hand and began to peer through every page. I had several nude pictures of my beautiful young wife in the album, and I was very embarrassed.

When they finally left, I practically collapsed in bed for a greatly needed sleep. It seemed like I'd barely had time to fall asleep when a new boat thumped against my side and two new uniformed men came onboard. They excused themselves and hoped I wouldn't mind if they asked me a few questions.

Although I was half-dazed, not only from lack of sleep but also, I suspect, from the shot I'd been given in the hospital, I still recognised the same questions that had been asked by the previous crew. I told them so, saying I was very tired and if they wanted answers to those questions all they had to do was to see their colleagues and get a copy of my answers.

Much to my annoyance, the men said they belonged to a different division and didn't have access to the other department's reports, so they had to get the interview directly with me.

Again it took forever. One officer asked questions while another wrote down my answers in longhand. Finally they reread my statement to me and asked me to sign it. I don't remember how late it was when they at long last left, but shortly thereafter the sun came up and a couple of new police investigators came and started all over again. How long did they stay? Perhaps two hours, perhaps three, but when they finally left, it seemed like only a few minutes had passed before I was again boarded by new policemen. In my naivety, I at first thought that the officials just didn't know their business. It was several days later before I understood and realised that, far from being disorganised, the police knew exactly what they were doing. The apparently confused repeat interrogations were just routine police procedure.

I didn't realise all of this yet on the second day when, after a lengthy questioning, a new crew came onboard. This time they were civilians. I asked them why they weren't in uniform. One of them laughed and said they weren't policemen, but reporters for a daily newspaper and, without wasting any time, went right to work asking me all the same questions once again.

The interview had hardly begun, when I became angry at seeing how eager they seemed. They were actually happy to get a good story out of my misfortune. I cut off the interview right there and told them to leave me alone. I resented people who were there solely for the purpose of cashing in on my tragedy. They left with sullen, if not hateful, expressions, clearly resenting my rudeness.

As soon as they left, before any new visitors could corner me, I rushed ashore to try to find peace and quiet. I remembered Rowan had spoken of a friend in Brunei before we left Cebu. I needed a friend to talk to and a place to rest, free from all those awful questions.

I looked him up, and both he and his wife could not have been nicer to us. He was an officer in the English military, stationed at the base in Brunei. True to most English officers, he couldn't have been more hospitable and considerate when I told him of our common friend and my tragedy. Realising how run down I was and seeing the pitiful face of my little son, he suggested we be his guests for the evening. He also invited the base's chief doctor over to doublecheck on my son, as well as another friend, a sailing enthusiast who'd said he'd like to meet me. The kindly officer did everything to cheer me up, and I was quite relieved and relaxed to have found someone who really seemed to care.

The doctor was the first of the guests to arrive. He was a very friendly and charming Englishman who insisted on first having a look at Thomas. After a thorough examination, he fully agreed with the diagnosis reached by the hospital staff, but he was not very impressed with the medicines they had prescribed.

"It's not my habit to criticise other doctors," he said, "but in this case I would strongly recommend that you disregard their treatment altogether and use a medicine I will prescribe for your little boy. In no more than three days you'll see a cure, although you must promise me not to stop the treatment for a full week. Inflammation of the intestines is very serious if it's not treated correctly. I don't have the medicine with me, but I'll drive home right now and get it. I'll be back within half an hour. Just wait here."

Half an hour later he was back with a bottle and seven doses of medicine. I was very grateful to him. Thomas regained his health quickly, just as the doctor said, and to this day has never relapsed.

The other guests, also military officers, began to arrive from the base. They made me feel good, each of them trying their best to comfort me. They were friendly and considerate.

We were just going to the dinner table when we heard the telephone ring. Our host answered and, when he learned who was calling, made signs to turn down the radio and for everyone to talk softly. We stopped talking altogether, so we couldn't help but hear the telephone conversation. Our host began to look surprised and uncomfortable as the conversation progressed. He almost looked as though he was standing at attention.

"Yes, sir, they're here....But, sir, I can't do that. He's a friend and in dire need of comfort....I'm sorry, sir, it's too late to cancel now. We are just going to sit down at the table. Dinner is being served right now....Very well, sir, I'll be there first thing in the morning."

He hung up the phone with a puzzled look. "I can't understand what went into his head," he said, addressing all of us. "That was our

C.O. He said he'd heard that I intended holding a party for a man who claimed to have been attacked by pirates and he told me to have nothing to do with him. When I told him that you were already here and we were about to have dinner, he could hardly hold his temper. He told me to be in his office first thing in the morning. I wonder what's gotten into him. He really sounded mad and didn't want the base to get entangled in pirate stories."

My host explained that C.O. meant commanding officer and, from what I understood, he was the big boss whom everyone feared. But after discussing it for a while, the group dismissed the matter, saying that the C.O. must have been in a bad mood and had a couple of drinks too many. We soon forgot the interruption altogether and I thoroughly enjoyed the evening. The meal was the most excellent I could remember and tasted doubly good because, after the attack in the Sulu Sea, I had hardly cooked a single decent meal and must have been half-starved.

Some of the officers drove me to the dock late that night. We agreed to rendezvous the next morning at 10 a.m. They had offered to drive me around and show me a little bit of the countryside, as well as the capital, which I'd seen only during my hospital visit.

Back at the boat, the police left me alone that night, but early the next morning they were back. This time it was the officers who had interrogated me when I first came in. After excusing themselves for bothering me, they said they had a few more questions they'd forgotten to ask me the first day and hoped I wouldn't mind helping them make their report more complete. But to my surprise, except for a couple of new questions, most of them were the same old questions they had pestered me with ever since I entered the harbour. They were polite enough that I couldn't complain, but they were so persistent that my nerves were constantly on edge. They focused on the smallest of details, which to me were a remembrance of a tragedy

I was trying to forget, to protect my mind from going to pieces.

When they had finally left and were out of sight, I rushed ashore before the next investigators could corner me onboard and make me miss my date with my new friends. I still had nearly an hour to wait for them, but I feared if I waited onboard I would get stuck there with new interrogations, so I decided to wait ashore for them.

The time of our planned meeting came and my friends had not arrived, so I waited. I waited 20 minutes, 30 minutes, then a full hour had gone by. I wondered why they hadn't come as they'd agreed. Perhaps they'd forgotten, so I took the long walk over to their house. No one was there and everything was closed. I asked neighbours if they knew where they were, but I was met with unfriendly stares before they shut their doors.

On my way back to port, I stopped at the local store and a newspaper headline caught my eyes: "Pirate Attack, or the (Nearly) Perfect Matrimonial Murder?" It was my story with my name! I was horrified. It explained the police's persistence. They weren't merely making a report to mark down the facts in their records—they actually suspected me of having murdered my beautiful wife, someone I loved so much, who had meant everything to me.

Only then did I realise that their tiring, repeated interrogations were just a police tactic to see if, with my fatigue, I'd start to contradict myself and thus incriminate myself.

As I read the article I was shocked at its meanness, as if it were written by someone who hated me and really wanted to do me harm. Then I remembered those reporters and how rude I'd been to them. They were getting even with me! It's unwise to make an enemy of a journalist. The printed word has tremendous power. All too many people think that if something is in print, it must be true.

To make matters worse, this nasty newspaper article was not going to remain local. Due to the normal procedure of news distribution, it was going to be published in many countries including France, Lydia's home. In fact, that same day, I got a message from the telegraph office with a request to present myself as soon as possible for a phone call from Paris.

It was Monsieur Grosset, the director of the press agency who had been so nice to me when I'd visited his office in Paris several years before. He told me he was saddened to read about my wife's death and horrified about the nasty way the reporter had handled the story. He was calling me so I could tell him what really happened. Fortunately for me, over the course of many years of correspondence, I'd made a real friend, and also fortunately for me, his word carried far more weight than that of a small-time reporter in Brunei.

The next day, another story appeared in the newspaper, this one based on the facts. The story also helped readers understand that pirates were far more prevalent in some parts of the world than was commonly believed. Several other recent pirate stories were included that previously had not attracted much attention from the press.

I was so grateful to him for putting the story straight. I'd been feeling terrible, thinking about my wife's family and what they must have thought reading the first article with its nasty accusations. I later received tender and thoughtful letters from all of Lydia's family. Although they'd never been too happy about our union (which was understandable because of the difference in our ages and my lack of financial security), they joined me in my sorrow and stood by me, offering me any help they could give. I'll forever be grateful to them for the consolation and support they gave me when I needed it most.

But in Brunei, I was on my own. My new friends were to fail me completely, perhaps because the story published by Monsieur Grosset never appeared. On the contrary, the local newspaper insisted on printing only their own version in the days that followed, included nasty suppositions and hidden accusations.

My nerves were completely on edge. When I came back to my boat and found yet another police officer waiting for me with the usual male secretary there to write everything down, I blew into a fit. I told him in no uncertain terms what I thought of them and their insulting suspicions. I said they no doubt resented having to admit to the world that there were still pirates in their part of the world and they'd been unable to stop such activities. I told him they were unworthy of the 20th century when any well-organised country with radios, helicopters and coast guard should have been able to erase such activities long ago. I said they much preferred to prove that it was just a cheap matrimonial murder between two foreigners having nothing to do with them. I lost more and more control of myself until I couldn't speak and fell into tears. I was having a nervous breakdown and the officers realised it. Far from harshly answering me in the same tone and ordering me to keep my opinions to myself, they patiently waited for the storm to blow over.

When I had calmed down somewhat, they assured me in a friendly tone that they had nothing to do with the newspaper article. Their records are kept confidential and certainly were not available to reporters. They insisted they had no preconceived ideas about what had happened. They were just trying to make as thorough a report as possible and would try to reach a conclusion only after it was complete. They would try to verify and analyse the information in as objective a manner as possible.

Their friendliness soothed me. I now believed that they earnestly were trying to find the truth. Despite those nasty suspicions printed in the newspaper, which had been dreamed up by some vengeful newspaper man in search of a sensational story, they had no pre-conceived ideas. I suddenly calmed down completely and decided to cooperate with them in all respects.

They remained polite and courteous and said they had two

requests to make of me. First, they wanted to question my three-year-old son out of my presence, promising to try not to upset him too much, and second, they would like me to allow them to make a photographic reconstruction of the attack. I readily agreed, but I reminded them that Thomas spoke only French and no English at all. They said that was no problem because the wife of the chief of police spoke perfect French and would be their interpreter.

When Thomas and I arrived at police headquarters, I was very relieved when the officers introduced me to our interpreter, an extremely charming and beautiful woman. She was someone I hadn't expected from my preconceived notion of what a police chief's wife would be like. After making friends with Thomas, they did take him into another room and made me wait for what seemed like hours in a cold-looking waiting room. They eventually brought him back and, to my relief, he didn't seem distressed at all by the experience. I earnestly thanked them for not upsetting Thomas.

The next day, they came back with a crew. In addition to several police officers and their secretaries, they brought a photographer and his helpers, as well as a model who was to stand in for Lydia. They asked me to pose in various situations so they could reconstruct the attack. I especially remember one picture they wanted to take from the eye level of the pirate who'd sighted his gun at me. I stood at the tiller while Thomas clung to my leg. Another picture I could hardly bear to assist with was one of Lydia falling into the sea while she lost her grip on the gun, which then fell to the deck. There were several other pictures which I was able to bear only because of my firm determination to cooperate with the police. I was almost beginning to consider them as friends trying to find the truth—the opposite of those mean and dishonest reporters.

All the interrogations and photography had been going on for about two weeks, off and on, during which time none of my friends from that dinner party came to visit me. I hadn't been able to find them at home or reach them on the phone until one day, I ran into the host of the dinner party at the market. Far from greeting me with a smile as I expected, he kept a rather gloomy and aloof face and answered me abruptly before turning and disappearing in his car.

It was all too obvious that he didn't want anything more to do with me. What had gone wrong? Was it the newspaper article which made him believe he'd been befriending a murderer? Perhaps, more likely, his C.O. had been serious in his order not to get anyone on his base entangled with any kind of pirate story.

In any case, with very few exceptions during my whole stay in Brunei, except for the police, I hardly spoke to anyone. The most I'd get if I tried to meet anyone was a short yes or no. It embittered me to think that, just when I most needed friends, I was let down. I felt tired and sick and so terribly lonely without my wife. I had no friends and was alone with my little son in a faraway country with a culture so different from our own.

Then on the 14th day, one of the head policemen came over to my boat with a big smile, saying he had good news for me. I just stared back at him, not comprehending what he meant. As far as I was concerned, the only good news he could bring me was that Lydia wasn't dead—that she was alive and that it had all been just a bad dream. Failing that, I could imagine no good news.

"I have good news for you," he insisted with a friendly smile. "We have closed your case and you are free to leave anytime you wish."

Only then did I fully realise that I'd really been under arrest even if I'd been permitted to remain on my boat. His friendly smile, so different from the austere, if courteous, looks I'd gotten from the police before, also told me that I was no longer a suspect, but rather a victim whom he wished he could help.

Despite the fact that he was still in uniform, he ventured to talk to me as a friend. "We were never surprised at the possibility of your wife's being killed by pirates. We were just surprised that you hadn't been killed, too. We estimate that there are about 300 attacks in this part of the world each year. That is between Singapore and up to and including the Philippines.

"You look surprised," he added, seeing my disbelief. "Yes, that's right, nearly one every day."

"In that case, why did you suspect me of not telling the truth?" I exclaimed indignantly.

"As I told you," he said, "because you weren't killed. You see the normal procedure of the pirate is to come alongside, jump onboard and take control of the boat. They then kill everyone onboard so they can take their sweet time to empty the ship of all its valuables. They even unbolt the main engine and transfer it to their own boat. Then, when everything sellable or of value has been transferred to their boat, they sink the boat with the bodies locked inside."

"Thus there are no witnesses and no possibility of ever catching the bandits. You baffled us. As far as we could make out, everything you said checked out, yet they didn't kill you, especially when you were a dangerous witness who could testify to the murder. We got the explanation when we studied the pictures we took. The picture of that little blond boy clinging to you, to his father's leg, looking so innocently into the murderer's eyes, could soften anyone's heart. He must have been the reason why the pirate didn't have the courage to shoot you. Even a hardened criminal can have a soft heart for children. We believe your son saved your life.

"That was the reason the criminals took only your money. They didn't want to be traced through a stolen receiver or other personal items. They did take your gun, which could become a clue against them if it were found. But it's our guess that the man who took the gun merely did so to ensure that you couldn't grab it and shoot them with it when they departed. In all probability they threw it overboard later on. The man who picked it up probably didn't throw it immediately from your boat because he didn't want to take the responsibility and wanted his boss to do it himself."

I was relieved that the seemingly never-ending police interrogations had ended, but I should have been more relieved to know that I wasn't a suspect anymore and ran no risk of being put in jail. I should have been more relieved, but I really didn't care. I had lost my wife. Whether I was onboard my ship or in jail or anywhere else hardly seemed to matter to me. The one thing I did care about, though, was finding the men who had killed Lydia.

"I'm relieved that you believe me," I said, "but why close the case without even trying to find the bandits? I guarantee that I'll be able to identify their boat, even among a thousand. Why not take me from port to port until we find the boat?"

He shook his head and answered, "Don't think we've done nothing during these two weeks but interrogate you. We've checked on you, on your sailing and on your family life. We've checked to see whether you have any life insurance. We know more about you than you can imagine. It hasn't always been easy. You have not always followed the prescribed regulations and you often leave a port without bothering to clear out. For example, at your last port before the attack, you left Cebu without making the proper exit formalities. Indeed in Cebu, you didn't even make the entry formalities, so at first we thought you'd never been there and were lying to us. Yet by persisting, we were able to contact a coast guard officer who remembered showing you a suitable place to anchor after you'd gone to their office to ask for advice!"

I must have looked a bit embarrassed at this point, but he continued. "We have also checked on shipping activities along the shores of northern Borneo and the Southern Philippines, which are the closest shores to where you were attacked. Although it may sound easy to you, it will be a never-ending hunt. All too many boats fit your general description, and most of these boats are not sitting in harbour—most of the time they're working at sea.

"They don't always come back to their same port, but may go from port to port. How long would it take for us to see them all? We're not even sure that they didn't come from far away. And then we have administration problems. You reported the crime in Brunei, but the attack happened in the Sulu Sea. We have no jurisdiction there unless it's considered the open sea and we were your first port of call. But we still may not be able to claim it's the open sea, because the Philippines claims it's an interior sea belonging to them. And officials on the northern coast of Borneo don't want to work with us, despite the attack's having happened much closer to their shores than to someone else's. We consider that we have very little chance of finding the boat and even less chance of having the crew punished, so we've dropped the case."

My friends since that time have told me that had it been them, they would have searched for the bandits on their own, spending years to do it if necessary. They would either kill them themselves or bring them to court where they would be judged and hung and Lydia's death would be avenged.

I've thought about it many times, trying to visualise what would happen. Suppose I did find the boat. Suppose I had the crew arrested. If on the day of the trial the judge were to ask me, "Can you identify the murderer of your wife?' I would look at him and perhaps remember him as he sighted me along his gun. But this time I would see him scared and know that his life might rest with me. He would be at my mercy. My testimony could hang him, could kill him as surely as he could have killed me and my three-year-old son. I would see his scared eyes and I would realise that the only reason I could testify against him at all was because he had mercy for me and my son. Should I now repay him by having him killed? I know I could not feel right about it. I would probably say, "I'm sorry, I can't identify him," and he would have gone free—just as he had let me go free.

It wasn't that I didn't love my wife, that I didn't mourn her death, and want a murderer punished. I just didn't want him condemned for the one act of mercy he had shown. Should I, who consider myself an honest and decent citizen, show less mercy than this criminal?

After thinking it over, I was rather grateful for the police's decision to abandon the case. As for me, I decided to return home and to try to forget my life in Asia, which had been nothing but disappointment and sorrow from beginning to end.

In earthly goods, I still had my boat and two years' worth of savings from my work in China. To sell the boat right there and fly home would have been the best thing for us. With my savings and the money I got from the boat, I could buy a home back in my own country, and still have enough to live on until I could get my health back and look for a job.

It was a sensible plan. The only hitch was that I was unable to find a buyer. Or rather, the only man interested in buying my boat also fully realised the difficult position I was in and offered me a ridiculously low price. That revolted me and made me lose all intentions of selling it, if for no reason other than spite. I was not going to give the boat away to an opportunist after all the love and work Lydia and I had put into it. I decided that somehow I would manage to get the boat back to the western world and eventually sell it there at a decent price. It was not just a matter of whether to sell or not to sell. If I could get a fair price, I would not feel all our work had been wasted. I would merely transform the work put into the boat into a house, which would be more suitable now. Selling it at a give-away price to a man who wanted to take advantage of my bad luck made me feel like I would be failing Lydia who had worked so hard on the boat and who, more than once, had said it would be our inheritance to Thomas, if nothing else.

But bringing the boat back home seemed a formidable project. While long-distance sailing is fun when everything is right, it becomes a seemingly impossible task when conditions are against us, as they were now. The ship didn't steer properly, I had a small child to care for, I had no crew and, worst of all, I was on the verge of a nervous breakdown.

The obvious solution would be to get a crew to help me, so I put an advertisement in the local paper and received three responses. The first was an Englishman who was finishing a contract in Brunei and thought sailing home would be more fun than flying home as most people do. He was pleasant enough, but admitted he had never sailed before—something I could have guessed by the way he entered the dinghy, nearly capsizing it. He showed quite a bit of surprise to hear that I would expect my crew to take turns steering night and day.

"Do you mean that this sailing goes on also at night?" he asked, obviously losing interest in the project.

The two others were entirely different types of applicants. Both were professional seamen, but neither had been on a sailboat before. They'd only been on fast inshore outboard-powered fishing boats. They applied because they expected to obtain higher wages from me than they would get on a fishing boat and specified that they would be willing to risk the danger of sailing the high seas in a boat without a motor only if I would hire a large enough crew so they wouldn't have to work more than 40 hours a week. They also expected to be flown home as soon as we arrived at our destination. When I told them I wanted only two men at most and I would pay for only their food and return tickets—I didn't intend to pay any wages whatsoever—they looked at me in disbelief and quickly went ashore.

In most harbours around the world, it's quite common for yacht skippers and idle tourists to meet and to be of mutual service. The yacht owner offers a nice sailing cruise against room and board, while the new crew member offers his muscles to help run the yacht and earn his keep. Unfortunately, in this part of the world, I had practically no chance of finding such an arrangement. There were virtually no tourists and, if there had been, they would probably not have thought to look in the port as yachts rarely stopped there.

Since the boat didn't self-steer with its new rig, except under especially favourable conditions, the only practical way of continuing my voyage would be to design and have made a special self-steering gear which could pilot my boat while I got some rest.

I spent several days designing an adequate self-steering gear, and drew up proper industrial drawings that any mechanical workshop should be able to understand. I felt sure the gear would work this time, but when I tried to find a workshop, I soon discovered that, despite Brunei's being a rich country, there wasn't a single workshop able to make my gear. I could hardly believe it until I considered Brunei's rather unique situation. In a country where wealth flows in from the oil pumped from its soil, there is little need for the population to strive to build their own industry, or to build anything at all for that matter. They are able to buy and pay for imported goods of any kind.

I didn't know how I was going to get out of my dead-end situation, when a messenger came to me with the order to present myself immediately to the British High Commissioner. I wondered what it was all about, never having heard of any such office before. It was explained to me that the British High Commissioner was the highest authority in the country, second only to the Sultan himself, and I'd therefore better not keep him waiting.

Once I arrived, the secretary ushered me into the private office of the High Commissioner, who proved to be a most charming and considerate man. He expressed his condolences and regrets for the tragedy which had befallen me and said that the reason he'd called me was to tell me that one of my old friends, the Count Guillaume de Montravel, had tried to contact me through him.

The Count had offered to take care of my son, Thomas, and to adopt him in case I didn't feel able to raise him myself now that I was alone. I was grateful to Guillaume for his concern but, as I explained to the High Commissioner, even if Thomas would certainly be better off, both financially and socially, if raised by de Montravel, no father, however poor, would be willing to give up his own son. I added bitterly, "I've lost my wife. Do you want me to also lose my son?"

The High Commissioner smiled sadly, saying he could fully understand my feelings. He pointed out that the idea was not his; he was just relaying the information. We then had a long, soothing talk. It felt good for me to meet a truly understanding man with personality and strength of character, who was far above being influenced by a cheap newspaper article. When he asked me if there were anything he could help me with, I told him of my difficulties in finding a crew and about the trouble I'd encountered in having an automatic pilot made to my specifications.

"Regarding a crew, I don't think I can help you if you don't want professional seamen, but I do know where you can get the pilot made," the Commissioner said. "There is only one place capable of doing it—the workshop of the naval base. They are very well equipped, they have excellent engineers and, best of all, they have plenty of time to do extra jobs."

I told him about the C.O.'s order for his personnel to stay clear of me, which made him rather indignant at first. After thinking it over, he said that, no doubt, they had probably felt a bit worried about the case getting too much publicity. If it were to reach their main office in London they might be confronted with questions like, "How come you haven't been able to stop small, primitive boats engaged in piracy in that part of the world with your powerful ships and expensive equipment. What are you doing there?"

"Actually, all they're trying to do in this case is hide their heads in the sand like an ostrich," he said. "I don't want to interfere with this policy matter, however much I disagree with it, but I will try to get him to at least make the gear for you. Just wait, I'll call him right now."

He took the phone while I was there and got the commissioner on the line. "This is M.H. D'ath from the British High Commission," he said. "I'm calling on behalf of Mr. Tangvald, of whom, I understand, you've heard." He went on with a faint smile. "As you know, he has suffered a great hardship. He needs special gear for his boat so that he'll be able to sail his ship single-handed, now that he no longer has his wife as crew. He has not been able to find a workshop in town able to build it for him, and I believe you are the only one equipped to do so. I will consider it a personal favour if you would make this gear for Mr. Tangvald so that he'll be able to safely continue his voyage home."

Apparently the C.O. didn't dare argue with the High Commissioner and agreed to do as he requested. I went straight to the base to get the work started. The base was far away and there were no buses, so I found a taxi and got there as fast as anyone could have expected. Yet the man in charge had already gone for the day. "Could I come back tomorrow?" I asked. They said I could and I did, both the next day and the day after. But each time the man in charge was either out or in an important meeting.

No, I was told. I couldn't talk with the second in command or the C.O. himself. That was completely out of the question. They all resumed their business curtly, obviously wanting nothing to do with me. I was just about to give up when, by chance, I cornered the officer in question. I handed him a pile of my drawings, but he hardly looked at them. He said he was extremely busy for the moment. Perhaps I could come back in a few weeks' time when they might be less rushed. He excused himself and made a sign to one of his soldiers to accompany me back to the gate. I tried to get some information from the soldier as to whether they were in fact so busy or if just trying to discourage me, but the soldier only looked straight ahead. He wouldn't even give me the usual yes or no, which I'd at least gotten from the others.

It was all too obvious that the C.O. had not dared openly refuse to obey the request of the High Commissioner, but he still had no intention of making anything for me. He was taking the easy way out by discouraging me little by little without my being able to go back to the Commissioner with a firm complaint.

In any case, I was getting tired of it all—tired of these small-minded people and tired of all the unpleasant memories I will always have of Brunei. I had just one thing on my mind now, and that was to get out to sea again. Somehow I would manage.

First I would have to paint the bottom of the ship with anti-fouling paint. The bottom had now grown so full of shells and other marine growth that it would slow us down beyond reason. I obtained permission from the harbour authorities to use a beach close by which, with the help of a huge tidal range, would be suitable for drying out the boat. But this nearly caused me a new disaster.

Just next to where I beached the boat was a vast, nearly deserted parking lot for the military. I thought it would be safe for Thomas to play there with his tricycle while I worked. One day, while I worked on the boat, I heard the sounds of screeching tires and broken steel, followed immediately by car doors opening. A woman cried out, "Oh my God," and I heard a man's voice, whose words I couldn't discern but which sounded panicky. Frightened for Thomas, I sprang up on the deck to see a car with all four of its doors open wide and its panicky occupants peering underneath. My heart stood still when I saw Thomas's little tricycle all twisted under the car. I rushed over, but as I got closer I got a view of Thomas, not crushed under the car, but peeking out with a scared look from behind a neighbouring car.

It turned out that when he saw the car backing out at too great a speed towards him, he jumped off his bike just in time to take refuge behind the parked car. The backing car, which couldn't see the low tricycle, just ran over it and crushed it.

When Thomas saw me, he ran to me and jumped up to hug me, his arms around my neck and legs tightly around my waist. I carried him back to the boat, half-blinded by tears from the emotion. The car's occupants offered to repair the bike.

"Never mind the bike," I told him. "I've got my child alive. Never mind the bike."

The next day, one of them did come down to the boat with the tricycle completely repaired—quite an achievement, considering how it had looked the day before. He said just three words, "I am sorry," and then took off. He didn't want to take the chance of disobeying orders not to have anything to do with me.

After I painted the boat and refloated her, I went to the local grocery shop where I bought enough food and supplies to go to sea. This time I made sure to clear with all the authorities—customs, the police, the harbourmaster, and immigration before finally hoisting my sails for the open sea.

# 19

# Alone With Thomas

*A*ll I had in mind by now was to get home, back to the western world with my son and my ship. First of all, I wanted to get the South China Sea behind me. Singapore, located at the separation of the South China Sea and the Indian Ocean, would probably have been the first logical stop, but I strongly disliked its police state. I decided to bypass it and sail directly into the Malacca Strait, which led to the Indian Ocean. I'd heard a lot of good about Malacca, which lay in the strait just past Singapore, so I decided to sail there as my first stage of the way home.

The shortest way from Brunei would have been to follow the coast of Borneo, which had the added advantage of offering places to stop and anchor along the way if I got too tired. But I'd gotten such a fright in that part of the world that I preferred to put straight towards open sea. There I would meet many fewer boats and could sail on towards my destination by a long, sweeping curve, which would keep me far from those inhospitable and dangerous shores. It would take much longer, but I would feel more secure for both myself and my son, and would endure much less nervous tension.

The weather stayed good for the first few days of April, and I managed to keep the boat sailing reasonably well on its own. The wind was light and with my make-shift rig, our speed was slow. But we covered nearly a hundred miles each day, which satisfied me as long as we were having an easy ride.

On Friday the 13th, the sky clouded over, which might have worried a superstitious sailor, but nothing terribly harmful happened to us that day, other than that I couldn't take any celestial sight due to the clouds.

The days passed easily and we made steady progress over a seemingly deserted sea until, suddenly, the ocean became full of traffic. We spotted as many as four ships simultaneously, large tankers and freighters in the Singapore-Hong Kong shipping lane.

It may seem strange to newcomers that the ocean can be so empty in some places and so crowded in others. The reason is that, with modern motorships able to keep an accurate course regardless of winds and currents, there is one course which is the shortest (quickest and cheapest) from one port to the next. So between these ports there will always be a steady stream of vessels. Outside the shipping lanes there is likely to be no traffic at all, except for the occasional small yacht, fishing boat or odd freighter going to a little-frequented port. Outside of the major shipping lanes, one can sail for weeks without seeing a single boat.

I had stayed clear of the coastal traffic because I was afraid I might again cross the track of a pirate, but seeing these large ships didn't worry me at all. On the contrary, after several days alone at sea, we felt quite cheered at the sight of other ships and other human beings. But the pleasure of passing those ships lasted only a few hours. Once I had crossed the line, the row of boats soon dwindled, and once more we were alone on the empty ocean.

The weather stayed light and pleasant until we got closer to the end of the South China Sea. The wind became very squally and sometimes quite stormy, forcing me to reef down despite my short canvas. It made for very rough going as the wind had turned against us, forcing us to beat into the seas with spray flying all over the ship.

On the 25th I wrote in my log:

*Gale from SW again, rain and heavy seas. Reefed down. Miserable.*

And the next day:

*Saw glow of light over Singapore last night although distance of 90 miles. Heard military planes exercising and three bangs of sound barrier. Almost becalmed.*

I was getting into doldrums weather, which is common in those parts of the world at certain times of the year. In all times, sailors have always hated the doldrums. The weather pattern there is exactly the opposite of what is most favourable for a sailing vessel. Instead of a steady following breeze and clear sky, we have to suffer alternating conditions, from total calms where a sailing ship lies helpless to violent squalls which can easily tear sails and break masts. Even more frustrating is the short duration of each; by the time adjustments are made and the ship can at least make some progress, the weather has changed again.

With perseverance, however, in each squall some progress is made, and even during the calms a good sailboat will often coast on its way. Even traveling at a snail's pace, it will not stop completely, and eventually the ship will get out of the doldrums and into more stable winds.

I did my best to keep the ship going and was finally rewarded by a glow of light far ahead that could only be the lights of Singapore reflected high in the sky. Under clear conditions, the glow of light from a big city can be seen at very great distances even though the city and its lights may still be far below the curvature of the earth and the horizon. Singapore was still some 90 miles away, but the light was unmistakable. A check with my calculation showed it to be coming from where Singapore should be. And if that hadn't been proof enough, the supersonic military planes constantly practicing around Singapore would have been a sufficient sign.

At Any Cost

I was indeed approaching the big commercial capital of the east. While I didn't want to stop there, Singapore represented a milestone for me. It separated the South China Sea and the real Far East from the Indian Ocean, which was already much too close to the western world. I continued out of the open South China Sea into the crowded waters leading into the Straits, which would take me to the Indian Ocean and, eventually, home to the western world.

But now, I had to watch not just for the countless ships, but also for the many islets and reefs of that region, so sleep became a problem. Soon I was in such congested water that I couldn't leave the tiller at all. As soon as I avoided one ship, I had to start worrying about the next one.

Which course is that one keeping? Will she pass to my right or left? Ahead of me or aft of me? Will she go clear or should I change course to be sure to avoid a collision? So my thoughts went, while I grew sleepier and sleepier. Of course, in theory, a sailboat has the right of way over mechanical propulsion vessels, but that's only in theory. In practice, big ships sometimes don't keep proper watch. So how would I know whether the ship headed towards me is properly run or not? I had to be cautious at all times. I kept a good watch day and night until I was through the most critical part and until I had cleared Singapore territory.

I knew how well patroled that country was, so I didn't even consider anchoring anywhere close to its shores. That is strictly forbidden in most countries until we have "cleared," and this can only be done in a few accepted places. Of course there is so-called "international law," which states that under true emergencies any vessel can anchor anywhere. But again, that's just in theory. In practice it all works out very differently. International law invariably originated in the western world at a time when it ruled the world. A good many present day countries disregard these laws altogether.

Even if they should accept the excuse of an emergency (in this case, needing sleep), officials would first seize my boat and throw me in jail while they investigated my case. In many far-away countries that can take a very long time. When I finally was released, my boat could be in sad shape, probably plundered and maybe even sunk. It has happened to countless unfortunate sailors and still occurs today.

Fortunately all countries are not as rigid in their policing and, while I knew Singapore was very strict, I also knew that their next door neighbour, Malaysia, was far more lenient and understanding. If I could just reach their border, I would be safe to anchor off their shore. I knew the strait was shallow and had many anchorages.

Thus, a little later I wrote in the log:

*Monday 30 April*
*Have been at tiller two nights-sleeping sometimes 10 minutes. Very tired. Good wind at last. Passed Singapore last night. Setting course north again with Indian Ocean before me and China Sea behind me. Sad to think about the expectations we had about getting into the China Sea, three years ago with our newborn Thomas and everything has gone so wrong.*

*Anchored as night fell in seven fathoms, nine miles from shore and 20 miles from Malacca. Too tired to continue."*

I was then well past Singapore, but I still didn't want to take too many chances on the Malaysian coast, so I anchored a full nine miles out to sea which, in any case, is considered outside of the territorial waters of most countries. I still remember today, several years afterwards, how blissful it felt to sleep in relative safety with the South China Sea well behind me.

Next day I wrote:

*First of May. Becalmed this morning—will rest at anchor until wind comes. Very strong current alternating by flood and ebb—many fishing stakes—Sailed by noon in light airs—anchored five miles from Malacca in 20 fathoms.*

The next day the log read:

*Second of May. Anchored outside of Malacca's breakwater in two fathoms at 0730-20 days from Brunei—40 miles a day average!*

I had traveled safely the first leg of the way home, though at the slowest average speed I had ever done in my life. Considering the sailing conditions, my run-down health, my makeshift rig, my lack of motor and no crew, I had every reason to be well satisfied for not having done worse.

# 20

# Life As A Widower

We had no detailed charts of the harbour, which was a great river. Since it was subjected to a strong tidal influence, I had to wait for the right conditions of tide and wind before sailing in, using my powerful binoculars to learn the layout of the harbour.

Soon, much to my satisfaction, I saw a sail coming up over the horizon headed our way. As it grew bigger, I saw it was a native cargo sailing ship. Most are not equipped with motors, but are true sailboats like my own. The ship was traveling at a good speed in the freshening breeze and soon headed for the entrance to the harbour. It entered under full sails until its crew lowered them to slow the boat down. It came to a halt along the dock where it made fast. I was in luck. Having observed the whole manoeuvre through my binoculars from up in the mast, all I had to do was duplicate exactly what they'd done. So I hoisted all my sails, took up the anchor and headed for the narrow entrance, feeling confident despite my lack of proper charts.

Thomas is normally locked in his cabin while at sea because I fear losing him over the side in a moment of inattention. But I didn't want to deprive him of the joy of the sight of new land after a long sea trip. I put his lifejacket on him and let him take up his favourite position on the boat all the way forward, comfortably seated in the triangle formed by the two bulwarks meeting in the bow.

After three weeks of seeing only the walls of his cabin, or the empty sea whenever I did take him up on deck and held him in my arms, he now stared with amazement at the new land and the harbour which soon opened up for us. Just as I was concentrating on the sail and the proper manoeuvre to get safely along the quay, Thomas spotted a motorcycle, which fascinated him.

He called out to me, "Papa, look at the red motorcycle, look at the red motorcycle, Papa, it's all red, look, Papa! It's red, all red. Look, Papa. Why don't you look?"

Despite my assuring him that I'd seen it and telling him to keep quiet so I could concentrate on my manoeuvres, he kept talking. Even after watching the native boat precede me under sails alone, getting in safely was tricky in a strange harbour without a crew. I was rather regretting not having left Thomas in his cabin until we were safely tied up. Fortunately the wind was just right, so I easily overcame the current and slid safely to a stop along the dock, taking the power out of my sail by dropping the peak of its gaff.

I threw a line to a passerby, who calmly took it and tied it casually to one of the quay's bollards before continuing about his own business. I was surprised at the lack of attention I received. In most ports, a foreign boat coming in under sail would stir a crowd. When I saw the whole fleet of native sailboats moored a little further into the river, I soon realised that this was a common sight here, and my boat with its traditional working boat lines was not very much different from many of their own.

I tied up securely in a port which looked safe—in a new country in a new part of the world. I was no longer in the South China Sea region. I had passed Singapore and was now in Malaysia, bordering the Indian Ocean—where we'd come from three years before. I had never been in this town before, but we had sailed close past it on our way to China. Thomas had been about a week old at the time and Lydia was in bed after his difficult birth. We didn't have a cent to our names, but we had such great expectations and were happy just to have each other.

Now I had some money, but I no longer had my wife and, far from having great expectations about the future, I was very depressed and on the constant verge of a nervous breakdown. Only the knowledge that I was the only parent Thomas had left and my determination not to let him down kept me from thoughts of suicide.

Having just entered a new country, my immediate concern was to get cleared by the authorities. No one paid much attention to my yellow flag, which is the international sign to declare we are coming from a foreign country and are requesting clearance. I hailed a uniformed man who proved to be a maritime policeman and advised me to go to the administration building overlooking the harbour, where I would find the harbour police, customs and immigration.

I went there immediately. I had hoped that being in a new country would help me to forget what had happened and start a new life, but I was mistaken. I realised it as soon as each of the three offices pointed out that I was breaking the law by taking my son ashore. I should know, they said, that international law forbids anyone coming ashore except the skipper until given "pratique" (clearance).

"I'm sorry," I explained each time, "but I have a small child and can't leave him alone onboard. I have to take him wherever I go."

"How come you're alone with your son? Where's your wife?"

"She's dead," I had to answer reluctantly.

Then I was to suffer the lack of discretion so typical in the east. It was caused not by rudeness, but, on the contrary, by genuine concern and interest. But as they pried into my private life with too-direct questions, I felt trapped by the continual reminders. They would invariably continue, "But how did she die? With such a young child, she must have been young. Was it an accident?"

Not wanting to recount everything, I would vaguely say, "Yes, it was an accident of sorts," and hope it would stop.

"How sad for you, but at least you and your baby didn't get hurt. Was it a car accident, maybe? Was she alone in the car?"

"No, it wasn't a car accident," I would say and try to cut short the questions by showing my papers and asking for clearance.

"If it wasn't a car accident, perhaps it was an accident at sea?"

"Yes, it was an accident at sea," I said, becoming more and more annoyed with their insensitivity.

"But if it's an accident at sea it must be reported. When and how did it happen?" I was feeling more and more uncomfortable and I realised that I was never going to be left in peace, so I said, rather curtly, "It happened a long time before I came here and it's all been reported and investigated by the police."

Then when they saw the name of my boat on my papers, they would exclaim, "So you are the one who suffered that attack in the Sulu Sea. We're so sorry that such an awful thing happened to you. That is indeed far from here, but we also have pirates. Did you notice that power boat half-sunk, next to where you're moored with all the bullet holes through its sides and through its deckhouse?"

I shook my head, miserably.

"Well on the way back, do take a look at it. It had been engaged in a fight with pirates from Indonesia who fled when they saw our patrol boat. We towed the boat here in a sinking condition. We patrol our side of the Malacca Strait very efficiently so the risk of an attack on this side is very small. But the day you leave, be sure not to get close to the Indonesian side of the strait. You'd have a good chance of getting attacked there. We're sorry about what happened to you, but we can promise one thing—you'll be perfectly safe as long as you stay here. We're going to make 100-percent sure that you'll not be attacked in our port," they assured me.

"We want you to move your boat from where you are now to the spot between the customs dock and the police dock. There should be just room enough for you. The police and customs boats have 24-hour guards who will watch over you. Furthermore, we want you to moor away from land to make it even more difficult for would-be criminals to try and get onboard your boat unnoticed. We'll do our utmost so that you'll remember Malacca fondly."

I was disappointed to see that I wouldn't be able to pass unnoticed here and left alone. My story had also been in the papers here. But I was greatly relieved to see the friendliness of these people, which proved to me that the papers must have picked up the story published in Paris from my telephone interview with Monsieur Grosset and not the one written by the vengeful Brunei reporter.

So if I couldn't forget, at least I was here among friends and I was safe with my child. Still, when a reporter came to "get my story," I was able to stay calm only because I knew that if the reporter took a dislike to me, he could publish a nasty article. I answered all his questions.

I was in a safe harbour and had been legally admitted to the country for a stay of up to three months. What I had to do now was try to organise my life and get my wits back, which wasn't going to be easy.

One of the first visits I made was to the post office, which is usually the first place most travelers go as soon as the official paperwork has been straightened out with the authorities. As I was standing in line with Thomas, it soon became apparent how difficult it was going to be to forget what had happened.

I was waiting in line to see if any mail had been held for me when the woman next to me smiled at Thomas and stroked his blond hair. Blond hair never ceases to surprise and charm all the people in the east. She soon asked me where his mother was. It appeared that I would not be allowed any peace, despite my attempts to avoid being dragged into conversation.

One way to avoid it would have been simply not to answer, to look straight ahead and ignore the unwelcome intruder. But the people in the east are so friendly that such a rude response would really hurt them, which didn't seem fair since they meant no harm. I also didn't want to take the chance of making them "lose face." I would make enemies of them, something I especially didn't want since I intended to remain here for a while to rest before I went back to sea. I wanted to be able to stay here and not have to think. When I felt better, I would continue my voyage.

So again came the dreaded question, "Where's his mama?"

I could have lied and said that she was at home and let it go at that, but I was unable to lie, especially with Thomas listening. He knew only too well that he had no mama waiting for him anymore. I tried to satisfy her with a weak, "She's not here," but the woman wouldn't take that for an answer.

"So she must be at work, perhaps, while she lets you take care of that little boy. What kind of work does she do?"

"She's not working," I said, getting more and more annoyed.

"Oh, I get it. She's out having fun and lets you worry about the boy. Yes, I know," she added, "it's common in your country, but here no man would allow that."

I was getting more and more exasperated and could see no end to the line which was moving at a snail's pace and I exploded, "She's not playing, she's dead!"

"Oh, I'm so sorry. I suppose it must have been an accident."

She went on and on until I had to tell the woman the whole story about the attack. Then, as if that weren't enough, the woman began to lament, "But then your wife has not been properly buried! My God, she's just lying there in the sea. My God, why didn't you try to find her so she could be properly buried? You know it's a very serious matter for a Christian not to be properly buried. I presume she was a Christian, wasn't she?"

I couldn't stand anymore and suddenly excused myself. I said I didn't have time to stand in line any longer and would get my mail later. I went to sit in the park to try and soothe my nerves, wondering how I was going to avoid this day after day. After a while, I calmed down and regretted letting myself be so easily upset by a stranger. I went back to the post office to get my mail, but apparently I was far from being calmed down. No sooner had I taken my place in line, this time with new people, of course, than I heard, as if through a daze, "Oh, what a cute little boy you have. But where is his mother?"

I turned toward the voice and just exploded, screaming, "If you really want to know, his mother is lying in the bottom of the Sulu Sea with a bullet hole through her head!" Grabbing Thomas I fled into the street, half-blinded by the tears flooding down my face. Only after I was once again back in the boat with the gangplank drawn did I feel safe and able to relax.

I stayed in the boat for several days, not daring to talk to anyone. I tried to think about how I might arrange my life without going into a nervous depression for good. Despite my rundown condition, I even considered the possibility of putting back to sea immediately to try to reach home.

I studied my pilot charts, but had to admit that it would be near impossible to fight the wrong monsoon which I knew we would face as soon as I cleared the Malacca Strait. I'd just have to wait eight or nine months, like it or not, for the right monsoon to come back and push me across the Indian Ocean and back to Europe and America.

I must admit that, in any case, I was not fit for a long voyage until I got my health back. The three-month visa I'd been given could be extended since I had good reason. The answer, I felt, lay in not giving people the opportunity to ask those dreaded questions about Lydia. It suddenly dawned on me that I could put Thomas in a nursery during the day. Nobody would have much reason to start a conversation with a lone man. In the afternoons I could pick him up on my bicycle, and at night we could just lock ourselves inside the boat.

I took Thomas to the first school I could find and asked them if he could start right away, but we ran into bureaucratic difficulties right from the start. The school was supported by the government and could be used only by taxpayers. Since I was a foreigner, Thomas could not attend. I tried the next school, hoping for perhaps a different rule or a more understanding principal, but with no luck. We were tourists and the schools were only for residents and citizens of the country.

In despair I returned to the harbour authorities who had been so nice and understanding and asked their advice. One of them, a Chinese immigration officer, asked if I'd tried the Salvation Army school. I told him I hadn't.

"In that case, It might be well worth it to go there. Religious schools often disregard some of the laws made by the governments as they live separately from the population and obey their own rules. I know the headmistress. In fact, I'll drive you there and put in a good word for you. Maybe she'll accept Thomas in this case."

Not many immigration officers are that kind, but I was lucky to hit upon one of them. He took me to the Salvation Army school in his car and introduced me to the headmistress, a small, trim, very young Chinese woman. At first glance she looked to be barely in her 20s, but after talking with her and seeing her assurance and authority, I realised she must easily be 30.

Had I looked at her the way a man normally looks at a woman, I would have found her quite pretty with her big, almond-shaped eyes and smooth skin. But sitting behind the large, imposing desk with her spotless white uniform and her unsmiling face, she just looked like an important authority whose assistance I needed.

She looked at Thomas and me while she listened to the immigration officer. They weren't speaking in English, so I stood quietly and hoped for the best. When he had finished his speech on our behalf, she finally addressed me. She very curtly announced that I could bring Thomas to her next morning. He would get his midday meal there and I could pick him up every afternoon at 4 o'clock. She then rang a bell and a servant came in at the same instant (she must have been waiting on the other side of the door) to escort us out.

Little did I know at the time that this short interview was not only going to ease my immediate situation, but that this little woman was going to change my whole life.

As soon as I got back on the boat, I tried to repair my French racing bike. I borrowed parts from Lydia's bike, but I needed still more spare parts, which were impossible to get anywhere in Malaysia. I then remembered the harbourmaster telling me he'd tried to sell his bike. I went to his office where he showed me a bike which was as good as new and for which he was asking only $18 U.S.—everything is incredibly cheap in Asia. I bought it without a moment's hesitation and added a child's seat made of thatched bamboo for an extra dollar.

I now had no problems getting Thomas to school. I could get there rapidly and in complete peace from people's questions. Nobody starts a conversation with a cyclist whizzing by, even if his passenger is a cute blond boy.

From then on, my days became restful with no surprises. I got up at sunup to fix breakfast for Thomas and myself. Then I'd get my gangplank in position so I could get ashore with Thomas. We'd get on the bike and could be at the school 15 minutes later. I would sometimes see the headmistress, but most often the teacher, a most beautiful Indian woman who dressed in saris and painted a black dot on her forehead, which is typical for some women in India.

Malaysia is a multiple-race country with a population which is about 55-percent Malay. They claim to be the original inhabitants of the country, although that's not quite true. It's well established that the original inhabitants were the aborigines, who now lived back in the mountains. They rarely, if ever, came to town since they were invaded by the Malays, who look more like a Polynesian race. The Chinese account for another 30 percent of the population. Most of those are second or third generation, after the big wave of immigration when the communists took over in China. Finally there are the Indians, who account for 15 percent of the population.

The Malays, who are in the majority, have the power and are given preference for all the civil service jobs. The Chinese and Indians run most of the business and have most of the money which, of course, creates a lot of friction and difficulties.

During the school day I was free to do all my errands, write letters and maintain my boat. At noon I would go to one of the small Malay, Chinese or Indian restaurants. Most of them were very good and all of them cheap. A sidewalk "restaurant" was often just a huge tricycle with a kitchen installed, like they had in China. Customers would sit on small stools and a meal cost the equivalent of 30 cents American. A fancier meal in a "proper" restaurant would never cost more than a dollar or, perhaps, a dollar and a half in a really fancy place.

After my meal, I would return to the boat where I would either finish sewing my new mainsail, redo some painting, which really suffered in the equatorial climate with its steaming heat and broiling sun, or work on designing yet another sailing yacht. I had in mind to make a small portfolio of stock yacht designs for future sale and thus have it as a regular income. I completely disregarded the modern trends and designed very classic boats, all of them much along the lines of my own *L'Artemis de Pytheas* and all inspired from around the 1850 time period, which I consider the apogee of sailing.

Just before 4 o'clock, I'd bike back to the school and see either one of the teachers or the headmistress herself, since no one was permitted to take a child without talking to someone on the school staff. For safety reasons, each child was surrendered personally only to the child's parent or approved guardian. Sometimes I exchanged a few words with one of the smiling and friendly teachers, but my conversations with the headmistress never went any farther than hello and goodbye.

From there I would bicycle straight back to the boat, where we were at peace and had our privacy. I would read to Thomas or just talk to him, then fix our evening meal. Soon after that I'd put Thomas to bed, which most of the time amounted to my going to bed, too. He always liked me to hold his hand until he fell asleep.

Since Lydia's death, I'd never returned to our big double bed. In fact, the whole bedroom had just become a huge locker for all my unwanted gear. I preferred to sleep on the saloon settee, despite the fact that it was very narrow and had no cushions. I slept on the bare wood, which feels cooler in the tropics than our deep, soft mattresses. Since Thomas didn't like to sleep alone in his own cabin, which was all the way forward, I finally gave in and let him sleep in the saloon on the settee with me. He slept on the part forming the bottom of the U, while I slept on the settee at a right angle to him. He wanted me to lie down with my head close to his and my hand grasped by both of his until he fell asleep. I tried using various teddy bears, but he firmly declared that clutching my hand was far preferable.

Each evening around 8 o'clock, I put out all the lights and lay down with him, secretly deciding that, once he fell asleep, I'd get up, relight the lamps and have some time for myself. But each night I was the one fooled, falling asleep before he did and never waking up until morning, sometimes with my hand still clutched in his.

Thus life went on, week after week, month after month. Not very exciting, perhaps, but I was looking for peace, not excitement.

Then one day, I got a wonderful surprise and perhaps the best medicine any man could wish for—a visit from an old friend. I'd been below, writing some letters, when I heard a familiar voice which I couldn't immediately place, but which brought me back into the past. A typically distinguished British voice hailed me from the dock, "Ahoy, *L'Artemis*, ahoy!"

Peeking out, who did I see but my old friend Edward Allcard, now in his middle 60s, but still as trim and fit-looking as I'd always known him. The only change I could see was that his long, always well-groomed beard had now become snow-white. It had been grey the last time I'd seen him, when he anchored next to me in Kourou during his circumnavigation about eight years ago, when I'd first had *L'Artemis* in the water.

I had met Allcard first in the Canary Islands many years before, when we'd raced the Atlantic against each other. He was in his early 40s then, with a dark brown beard. Except for the colour of his beard, he was the same man, with the same gentle smile. He walked across my wobbly and unstable gangplank with the ease and agility he'd always had, though that gangplank had scared off most other would-be visitors, even those in their 20s.

I was so surprised to see him I had trouble finding words. I had thought he was on the other side of the world and must have sounded pretty stupid, asking all manner of silly questions. I never suspected that he'd come to Malacca for the sole purpose of visiting me and seeing what he could do to help.

"What are you doing here?" I asked.

"I just came to visit you," he answered matter of factly. "I'm very sorry I didn't come long ago, but I heard about your misfortune only a couple of days ago while we were anchored in Seychelles. I immediately booked a plane to come and see you. I thought perhaps you'd be feeling lonely. My wife stayed onboard to watch my ship."

He'd flown clear across the Indian Ocean from those islands close to Africa just to see me and try to cheer me up! I had trouble fighting back tears, I was so touched by his spontaneous display of friendship. Just one friend like him compensated for all the unfriendliness shown me by the small-minded people in Brunei. He stayed with me a whole week onboard, and it was the happiest week I'd had since that fateful day in the Sulu Sea. We talked about the old days when we'd raced across the Atlantic and about our adventures in the West Indies 20 years earlier when we both were chartering our boats.

He tried to talk to me about the future. I needed to start to live again and assure a future for my son. His visit passed all too quickly, but even after his departure the spirit of optimism which he'd brought remained with me, making me look at life a little brighter.

Then one day, as everything seemed to be going so much better, disaster struck. It was a Sunday morning so Thomas wasn't in school. He was playing on the deck while I was typing some letters down below in the saloon. The quay, normally quiet during the week except for the police and customs crew, was now filled with Sunday strollers taking a look at the harbour and enjoying a walk on the jetty. Some of them stopped to play with Thomas, simulating either a war or perhaps a pirate attack by pretending to aim an imaginary gun at Thomas and yelling "Bang, bang!" Thomas answered in the same manner and was running wildly up and down the deck. I would have been extremely exasperated just after the accident, but I was trying to calm down and ignore it all at that time, though it wasn't exactly the type of play I appreciated.

All of a sudden I heard a splash and complete silence from Thomas, while alarmed cries echoed from shore. I immediately guessed that Thomas had slipped and fallen over the side, so I jumped up on deck. I saw no trace of Thomas, but the crowd was pointing at the water and shouting. Only seconds had elapsed since he'd fallen in and I could still see the rings in the water where he must have fallen. Yet the current was so strong, the rings had already moved from where the crowd was pointing.

Presuming that Thomas was under the rings, being swept toward the sea at the same speed as the rings at the surface, I disregarded the crowd telling me to dive in abreast of the bow of my boat and instead dived in much farther back. The water was murky and black and, in my haste to dive in, I inadvertently swallowed some of it. It was the most evil-tasting water I have ever had the misfortune to taste. The river, like most rivers in Asia, served as the town's sewer. It was not only evil-tasting, but worse, was so murky and opaque that I could hardly see my own hands in front of me.

The seconds passed and there was no sign of my child. I swam back and forth, searching desperately in the dark water, knowing that if I didn't get him on the first try, my chances would be nil on a second try because I'd be unable to estimate where the current had taken him. I was running out of breath and had to come up, but just then I saw a whitish spot below me. Swimming down, I reached for it. It was Thomas's blond hair. Almost out of my mind with happiness, I shot to the surface with him, gasping for air. With a force I never knew I possessed, I tumbled him violently over the rail into the boat and followed him in. I lifted him up by his legs and held him upside down in an effort to get the water out of his lungs, then alternately compressed and extended his legs to get the rest of the water out. He started to breathe on his own with a noisy, strained sound and I knew he would be all right.

I took him down below, but couldn't help thinking that while the crowd had shouted for me, not one of them had dived in to try and save him. I locked the latch behind me so Thomas couldn't get back on deck again and collapsed on the settee, sobbing from exhaustion and nervous strain, but happy to know my child was alive.

When I came to my senses and could think clearly again, it suddenly dawned on me that no man should ever cry for what he loses but should remain thankful and happy for what he can keep. I had lost my wife, perhaps the greatest tragedy any man can suffer. But it had happened and couldn't be remedied. Spending the rest of my life crying would do neither me nor anyone else any good. On the contrary, long-lasting sorrows are destructive to ourselves. I now realised that my distress at losing my wife could have been far worse still—I could also have lost my son. Now I believed I should try to feel as if my life with Lydia had been like a chapter of my life which had come to an end. I had to keep on turning the pages. And if so, why not rejoice at having my wonderful little boy still safe with me now and, hopefully, for many years to come.

All of a sudden as I lay there, a feeling of shame invaded me. I was ashamed of my endless tears, for not being able to fight adversity just because I'd had one hard blow. A man who has been knocked down should be able to raise himself up again if he is a man worthy of the word, and not just a weakling.

My whole outlook on life changed. At 54 I had to admit that I wasn't young anymore, but on the other hand I wasn't old, and could still hope to have many years ahead of me in which to enjoy watching my child grow to manhood. I should also be able to organise my life so that it would be a pleasurable one.

Analyzing the immediate situation, I thought that first off, since we were living on a boat and the chance of Thomas falling over the side again was always there, I needed to teach him to swim. I now knew for sure that the general belief that a child who falls, or is thrown into the water will naturally float up to the surface is not always true. At least it hadn't been for Thomas, whom I had found close to the bottom of the river. I also thought that people could now ask me all the questions they would like—I was immune from more sorrow. I would no longer hide away from them hoping to avoid their questions. I'd take Thomas to the pool every day and teach him how to swim. That would take care of our immediate needs.

As for the future, I'd have to study a little more seriously how to get home and prepare the ship properly for the voyage. Once back in the States, I'd just have to get organised for as good a life as possible for my son and me . Not many men are widowed with a small child, but many children are raised by single parents because of the many divorces in the Western world. Admittedly, it's the mother who generally takes care of the children, but why should it be any harder for a man? I felt confident that I could raise my son on my own and certainly would do my best so that when Thomas reached adulthood, he would not look back on his childhood as an unhappy one.

I studied my pilot books, which described wind, current and weather conditions all over the world and decided that the best time of the year to sail would be from mid-December until mid-January. I then went to work in earnest to get my ship properly seaworthy for the long trip home.

In my lighter frame of mind, the work on the boat progressed much faster and relatively painlessly. The weeks passed one after the other, and the day of my planned departure was nearing. At the beginning of December I went to the school and asked to see the headmistress to tell her we'd be leaving soon and thank her for having taken such good care of my son. I was shown into her office where she was, as usual, sitting behind her imposing desk in her spotless white Salvation Army uniform. There was no chair in front of her desk for a visitor to sit on, nor did she offer to get me one. She just let me stand there, somewhat uncomfortable in front of her, while she calmly scrutinised me with her almond eyes. Her face was expressionless and unsmiling as she listened to me tell her I would be taking Thomas out of school by the end of the month.

She let me talk without interrupting, but then, when I thought that nothing more had to be said, she surprised me by saying, "So you're going to sail all the way back to the western world all by yourself with a three-and-a-half-year-old child. I think you're making a mistake. It would be much better for both you and your son if you take a woman with you. Why don't you do so?"

I was surprised that this stern and cold-looking woman should try to interfere with my private life. But as the principal of the school which Thomas had attended for so long and also as an officer in a religious institution like the Salvation Army, she was really rather like a priest and was entitled to advise me in my private life. Indeed, it was perhaps even her duty.

I admitted that I would much prefer to have a woman with me, as I certainly was not the type of man who thrived on being a bachelor. But the reason I was sailing alone was very simple—I knew of no woman who wanted to go with me. I expected her to say it was regrettable and she hoped I would manage as well as possible under the circumstances, but what she said next made me believe I hadn't heard her correctly. She calmly replied, "You're wrong. You know at least one woman who would be very happy to go with you—me."

Either I was dreaming, or she was joking all of a sudden. I had to have heard wrong. Looking at her, I tried to get a clue as to whether she had really said what I thought I'd heard. The seconds passed in silence until finally, feeling quite stupid and probably looking it, too, I said, "I beg your pardon?"

With a faint smile, oh, a very faint smile, but still enough to take away her severe look and reveal the beauty of her almond eyes and the softness of a woman, she repeated calmly, "I said you're wrong in thinking that no woman would go with you. I will. Since you said that you wish you could have a woman with you, I don't have to ask for your acceptance. The only thing I ask is for you to wait a month for our departure so I can give 30 days' notice and find a new headmistress to train for this job."

I stood there completely dumbfounded in front of this little woman who was actually proposing to me from behind her big desk without giving me a chance to accept or decline. Seeing my bewilderment, she smiled—a real smile this time. It was the first time I had ever seen her beautiful smile.

"It's rather sudden, isn't it," she said. "But you'll see. I'll be a good wife to you." Before I had time to find an answer, she rang the bell and the servant entered instantly (she must really be glued to that door, I thought) to escort me out. I stood there in the street with my bike, still wondering if it was all a dream.

# 21

# To The Occident With Ann

nn came to my boat on the day we were to leave. A large car stopped alongside the dock, and Ann Ho Sau Chew arrived with everything she possessed in this world. I knew she'd quit her job, but it wasn't until much later that I learned she'd burned all her bridges behind her when she came aboard my ship. She had given up her future with the Salvation Army, where she'd been due for an advancement from lieutenant to captain the following month, and she'd broken all ties with her family. They wanted nothing more to do with her now that she'd brought shame on the family by getting involved with a "white devil." She was no longer considered a member of the family.

"I don't understand it," Ann was to say many times in the following years. "You're not young, you're not beautiful, and you're not even rich. So, how come I'm so much in love with you?"

I never knew whether to be flattered or offended by that statement, which she often dreamily repeated, but I'll admit that it was surprising. At 32, Ann was old enough to know what she was doing. She wasn't the type to try different men. On the contrary, Ann had never known any man before me. She had gone directly from her parents to the Salvation Army.

As for me, I slowly began to fall more and more in love with this woman. In addition to all the love she showed me, she was an excellent cook and a clever housewife, able to get the most on a minimum of money.

On January 2, we hoisted sails and set the course for Galle in Sri

Lanka. Poor Ann became awfully seasick during the voyage. Nevertheless, she insisted on taking care of everything in the galley and I never missed a single meal. It was in her best interest, she claimed. Who else could get her safely to port if, through neglect, I should fall sick? She not only did more than her share onboard, but she didn't want me to feel the least bit guilty about it.

In Galle we met three young tourists who asked if they could come with us as a paying crew and offered to pay ten dollars a day until we reached Europe or they disembarked. We didn't need the money and we needed a crew even less. I knew from earlier experiences that such haphazard crews are generally pretty worthless, but Ann rapidly calculated that she could easily feed them for just $5 a day, which meant that their money would pay for all our food and we wouldn't have to spend the money I'd saved while in Taiwan.

So on February 10, 1980, we continued our trip with three extra onboard: a 20-year-old French medical student, a 19-year-old Danish farmer and a 19-year-old farmer from Texas. One condition that I set was that I wanted no smoking onboard, not even on deck. They respected this rule, but proved pretty useless for the duration of the trip. They were an endless source of irritation for Ann and for me— an unfortunate but common occurrence when unknown and inexperienced strangers come into your home and live day after day.

To ward off boredom and keep them busy, I neglected to tell them that the boat could steer itself reasonably well and proposed that we all share in steering, except for Thomas, who was too young, and Ann, who was more than busy enough cooking for all of us.

The three men and myself would take turns steering for three hours each, and then have nine hours off, which shouldn't have worn anyone out. Yet it wasn't very long before they started to complain and more than once I'd catch one of them fast asleep while the boat was going badly off course.

Nor were they much help when we really needed them. One time it was the middle of the day in nearly a flat calm sea under a scorching sun. At sea I normally keep all the side portholes closed for safety reasons and content myself with the draft offered by the two centre hatches. But that day I'd given in to their nagging about extra ventilation because "there was no danger now that we had practically no wind." All of a sudden we heard a strange, frightening sound as from an invisible gale. At first I didn't understand because there wasn't a single cloud in the sky, but then I saw a dark spot in the water not 50 yards from us. It was one of those dreaded "white squalls"—tiny but violent storms which have caused the floundering of so many ships and planes. The black spot I saw was the sea being whipped up by the wind. These tiny local storms can reach hurricane force. Logically the sea should have become white, but I just recall that black spot racing towards us at high speed.

I shouted to two of them to rush down below and close all the portholes. I told the third to hurry and help me get the sails down. By the time they got around to moving, the wind had hit us with such violence that the boat heeled over until the masts were nearly horizontal and the sea rushed through the portholes—portholes which would have been closed if they hadn't been onboard. Instead of helping me, all three of them simply froze, terrified, grasping the handrails and screaming for me to launch the dinghy.

It was little Ann who fought her way down below to close all the portholes. I still can't understand how that tiny, 85-pound woman was able to close those portholes against the water pressure. But she managed to do so in record time, which was fortunate because, otherwise, we would have sunk. We had already taken on so much water that the floorboards were flooded and everything was soaked, including little Thomas. He must have wondered what in the world was happening to his secure and snug cabin.

While Ann had been fighting the waters down below, I had to get the sails down on my own, which wasn't an easy task on a boat lying on its side. I was glad I had a gaff rig. With a modern Bermudian rig,the sails travel in a rail or sometimes in a mast groove, and all the friction would have made the job much harder, if not impossible.

When the squall had passed and we were again in a calm, I expected to see those husky guys rather embarrassed over their cowardice, but far from it—those three idiots started to reproach me, saying I was an irresponsible person to dare take passengers on such an unstable boat!

It was difficult to stay calm. In my indignation I tried hard to think about the $30 I was getting from them each day. As time went on, it became more and more difficult to stand living with them. One day they started to complain about the food which Ann had taken pains to make for them. They even complained about the excellent homemade bread she made for us every day. That was the last straw. She was furious and announced they would have to disembark at the next port or she would.

I really didn't think she would have fulfilled her threat, but I didn't want to take the chance of destroying the happiness I'd found with her. I was also getting pretty tired of those strangers and the lack of privacy in our home. I promised her I would get rid of them as soon as possible. The difficulty lay in finding a suitable port. In the part of the world we were in, regulations are strict and there are few places that passengers are allowed to disembark. The closest port was Aden, but it was generally considered an unsafe place for a foreign yacht.

The next possibility was Djibouti, which I hadn't liked the last time I was there, but the authorities had been very relaxed. I thought it would be a safe place to put my crew ashore without risking any trouble. In most countries, maritime laws hold any skipper respon-sible for everything and everybody onboard. This means that if a crew member disembarks, the skipper is responsible for his fare back to his home country should he be unable to, or claim to be unable to pay for it himself. That would mean one airplane ticket to Texas, one to France and one to Denmark, which would cost far more than I'd earned from taking them across the Indian Ocean. Of course any honest and fair man would pay his own fare, but I had heard of enough cases where a dissatisfied crew took advantage of this law to save themselves the money and get even with the skipper.

But in Djibouti, I felt confident that the authorities wouldn't give me any trouble, so I laid the course for that harbour. My conscience didn't bother me about not taking them all the way to Europe as agreed on originally. They were old enough to manage on their own—at least that's what they'd been doing for the last six months while they traveled and lived in India. Besides, they thought Djibouti, Somaliland, with its camels sounded exciting.

While we were still in the Indian Ocean headed for Djibouti, which lies close to the southern entrance of the Red Sea, we spotted a sail far forward of us. It grew steadily bigger as we overtook it rapidly, and we recognised it as a yacht under spinnaker. (It had to be a yacht because native sailboats never use spinnakers anywhere in the world.)

It's always exciting to meet another yacht at sea, as such meetings don't happen very often. We watched eagerly as we came closer to see who its passengers would be. Soon we were alongside and recognised the catamaran, now on its way from Hong Kong to England. We'd seen the same yacht in Malaysia and then later in Galle. The captain had signed my guestbook, jokingly and somewhat ironically writing, "We'll race you to the Red Sea."

I had said innocently that I was going the same way and it would be fun to sail together, but I never thought I'd have the slightest chance of keeping up with this modern catamaran. Yet, although the skipper was under a huge balloon spinnaker and I had only my three working sails, I had easily bypassed the vessel, which had left Galle a couple of days before me. He arrived in Port Sudan, where we later met up again, after we did. I must say, to his credit, he didn't make the usual excuses some people make when being overhauled by a faster boat. He didn't say his bottom was foul or he'd just been fishing. On the contrary, he came towards me with an outstretched hand and said, "I must really congratulate this boat's designer, builder and skipper. I must admit I never, in all my life, have been as surprised as when I saw you effortlessly sail past my modern catamaran with your old-fashioned gaff rig!"

A sailor remembers such flattering words his whole life, especially when he's created his ship with his own hands. If my friend had seen me on my outward passage four years earlier in an unfavourable monsoon, he might have been less impressed. He also would have been much better off with his diesel auxiliary.

But on this trip, we had the right monsoon with the wind mostly on the quarter where the schooner rig is supreme and we really made good speed. We frequently made 185 miles a day with a best-day run of 202 miles, which is nearly an 8-1/2 knot average speed. That's no speed record, of course, but still very good for a boat designed as a cruising boat that could be handled by just a man and his wife, or even a single handler if necessary.

We arrived at Djibouti on March 4, and our three crew members disembarked without bothering with any of the formalities. During my last visit there, I'd had some trouble hunting up the authorities and they'd let me know that they had more important things to do than be troubled by small yachts passing through. But what I didn't know was that, since my last visit, Somalia had gotten its independence from France and this, of course, would make a difference.

No one takes their authority more seriously than recently established new governments and officials. As soon as I realised that, I lost no time in hoisting the sails, even though they were badly in need of repair. As we sailed past a beautiful island which formed the outer part of the anchorage, I noticed a narrow entrance into a lagoon. It was marked very shallow on the charts, but with high tide I thought it would be sufficient for me. I took a chance on shooting through the entrance and soon we were in a tiny, well-protected anchorage—the perfect place to repair my sails.

We stayed in the secluded anchorage where we were completely hidden among the mangroves for four wonderful days, just the three of us. Once the sails were repaired, we put out to sea again and arrived in Port Sudan, halfway up the Red Sea, on the 17th of March.

We had no idea what we'd narrowly escaped in Djibouti until we talked to the crews of two other yachts which had been lying in port in Djibouti and were now in Port Sudan.

"How in the world did you escape the gunboats?" they asked.

"What gunboats?" I asked, not understanding what they were talking about.

Slowly, they told us the whole story. Our three paying guests, or perhaps I should say paying crew, had gone to the authorities and told them they'd been set ashore from a foreign yacht which had not cleared with them. Apparently the authorities had gone at full speed to the dock to question us. When they discovered we'd already gone, they went into such a fury that they literally jumped up and down, waved their arms and screamed. They then sped off to organise a pursuit at sea and arrest us for the terrible crime of smuggling aliens into their country—a crime which could be punished by confiscation of the boat, heavy fines and even a prison sentence.

They weren't content to send an ordinary patrol boat after us. They sent a large warship. They'd been sure they'd find us, thanks to their huge and powerful radar equipment which could see even poor targets like us despite our wood and canvas and lack of steel parts. But to their surprise, they raced all the way to Ethiopia without finding the least trace of us. Two days later they returned to port, not understanding how we could have escaped them.

The truth was simple enough. While they searched everywhere at sea, we were peacefully at anchor, hidden from view in that beautiful lagoon just in front of their town. In fact, if they'd used their binoculars from their office windows, they probably could have seen the upper part of my masts sticking up above the mangroves.

When we left the lagoon after repairing our sails, the warship had already given up the chase and was back at the dock. I've never had greater luck. If I'd been caught, I not only would have lost my ship, and everything in her, but God only knows how long they might have kept me in that Somaliland jail. That is, presuming I would have survived a stay there. And what would have happened to Thomas?

I had avoided jail in Singapore, thanks to Lydia's pretending she was hysterical. Now, I'd been lucky again. But how long could I expect my luck to hold out in a part of the world where so much can go wrong? I longed more and more to get back to Europe and to more civilised conditions. I did my best to ready the boat for the second half of the Red Sea towards Suez—the last milestone to the west, or to the "Occident," as Ann called it.

# 22

# The Arab Countries

On the 26th of April, we sailed from Port Sudan towards Suez. Much has been written about the Red Sea, and many dream about it as the greatest adventure of them all. Certainly the underwater life there is fantastic, with beautiful coral reefs and myriad fishes of all sorts. But on the surface, we had to fight a very strong and persistent headwind from the north. On shore we saw nothing but sand, barbed wire and soldiers—not exactly my idea of paradise.

To save time by sailing at night, we kept our course far from shore, to avoid running into the unlit, unmarked reefs. We still had to keep a careful watch for the many other ships also trying to navigate past the reefs. Unfortunately, sailing against the wind in any boat on an open sea is very strenuous for everybody onboard. People who are not very resistant to seasickness can become violently ill. When I looked at poor Ann, who was so miserably seasick despite her efforts to hide it, I had to stop to give her some respite. Whenever the wind got too strong, I steered for shore and looked for a quiet anchorage so she could recover.

To avoid being pestered by the many soldiers patrolling these shores, I tried to find suitable anchorages far enough from shore among the reefs so we could be left in peace. All too often, though, we were disturbed by wild shouting from shore and always the same word: "Passport, passport!" The patrolling soldiers wanted us to come ashore and show our passports.

The first time it happened, I shouted back through my loudspeaker that I had no intention of disembarking and so they wouldn't need to see my passport But the soldier just aimed his gun at me and repeated in a menacing voice, "Passport!"

I didn't want to take the chance that he was bluffing and rowed ashore with all the passports. The soldier took them without looking at them, probably because he didn't know how to read—at least not our language—and ordered me to climb into his jeep, a rusty old Russian car. We drove nearly two hours before we arrived at his camp in the desert. There I was interrogated by some higher officers with a lot of gold on their shoulders who tried to contact headquarters to find out what to do with us, but the radio functioned poorly and they had to try repeatedly before getting through.

In the meantime, they served me horrible coffee, which, no matter how hard I tried, I was unable to swallow. I excused myself by saying that I never drank anything but water, milk and fruit juices. The officers didn't seem to believe me and were a little hostile. At long last they made contact with headquarters and, apparently, got the order that I was okay and they should drive me back to my boat.

The trip with the soldiers had taken most of the day. It was late afternoon by the time we got back to my landing place. Ann was frantic with worry. She didn't know what had happened to me or why it had taken so long for my return.

Our trip to the Red Sea was to continue like this with hard headwinds and troublesome soldiers. Sometimes the wind brought such fine sand that it appeared a fog had rolled in. Visibility was cut way down and we couldn't see ships until they were practically on top of us. Navigation became very difficult and dangerous. At other times we had almost no wind, especially at night. Sometimes we were able to anchor and be left alone, but all too often we were shouted at by soldiers and ordered to go with them again. I will never understand why the Egyptians are so worried and have such tight controls along their shores. As far as I'm concerned, they can keep all that sand, along with their barbed wire, camels and rusty jeeps.

On the 25th of June, at long last, we reached Suez. We'd barely anchored when the Egyptian customs boat *Gehad* rammed into our stern. It came towards us at full speed, planning to use the usual manoeuvre of engaging in reverse at the last minute to stop. In this case, they must have engaged the reverse a little too late. They rammed us so hard they broke our rail and put a large hole in our deck. When I asked for reimbursement for the damages, they simply shrugged their shoulders and ordered me to show them my papers.

I've always hated those risky manoeuvres done just to show off— why not just come gently alongside?. I had laid out my fenders for them, but to no avail. The customs boat had barely left when the police boat arrived. This boat was so big that they used huge truck tyres along the side. It was much higher than we were, and came alongside so brutally that they smashed our rail from aft all the way forward to my mast's chainplates.

Ann and Thomas were down below during the boarding and rushed up on deck in a panic, thinking the whole boat must have been smashed, judging from the horrible, shocking sound of broken wood. Fortunately, the hull itself was undamaged except for a couple of deep scars in the topsides. But with the rail and upper part of the transom smashed, we looked like a derelict. When I indignantly demanded who was going to pay for the damages, I was met by a roar of laughter from the boat's crew and officers.

In the beginning I was determined to get the authorities to pay for the damages, but in the days that followed I soon realised that I would be wasting time on a lost cause. The best I could do would be to resign myself to my bad luck and be thankful the damage wasn't worse. I could repair the damage myself with time and a little bit of money. The best thing I could do would be to get out of this country before any more hardships befell me.

But that was going to be easier said than done. I again was not allowed to transit the canal under sail, but had to take a tow. I did find a motorsailor with a powerful motor, who was more than willing to tow me, but when the appointed day came, the authorities declared that only one of their certified tugboats could do any towing.

We'd been there 13 days and I was still wondering how I was going to get through without spending $500 U.S. on an Egyptian tugboat ($500 presuming they were able to book a return tow, or I'd be liable for another $500 for the return). But luck began to smile on us when we saw a beautiful little tugboat come into the harbour. It was on its way back home to Holland after doing a tow to the east. It was an immaculate Dutch towboat, just the perfect boat for us. We went to see the captain to ask if he could tow us through the canal.

"I can pull you all the way to Holland if you like," he said. "We wouldn't even notice the difference with a small boat behind us. And you can have all your meals with us," he added with a smile. "It will be nice for us to have some company."

We couldn't have wished for better luck than that, though we didn't want to be towed any further than through the canal. But we were in for a disappointment when we went to the authorities.

"What flag does that tugboat of yours carry?" they asked.

"Dutch," I answered, not suspecting a trap.

"In that case, we can't give you permission to transit. You can only transit under the tow of a certified Egyptian tugboat. We can't take the chance of having an accident in our canal because a tugboat is not familiar with our waters."

It wasn't a valid argument. There are no difficulties in the canal, with its negligible current and no bridges or gates. But I knew there was no sense in arguing. These authorities were almighty and just wanted to get as much money as possible out of foreigners. On the other hand I wasn't going to give away $500, or even worse, $1000.

I returned to our ship disappointed and took out the charts for the Red Sea and down the coast of Africa. Ann looked a bit worried and asked why I was pulling out the charts.

"I'm trying to find out what kind of winds we can expect on the way to South Africa," I answered, worried about her reaction.

"I hope you're not trying to say we've been fighting our way up the Red Sea all for nothing? You want us to sail back down the way we've come and sail around a whole continent just because of these crooked civil servants?"

When I replied, rather weakly, that I could see no alternative, I saw Ann's beautiful almond eyes get narrower and hard. Without another word, she jumped in the dinghy and rowed hard to shore. There I saw her take very determined, short, rapid steps towards the authorities' control building. I was worried. I had seen Ann mad a couple of times before, when her fury knew no bounds. Time passed and I wondered if she'd been arrested, perhaps, for insulting an Egyptian official. I was wondering if I should go after her when, to my relief, I saw her walking calmly back towards the dinghy.

Back onboard she calmly announced that we should be ready to be towed by 10 o'clock that very night. "They will not be making the usual stop in Lake Ismailia," she said. "They will tow us directly to Port Said. We'll be there tomorrow before sundown."

"Don't you think you could have asked my opinion before paying them the $1000 they wanted?" I asked, rather annoyed. "Or did you manage to get the trip for $500, regardless of their return trip?"

"It won't cost a cent. You know I'm far too stingy to spend a single cent on those crooks," she smiled teasingly.

"But how in the world did you manage that?"

She laughed happily and threw herself into my arms. "You know yourself how scared everyone gets of me when I'm mad. I pounded my fists on the big boss's desk and he must have decided that the best thing he could do was get rid of me and get me out of his harbour as quickly as possible. He immediately called one of his tugboats to tow us through the canal right away and even apologised that he couldn't find anyone to take us before 10 o'clock. I also told him to order the crew not to bother us by begging for *baksheesh*. Furthermore, we didn't want to be towed side by side, but behind the tug on a long line. He promised to give the necessary orders to conform to our wishes."

It sounded almost too good to be true, but at 10 o'clock that night the tugboat arrived. They took our long tow rope with no discussion and towed us all the way to Port Said without a fuss. Outside the yacht club they let go our tow rope and headed back from whence they'd come. They never once tried begging for the usual *baksheesh*, nor did they bid us farewell, but that we could do without.

We had hardly let go the anchor and were busy warping ourselves to the dock, when a huge police boat steered for us and came alongside with a bang, shaking the whole boat. Fortunately there were no damages this time, although that would take only a matter of time if we continued to bang against them in the short waves of the harbour. I was tired and had lost all patience and told them in no uncertain terms to leave us alone until we had finished our manoeuvre and were safely tied alongside the dock. I told them I didn't want my starboard side smashed in, as their colleagues had done to my port side and stern. They sullenly observed my broken rail and backed off, docking their boat further down the harbour.

An officer came back on foot and waited for us to tie up at the yacht club's dock. When he asked for our passports, I was fed up and burst out, "I've had to continually give you guys my passports. I must have shown them more than a dozen times since entering your country and each time I lose a full day's time running around your offices and distributing *baksheesh* before I can get them back. Since you know that we've just transited the canal, you must also know that our passports are in order. Besides we have no intention of going ashore. All we want is to sleep before putting out to sea. I see no reason to give you our passports."

"Are you refusing to obey me, an Egyptian police officer?" he asked in a menacing tone.

"I'm not giving away my passports," I repeated.

"In that case, I'll have you arrested and thrown into jail," he roared in a fury. "We'll see who will have the last word in this matter."

Via walkie-talkie he requested a patrol car with two extra officers so he could make an arrest. The man he was talking to at headquarters must have been his superior, because he asked for more details about the arrest. Though we didn't understand the language, we noticed the police officer's gradual loss of confidence. In the end, the superior apparently felt there was no good reason to arrest us.

After replacing his radio in his belt, the officer said, "Okay, you don't have to show me your passports now, but I'll be back tomorrow morning at 8:00. If you're still here, you'll have two choices. You can either show me your passports, or all three of you can go to jail."

"I can promise you that by 8:00 tomorrow morning, we'll be safely out of your country," I said.

It was a promise we kept. Before sunup we let go the lines holding us to the dock and steered under full sails for the breakwater and the open sea. We set our course towards Cyprus. Our original idea had been to cruise up the Nile and explore that fabulous part of the world. It had sounded so romantic and exciting until we got to know Egypt a little better. Our only thought now was to get out of that police state as soon as possible. Both Ann and I were greatly relieved as Egypt's shoreline disappeared behind us and we could lay the course toward a free world.

We left July 9th and, just three days later, arrived outside Larnaca in Cyprus. Many people say it's hopeless to sail in the Mediterranean, where there are no tradewinds. But the distances are short, and those who claim that it's impossible to sail without a motor should remember that sailboats without motors have sailed the Mediterranean Sea for several thousand years.

Outside the harbour we were met by a beautiful police boat which was so immaculate it looked more like a yacht. Instead of coming alongside and risking damaging us, they stayed at a safe distance and asked in perfect English if everything were okay onboard. They must have wondered if we needed help after seeing our smashed rail and stern.

When we thanked them, assuring them that everything was all right, they bade us farewell and steamed away without bothering to ask any more questions. They didn't even ask our names. What a difference from the rusty, dirty Egyptian boats that never hesitated to slam into us at every opportunity.

Soon we were in Limassol Harbour and almost felt as if we'd come home. The authorities were still clearly influenced by the English, despite the fact that their country had attained independence. They wished us welcome and didn't submerge us with the usual exaggerated red tape so common in the east. We immediately relaxed and began to enjoy the little country, staying a whole month before finding the energy to continue our cruise. I wanted Ann to see more of the Mediterranean that I'd told her so much about.

I could find no suitable wood for repairing the rail and transom, but was able to buy a roll of canvas made for covering trucks at a British military base. It was of excellent quality, though a bit heavier than necessary, and would make very strong sails. I planned to sew new sails in the Greek Islands, hoping that my old sails would get us that far, though they were quite rotten by now.

We left Cyprus on the 13th of August, 1980, heading for Rhodes. Everything went well in the beginning but, long before reaching

Rhodes, the foresail tore from top to bottom in a sudden squall. We were just opposite the small island of Kastelhorizon which, although very close to Turkey and far from the main cluster of Greek Islands, is still considered politically, if not geographically, a Greek Island. We had no choice but to make the nearest port as best we could. Despite having to beat through the narrow entrance channel, we made it safely and were soon inside the cutest little harbour I'd ever seen.

I congratulated myself for having sewn all my sails with vertical panels instead of the usual modern way of laying them horizontally. The horizontal cut is supposed to be faster, but the vertical system is far stronger and has the added advantage of tearing up and down when it tears. Thus, I'd been left with two halves standing up. It was admittedly in very poor shape, but nevertheless usable. A horizontal cut would have meant the lower part would have collapsed on deck, the upper part remaining aloft like a flag waving in the wind.

We had managed to handle the boat despite the big split and were soon safely moored to the main street, where the cooks of small sidewalk restaurants were barbecuing just a few yards from us. On the other side of the street was a large, open building with beautiful arches. Under the upper story was a large enough area to lay out our sails and protect us from possible rain and the scorching sun. In summary, we had found the perfect place for sewing our new sails. During the weeks that followed, tourists often passed by and stopped to converse. Many wondered how we could sew such big sails without a sewing machine. Several of these impromptu conversations were to lead to lifelong friendships, and I still correspond with several of those people today.

We were happy there and Ann suggested that perhaps we should buy one of the small, abandoned houses around the harbour and make this our home port. We thought about it seriously for a while but finally concluded that we should buy a house in a place where we could truly feel at home. In our case that boiled down to only three countries: Norway, where I was born and where my family came from; France, where I had been raised; and the United States, which had become my new legal country and where I was a citizen. Malaysia, which was Ann's country, had to be scratched. Even if we got married, I was a white man and would never be able to obtain permanent residency there.

We would have liked to stay on the island a long time, but everybody warned us against the severe storms in winter, when the port would no longer be safe. After inquiring with friends and reading the various travel books, we decided to winter in Tunisia. I had seen many postcards with camels and palm trees, and expected the climate would be warm. I was to bitterly regret my decision.

We sailed out of the harbour on September 8th under our new sails, which proved to be excellent in all respects. It was a great relief to no longer have to worry about them tearing at the slightest excuse, but we left our little paradise with sadness. The voyage proved to be a slow and painful one—strong headwinds fought us the whole way and Ann was very seasick. We finally arrived and entered Sfax, a very dirty commercial port in East Tunisia. Even before we got our anchor down, we regretted coming to another Arab country, especially one that looked almost worse than Egypt.

The harbour was not only dirty, but also overcrowded, and I couldn't find a single suitable spot for my boat. Finally, in desperation, I settled for a berth between a stone dock and an old rusty hulk moored fore and aft. We had been there barely 20 minutes when a great big warship got out of control and slammed into the hulk next to us, breaking his rusty and worn anchor chain. (We later learned that one of the warship's two propellers had stalled and the ship lost control in the strong wind.)

The wind abroadship blowing hard, the two ships drifted towards us at a fast rate. In seconds they were on top of us, pushing us towards the stone dock with such pressure that I was completely unable to escape. We were drifting, completely helpless, towards those stones where the weight of the two big ships would crush us like an eggshell. I stood on the rail with Thomas in my arms, hoping I would be able to jump ashore the second we hit before we were smashed.

We were only about three feet from the stone deck when a miracle happened. Suddenly the two ships stopped and we lay in perfect calm between the dock and the towering wall of my rusty neighbour. The ships had gone aground while the shallowing water was still deep enough for us to float, completely unharmed.

We should have taken the incident as a warning, but I told myself that all industrial harbours were dirty and crowded. If we chose a small tourist town instead, we would find some better conditions. The local tourist bureau gave me a prospectus showing the island of Djerba, a beautiful paradise with girls in bikinis, men in long, exotic robes, camels and small white houses with arched windows and alleyways. The girls didn't interest me, since Ann was all I ever wished for, but if they wore bikinis, the climate had to be right.

When we arrived in Djerba, the place was nearly as nice as the photographs had shown except for two things—the photos must have been taken in the summer and at low tide, because the weather was too cold for bikinis, and at high tide the breakwaters protecting the harbour were completely submerged, giving one the impression of being anchored in the open sea for all the protection they offered.

# 23

# The Attack In Tunisia

lthough Djerba was rather pleasant, the lack of proper protection against the winter storms which would soon be upon us meant we would have to leave soon for a safer port. The harbourmaster recommended I look into Gabes , an entirely new harbour up the coast which had been made for a small fishing fleet. He said the port was not completely finished, so few boats had settled there, but it was an excellent and very safe port.

One day in early November we set sail for Gabes. We arrived the next morning. To our relief we saw the breakwaters were indeed both high and strong enough to protect us from even the worst storms. The inner harbour was already jammed and rather dirty, but the outer harbour was completely deserted and more than safe enough. We anchored there, a good distance from the breakwater. The harbour authorities soon gave us all the papers we needed to moor there and we got settled. I called a French teacher I had once met, who came to the dock and invited us to his home. We were to become very close friends during the months we stayed in Tunisia. He proved to be a member of an entire colony of French teachers and technicians who lived and worked there.

Tunisia has the reputation among Frenchmen to be the least Arab and the most French of all the Arab countries. It may have been true 50 years ago, when the French were in full control and French was the official language. But now that they'd acquired their independence, it looked like the authorities were doing their best to erase the French language as fast as possible. In fact, only the old people still spoke and understood French. All the younger generation spoke Arabic. Nevertheless, French was still taught to those who wanted to learn, and we found a French school for Thomas to attend. He would be able to have some playmates while we stayed the whole winter.

We had decided to wait out the bad season before setting out to sea again. But just when we thought we'd found a quiet and peaceful place, disaster struck again. On the night of November 11th, we awakened to find three men holding knives at our throats. I can't imagine a worse feeling than waking to find yourself completely at the mercy of criminals who could murder or mutilate you at their slightest whim.

They asked me in French where my money was. I had only a couple of hundred dollars and gave it to them, but they asked sharply where "the rest of the money" was. I assured them that I kept only small amounts on the boat at any time because I felt it was unsafe to have big amounts onboard. I thought they would have been the first ones to understand, but they answered me with a violent punch in the face, knocking me out.

When I'd regained consciousness, I was tied up and gagged so tightly that I had trouble breathing. They dragged me out of the double bed and threw me on the floor in the forward cabin. While one of the bandits stood watch over me with his knife, the other two ripped off Ann's nightgown and hit her in the face, saying this was just a taste of what was going to happen to her if she refused to tell them where the "real hiding place" was.

I had actually told the truth when I told them that I kept my money in a bank and I had no additional money onboard. I didn't want to think about Ann's personal money which she kept in one of her drawers. I felt I had no jurisdiction over her money. Ann was in a panic now, and proposed naively that if they promised to leave immediately and not harm us any further, she would give them all her money as well as all her jewelry. They had already torn off her gold chain, which she wore all the time. Her money we could make up later, but her jewelry, in addition to its monetary value, represented irreplaceable memories of her family and her childhood.

When they'd taken everything she had, far from leaving as she'd made them promise to do, they threatened to rape her if she didn't tell them where the "main hiding place" was. To show that they really meant it, one of the bandits pinned her down on the bed by holding her arms down while the other one took off his pants and lay down on top of her.

Ann was the type of woman who preferred to die rather than be raped. She went berserk and fought with all her might. They tried to subdue her by hitting her repeatedly in the face with such brutality they broke one of her teeth. Her face swelled so badly that she was almost unrecognizable and one eye was swollen shut, but she fought like a wildcat and, despite the fact that she only weighed 85 pounds, they were unable to fulfill their rape. Finally they gave up and left, but not without taking a four-speaker transistor radio, which Ann had brought onboard. It was to become their downfall later on.

After they had gone, Ann sobbed uncontrollably. They hadn't actually raped her, but she felt dirty and humiliated by their contact.

"I wish I was dead," she said.

"Don't talk like that," I protested. "Except for your broken tooth and your bruises, which will heal, nothing is changed between us."

As soon I as felt it was safe enough to leave her alone, I hurried ashore to the nearby police station. I had to knock a long while before a sleepy police officer finally opened up for me. While he wrote up the report, he let me use his phone to call for an ambulance for Ann, which arrived in just a few minutes.

The doctor onboard spoke perfect French. After taking Ann to the hospital and examining her, the doctor took me aside and confided that Ann was lucky to be alive. He said a good many people would not have been able to survive the beating she had suffered. Provided nothing unforeseen happened and provided she could get over the psychological trauma, she would completely recover except for some scars and, of course, the broken tooth. He gave me some aspirin for my jaw, but ordered Ann to stay in bed for three weeks.

Surprisingly enough, the police did find the criminals. They had many informers who wouldn't hesitate to give even a friend away if the police paid them enough for the information. The bandit who had stolen our radio was a poor fisherman. When his fellow workers suddenly saw him with an expensive radio, they told the police. He was immediately arrested and, while I didn't witness the interrogation, I can guess how it went, judging from the prisoner's appearance when I was called to identify him. I could see no wounds, but he was so weak he could hardly stand; when he begged the police for a cigarette, his hands trembled so badly they had to light it for him.

During the interrogation, he had not only confessed to the crime but also had given the names of his two accomplices. The police's efficiency impressed me even more when they found his accomplices hiding in a friend's apartment in Sfax. Sfax is quite a big town some distance away. The men had been caught just as they were trying to escape over the border to a neighbouring country. Both had fled when they saw their friend arrested, as they no doubt expected that he would turn them in, but the police were still able to catch them.

The police gave us back the radio, but not the money, the gold or the other jewelry. The two bandits that were arrested later claimed that, when they heard of their friend's arrest they had panicked and thrown both the money and the jewelry into the sea. But as the case progressed, I was convinced of quite a different story.

In the preliminary court hearing, we were called in to identify the criminals, even though they had confessed. They were condemned

At Any Cost

to two months of detention until their case came up in criminal court. One of the lawyers whispered to me that he expected them to get 20 years in jail for premeditated armed robbery and attempted rape, but they'd probably get out in 10 years on good behavior. The judge asked if they had any questions or remarks and one of them said, "Why are you trying to punish us when you are a Moslem and so are we, while those two," he said, pointing at us, "are just Christians?"

Those were scary words, indeed, showing just how little protection a foreigner has in Arab countries where it's believed that it's okay to harm a Christian. The judge was a well-educated man who, of course, could only answer that everyone is equal under the law.

I had still hoped that we'd be able to get our money and jewelry back. I didn't believe, of course, that the bandits had thrown them into the sea. Perhaps they would give it all back in hopes of getting a milder sentence. At any rate, we wanted to stay for the case. Winter was far from over and we had no desire to tempt any more Mediterranean storms. We attempted to renew our three-month visas— which we'd been told could be renewed with no problem—but were told now that we wouldn't get any extension at all.

"But you can't force us out to sea at this time of the year. Besides, we should be witnesses in criminal court, which will come up after our visas have expired," I insisted.

My arguments were of no use. Immigration insisted that we had to be out of the country before our visas expired; otherwise they would confiscate our boat and either put us in jail or deport us!

I rushed over to the judge, told him how unreasonable immigration had been with us and asked if he could please call and tell them that we needed to be witnesses in court and we needed an extension. The judge merely excused himself with a weak smile and said he had nothing to do with immigration. He thought it would be best if we followed immigration's orders and left the country. He added that we needn't worry—we'd already identified the criminals and didn't need to be in court for the trial. If the money and jewelry were recovered he would send it to us. In any case, he would keep us updated as to what the judgment would be.

We had no choice but to go to sea long before the case went to court. Of course I never heard from the judge.

In the months that followed, I wrote dozens of letters to the police, the judge, the prosecutor and even the priest who had assisted Ann in the hospital after the attack. A priest always answers. He had been very good to Ann and even made her a gift of a gold chain and gold cross to replace the one she'd lost. He was French, but had spent his entire life in Tunisia and knew the Arabs well. He wrote us a long, friendly and soothing letter, which really boiled down to his saying that there was no use crying over spilled milk. The best we could do was to forgive the criminals and not think about it any more.

I strongly suspected that the priest himself doubted we would ever get anything back. He probably suspected, as I finally did, that the gold and money had been surrendered by the criminals in exchange for their freedom and split between the police and the judge. That would explain why the police had made such an effort to catch them in the first place after we'd told them what was taken. It would also explain why they were so anxious to get us out of their country, why they never answered our letters and why the priest told us to forget the whole thing. The priest was getting no share in the take, but knew it would be useless for us to try to get anything back.

In countries such as this, even the press is not free. Not one of the newspapers mentioned the attack. No one in the country would benefit by scaring future tourists away, especially since half the national income comes from the tourist industry. In the Arab countries, the danger of being mugged, attacked or raped is far greater than most people realise.

# 24

# Norway Through Tropical Eyes

$\mathcal{W}$e sailed out of port on the 21st of March, long before the end of the winter storms, and set the course north towards Europe. We hoped to get to Ibiza, one of the Balearic Islands off the coast of Spain, where I had many friends. But two days after our departure the wind turned against us.

We were forced to beat against a short and rough sea at a slow speed. We kept fighting our way and cursing the Tunisian authorities, who had forced us to sea at this dangerous time of year. When we finally arrived in the middle of the Mediterranean, the wind gradually increased to force 9 and then to force 10. For 30 hours we lay hove-to in an unbelievably rough sea, hoping the ship would survive without damage. When the wind moderated to gale force 8, we made sail again, but lost courage to keep beating against the wind.

Instead we turned around with the wind aft, which gave us a far more comfortable ride. At this stage we felt any port would be welcome. The wind was pushing us to the south point of Sardinia, an Italian island south of Corsica, which didn't sound so bad. Indeed, it was to be one of the best stops we ever made, which proved again that it's difficult to know in advance what to expect. Even if you check with friends for help in choosing the right place, it doesn't necessarily work out. What makes one man happy may not necessarily be right for another.

On April 3rd, we entered the port of Cagliari and dropped the hook. We heard excited shouts from shore, which turned out to be my old friend Giorgio, whom I'd not seen in years. He had recognised my boat despite its new rig. Giorgio proved to be a big man in his hometown and doors opened up for us. As his guest, we were given a free slip at his yacht club and he regularly invited us to the town's most elegant restaurants. Ann was particularly impressed with the restaurants' elegance, good service and excellent Italian cuisine. She enjoyed every minute of those dinners, which must have been a welcome relief from her daily tasks onboard.

Giorgio also introduced us to many of his friends. We were to become very good friends with a man named Giambattista, a champion marksman. When he heard about the two aggressions we'd suffered, Giambattista offered us a beautiful automatic pistol, but I declined. I thought most authorities inflicted too many hassles on honest citizens who wanted to be able to defend themselves.

When Giambattista saw the damage the Egyptians' poor seamanship had inflicted on my boat, he asked me to make a list of the materials I would need so he could check around for their availability. The very next morning he came in a van and delivered everything to my boat. When I asked for the bill, he said the owner of the sawmill was a friend of his and didn't charge me because I was one of Giambattista's friends.

In the days that followed, Giambattista often came by to chat and see how the work was progressing. The work was often interrupted by invitations to restaurants and long drives in the country, but it still went along rapidly. My new rail and transom was finished within two to three weeks and the boat actually looked better than before. I made nice sweeping curves on the corners, which looked far better than the square corners I'd originally designed.

What impressed me most in Sardinia was the freedom and *joie de vivre* so evident everywhere in the country. I will never forget one evening when Giorgio invited us for dinner. Instead of picking us up in his big luxury car, he put us on his 1000-cc Moto Guzzi, a huge

Italian motorcycle with automatic drive. "The car is in for repairs," he explained, "and I won't get it back from the garage until tomorrow. But don't worry, the bike is big enough for all four of us and we'll get there much faster in the heavy traffic."

I thought he was joking, but all four of us got on that monster. Thomas was on the fuel tank, I was all the way aft and Ann was between him and me. I presumed he would just have some fun with us and drive us carefully around the parking lot, but I underestimated him. He opened up the throttle and we shot out of the parking lot and into the traffic. Ann was wearing one of her very long, tight dresses and had to sit sideways with both legs on the same side of the bike. Although this was very "ladylike," it's not the most secure way to ride a bike. When we came to a traffic jam, Giorgio jumped the sidewalk and continued down a parallel street. To my horror, it turned out to be a one-way street which we had gone down the wrong way at high speed!

Fortunately, we arrived at the restaurant without an accident. Giorgio tipped the haughty, uniformed doorman to park the bike for him, and the man didn't seem to show the least bit of surprise.

"Quite sincerely, Giorgio," I said, once we were seated at the table, "don't you think that was a bit much? Ann was sitting crosswise on the bike, none of us have a helmet and you were driving the wrong way down a one-way street. I even saw the speedometer topping 120 km in a 50 km zone. Don't you ever get any tickets? In fact, I'm rather surprised you still have your driver's license."

Giorgio laughed. "This is still a free country," he said. "I bought this 1000-cc to have fun, not to crawl along. The police's job in this country is to arrest criminals, not to pester honest citizens. Besides, they know me and generally leave me alone." He hesitated and then added, a bit embarrassed, "Well sometimes they do stop me, but after a few jokes and a small tip they generally let me go. They know a big bike is something to have fun with."

We did have fun in Italy. We were very happy among friends and in nice surroundings. I will never forget the wonderful Italian restaurants and their spaghetti, ice cream, cheeses and all the different breads which tasted so good. We even considered learning the language and settling there for good. One of our friends had the right contacts in immigration and could easily obtain permanent residency for us.

After the attack in Tunisia, Ann had been so depressed and miserable that I promised to marry her, sell the boat and settle down in a house as soon as we found the right place to live. The boat had meant everything to me, but now Ann was more important to me than anything in the world, except, of course, for Thomas. Since she was seasick so often, she didn't like sailing. I was willing to give up the sea for her because I'd fallen more and more in love with this little woman who had given up everything for my sake. She'd lost her career, her family, her friends and even her country, because I could never get residency there.

I hoped I could give her a new home, a family and a new country. We liked it in Italy, but thought it would be more logical to settle in America, where I was now a citizen. But since I had neither home nor family there, we decided first to try Norway, where I had a lot of family and which wasn't very far away.

On July 5th, 1981, we bade farewell to our friends and put back to sea, headed for Norway. Our first stop was Faro, in the south of Portugal. We arrived there after a pleasant voyage with light, shifting winds and a flat sea. Portugal is not nearly as free or open a country as Italy. There were many rules and regulations to obey and far too many soldiers for my taste. Nevertheless, Portugal is a pleasant country with very friendly people.

Our next stop was to be Falmouth, England. We should have

been able to expect following southerly winds, but as soon as we cleared the "Portuguese trades" blowing along the westerly shores of Portugal, we had to beat the whole way against persistently northern winds. By the time we rested up after the passage to England, the season was so far advanced we thought it best to wait until the following summer before attempting to cross the stormy North Sea. It wouldn't have done us much good to arrive in Norway just before winter, when we'd be miserable and unable to live onboard the boat. It would also be difficult to try to sell the boat then and buy a house.

We spent the winter in the Helford River, a tiny and beautiful river just outside of Falmouth, and waited for the winter storms to stop so we could cross the North Sea to Norway. In March 1982, an old friend offered me the use of her car so I could drive to Norway instead of waiting for summer to do the crossing in the boat. Her offer was doubly welcome because the big problem with sailing in the north is that the sailing season is so short. We'd have had to wait for good weather in order sail to Norway, and once there wouldn't have long before we'd have to leave again to go south in order to avoid spending the winter there.

The sailing season in Norway starts June 15th and ends around August 15th—just two months. Of course there's no law against sailing outside of those dates. Some hardy souls do start a few weeks before and hang on a few weeks after, but it's not very pleasurable and certainly wouldn't be for us. We were much too accustomed to the warmer weather.

On March 30th, we drove onto the ferry to Norway in our borrowed car. We'd thought England was cold, but we were shocked at how much colder it was in Norway. There was still snow every-where. Nevertheless, we were happy and excited to arrive in my old homeland and drove north towards Oslo with great expectations—and the heater going full blast.

On the way, we made a stop in Risor, a small town where an old friend, Lillerut Bryn, had invited us to stay for a few days. I had known Lillerut and her husband Nils in 1957. Nils later was to drown in the Mediterranean during a gale. We stayed aboard Lillerut's boat called *Stavanger*. Although it was an old ship, built at the end of the last century, it was still beautiful and I was quite excited to stay onboard her, even though most of my time was spent feeding the oven enough scraps of wood to keep us warm.

One day Ann opened up the hatch to go ashore, but then quickly slammed it shut with a look of horror, asking me what in the world was going on outside. "It's just a snowstorm," I said after taking a quick look.

"Never in my life could I have imagined a place this cold," she moaned, wiping the snow off her face. I didn't have the courage to tell her that it was probably only a few degrees below freezing (and quite mild by Norwegian standards).

A few days later we drove to Oslo. It was the beginning of April and everyone had left town for Easter vacation. None of my old friends or family were home. It seems the Norwegians work hard most of the year to earn enough money to escape the city as soon as they have a vacation. Most everyone had gone to either mountain cabins or seaside second residences.

As we drove around Oslo and its suburbs, I had trouble recognising things because the area had changed so much. Many new buildings and roads had been built since I'd left the country in 1949.

Eventually Easter vacation ended and I contacted members of my family. Each one invited us for dinner. It was nice to see them again, and they were interested in hearing about my travels, but it was all too evident that we didn't have very much in common anymore. Most of them were businessmen living lives far different from my own. They were uncomfortable around Ann because she came from an entirely different culture, and because she didn't speak Norwegian, they were forced to carry on our conversations in English.

We checked the real estate market to see what we could expect in case we wanted to buy a house. We also made the necessary arrangements to get married as soon as possible. In May we were finally married in the beautiful Church of Sagene in my hometown of Oslo. Ann was very beautiful in her Chinese ceremonial dress and I was very proud of her. I had hoped to get her integrated into a large and loving family to make up for the one she'd lost in Malaysia, but it wasn't to be. Only two people came to our wedding. Even the minister was a bit embarrassed to see his church so empty.

But we still had each other and Thomas. We could make new friends and Norway might still be a good country to live in. We decided to keep on exploring and get to know the country better.

On the 15th of May, Ann said something that would change our lives. I remember it was May 15th, because it was two days before the Norwegian National Day, and everybody was preparing to celebrate.

"You've shown me the country," she said, "but each time you show me its beauty and try to explain its advantages, I wonder if it's really me or yourself you're trying to convince. When we stood on that mountain high over the fjord, looking down into the water, did you really think it was beautiful? You sure were in a big hurry to get out of the wind and the cold and get back into the heated car.

"And how about later, when we drove along the water and looked up at the towering mountain wall. Were you really sincere in pointing out its beauty? I felt claustrophobic at the bottom of the fiord and dizzy at the top. Quite honestly, don't you think the beauty of palm trees and warm tradewinds is easier to appreciate? You've been telling me about the wonderful long days in the summer when the sun hardly goes down at all. I would long for the peace of darkness. We've never had so much trouble putting Thomas to bed as we've had since we've been here. And, I presume, we'll have much less daylight during the winter. I've never experienced a winter in the north, but I can well imagine how depressing it must be to live in darkness during the day. And what about the extra electric bills?

"I always told you, Peter, I would be willing to live wherever you chose, but I think you'd be unhappy here. Once we sold the boat to buy a house, it would be very difficult for us to try again somewhere else should we later regret it. Norway is a beautiful country, but it is a hard beauty, best appreciated by those who have been born and raised here and geared to the climate. You're going to be 58 years old soon, and of all those years you've only spent 14 here. You are a wandering soul, and I doubt you would be happy settled in a house. Maybe I'm wrong—maybe one day you will find a place where you could settle down, but how could you possibly thrive in a country where you'll have to be closed up in a house most of the cold winter?

"I have never known a Norwegian winter, but the spring has been bad enough for us. Don't forget that you've lived in warm climates almost as long as I have!"

I had, indeed. Ann was 34 years old, and I had lived in warm climates for 33 years.

"I fear it may even shorten your life," she continued in a worried tone. "You're always in good shape as long as the weather is warm, but as soon as it turns chilly you get your old bronchitis back. You cough so hard you almost lose your breath. I really doubt you could survive many winters here. And this country is so expensive. Why should we live in an expensive country and be forced to work hard when we can choose a cheap country, with a far better climate, earn less money and live happily? Even if I get seasick easily, I'd much rather keep on sailing with you than see you be unhappy here. Let's get back to the boat as soon as possible and set sail south to a place where the sun rises properly above the horizon."

I didn't answer, but simply took her in my arms without saying a word. Life was so strange. Here was someone from the other side of the world, from an entirely different culture, who had proved to be the one who understood me the best and the one I felt closest to.

I gave everything I had inherited from my parents to an auctioneering firm, bade a hasty farewell to the various members of my family and drove south to England and to the boat.

What a joy it was to be back on the boat. Thinking back to my narrow escape from a settled, "respectable" life in Norway, I thought again of the ashtray whose inscription had so troubled my childhood—"Whoever lives without folly is not as clever as he thinks."

Yes, I had tried to be responsible and do what a "mature grown-up" is supposed to do, but it must have been against my nature, judging from how relieved I felt to get back to my boat and my free life again. Ann, my understanding wife, had even managed to help me keep my wandering lifestyle without feeling guilty about it.

# 25

# Back Home to the Tropics

*T*he English climate has a bad reputation, but it's far better than Norway's climate. The sun rises higher in the sky and gives more warmth. When we arrived, there was no snow lying along the roadside and we could get out of the car without freezing. We liked England and decided to stay there for a while.

Since Ann was now in a country where she understood the language, things were easier for her. We lay in the Helford River next to Falmouth in the southwestern part of England, which for centuries has traditionally been the last port for departing England and the first port for homecoming ships. From here we could hoist the sails at any time and head south without first having to fight our way through the English Channel, so we relaxed and enjoyed ourselves in a friendly country so full of charm and history.

Often the three of us went to small restaurants serving the traditional fish and chips. Because we were next to the sea, the local places served fresh fish of the very best quality, which cost nothing compared to the outrageous prices of Norway. We also enjoyed walking through the narrow, charming streets of the old town where ship chandlers offered everything a yachtsman could wish for at very reasonable prices. We bought a whole roll of rope, and two anchors to supplement the three we already had. We also bought miscellaneous gear of all sorts, now that we had the chance.

But as much as we had enjoyed England in the summer, we knew that if we lingered too long winter would be upon us and make life miserable. We needed to get back to work and make the boat seaworthy again. We lay the boat alongside a small dock where we knew she would dry out when the tide ran out so we could paint her bottom again. We scraped the barnacles off the hull standing in the water as it went out. When we reached the bottom, we immediately started painting at the lower-most point and kept on painting upwards, racing the water following us up towards the waterline. Next day we turned the boat against the quay the other way so we could paint the opposite side. The whole job cost us only the price of the paint. In most other countries there is no substantial tide difference which forces us to be hauled out of the water at commercial yards and to pay whole fortunes for the privilege.

We left England on July 25th for the Canary Islands, sailing among a crowd of boats which had come to see the start of the Tall Ships race that same day. We left just before they did, expecting those big ships to soon overtake us, but we never saw them again. We made good speed with an average of 140 miles per day and arrived in the Canaries on August 4th.

The Canary Islands are a paradise for the yachtsman. The climate is perfect year-round—never too cold or too hot and very little rain. The people are friendly, the prices reasonable. We sailed from island to island, liked them all and could easily have remained there forever.

After a while restlessness set in again, so we hoisted sails for French Guiana to see the country where our little boat had been built. We left on the 19th of September and arrived at Cayenne on the 10th of October. *L'Artemis de Pytheas* had been the only boat there on my previous stay, but this time there were 10 or 15 other boats at anchor. Most of them were French. In French Guiana, it's easy to find work and many skippers take advantage of that fact to replenish their bank accounts before continuing their wanderings.

The harbourmaster hadn't changed and was very enthusiastic to see L'*Artemis* "come home." She was the only boat ever built in that country, at least, as far as anyone could remember. He telephoned the local television station and they rushed a crew right down to the dock with a fully equipped van to interview me. They told me the interview would appear later that evening and a friend invited us to his home so we could all see ourselves on television. The program proved to be a long one. It seemed strange for us all, especially Thomas, who finally exclaimed, "Gosh, I thought only important people appeared on television!"

Because of the television program, all my friends found out I was back and we received countless dinner invitations. They all wanted to hear about my adventures since I had sailed away several years before.

Of course Lydia's death prevented my return from being joyful and made it difficult for Ann, who must have felt like an intruder in Lydia's territory. Perhaps that was the main reason she discouraged me from starting a shipyard there. I had gotten the offer as a result of the television show. I also got offers from many would-be buyers who wanted me to build them a sistership to *L'Artemis*. In fact, three of them came together one day and offered me enough money as an advance payment to start a yard with no capital of my own. They also proposed to keep on paying me during the duration of the building.

It was a tempting offer. After the completion of these first three boats, other customers would surely follow, and even if they didn't, I could build on speculation and perhaps sell to America. I liked French Guiana and the thought of starting my own business, but as I checked further into things, I discovered that much had changed during the time I was away.

Now that the new Space Center was in operation, France seemed to take the whole country more seriously and enforced its regulations more, creating a lot of red tape. The last time, I had built my shed the way it pleased me and, except for the landlord's verbal authorization,

I hadn't worried about any other formalities. But now, I was warned that I couldn't erect any building of any kind without a permit.

"Where do I get a permit?" I asked.

"Well, first of all you have to get your drawings remade by a licensed architect," the state employee explained. "Then you have to submit the drawing to us for our approval."

"How long will that take?" I asked.

"About a year and a half," he said indifferently. Seeing my exasperation, he hurriedly added, "Well if you're really in a hurry, maybe we could do it in a year, provided, of course, we don't have too much other work to do."

Then I learned I could no longer build a boat I'd designed only in my head. My drawings first had to be approved by a committee who would determine if it would be safe enough. The fact that its prototype had sailed to the other side of the world apparently had nothing to do with it. In addition to getting my drawings approved, I would be subject to the committee's inspectors both during construction at regular intervals and at the launching of the boat.

I hated the lack of freedom imposed on us by these state employees and their rules and regulations. They seemed to feel entitled to rule over our lives. It was enough to make me lose all desire to remain in the country, which had lost all its charm for me. I had to decline the offer of my three would-be customers but, to my great joy, two of them asked to buy my plans. They wanted them exactly as I had drawn them without the state approval stamp. They were going to try to get the boats built outside of France's jurisdiction.

I sold the drawings as "stock drawings," which means drawings that have already been made and whose royalties remain my property. This meant I could keep selling the same drawings to other customers for $500 per set. That may seem like a lot of money for a dozen sheets of paper,. but it is actually cheap when you consider the weeks, if not months, of work it involves. To design a 50-footer especially for one customer would require thousands of dollars if the architect is to make a living out of it. As it was, with two customers I got $1000. Ann was used to the low prices and low salaries of the east and was very impressed.

When we sailed out of Cayenne on December 1st, Ann was very relieved that I'd decided not to remain there. She had waited until then to tell me about it because she didn't want to discourage me if I had thought it would be a good place for me.

"I don't like the country," she admitted as we sailed along the coast towards the West Indies. "First of all, I must admit that I'm a bit jealous and didn't like all the memories you had there of your late wife. I also didn't like the many Chinese there. They were unfriendly towards me because I married a white man. But most of all, I worried about the strain and fatigue you would have suffered had you started your own commercial yacht building business. You have good memories of your years of building *L'Artemis*, but don't forget, you were building for your own pleasure and had no one to satisfy but yourself. This time you would have been working to satisfy others. They would have frequently come to inspect your progress and give you orders. Sometimes you wouldn't have agreed with them. You'd also have had to comply with the many authorities and their regulations. In the evenings you would have been so tired and often frustrated that we would have had little time together to enjoy life. I'm really glad you gave it all up and I'm glad you made up your own mind rather than me nagging you about it.

"I think when you get rested and feeling like it, you should sit down at your drawing table and design a 40-footer along the lines of *L'Artemis*. I noticed that many of the people that admired her seemed scared off by her size. Make stock plans for a 40-footer and let people know wherever we sail that we have plans for our boat for sale and also plans for a smaller sister-ship. Once in a while we'll make a sale and we'll have money coming in without all the worries and restrictions a shipyard would cause us."

She was right, as always, and I did later design a 40-footer. But for now, we were approaching Devil's Island which is a beautiful spot, despite its ill-famed reputation. I suggested we stop there so Ann wouldn't leave French Guiana with only negative memories.

When we disembarked, Ann could hardly believe her eyes. We were in a tropical paradise with huge breadfruit trees and mango trees which gave us restful shade from the tropical sun. We could pick as much fruit as we could carry and the sea was full of fish. We could have stayed forever just living off the land and needing hardly any money. There were no harbourmasters, policemen, inspectors or civil servants to bother us. We stayed several days and ate ourselves almost sick on all the plentiful fruits. Ann also made jars of jam until we ran out of sugar.

"You're right," she said. "It's not French Guiana that I dislike. It's just Cayenne and life around town which I resent. Devil's Island is really paradise itself," she laughed, slightly embarrassed by her joke.

Devil's Island was certainly no paradise for all the prisoners who were sent there through the years. We walked through ruins of the many buildings now overgrown with vegetation. We saw graveyards where many of the prison guards and their families ended their lives, but we saw no graves of prisoners.

It wasn't that prisoners didn't die here. Many did. It was just that they were not considered worthy of a grave and were thrown into the sea for the sharks to finish off. The whole ceremony was a few words from a priest while a funeral bell rang and the corpse was thrown into the sea. It is said that the sharks recognised the bell and, when it started to ring, would rush over to the usual place, waiting for the dead to be thrown overboard.

From Devil's Island we then sailed to St. Laurent du Maroni, which is the only other town of importance in French Guiana, although now we should perhaps count the space town of Kourou. We sailed in several miles of river to reach the town which was both beautiful and peaceful. The town, which was built entirely by the forced labour of prisoners, still stands in good condition and is well-maintained but it gave the impression of a ghost town because so many of its residents have left to find work in Cayenne or Kourou.

We had intended only to stay a short time, but I still enrolled Thomas in a school which was just a block from where we disembarked. It would be a change of pace for Ann as well as for Thomas, and he would get some playmates. Ann liked it a lot better than she had in Cayenne because she didn't have to share me with all my old friends. Here I knew no one. No one approached me to build any boats for them, but time wasn't wasted. Thanks to the great range of tides, we were able to beach our boat and repaint the anti-fouling paint which had grown quite foul. The English anti-fouling paint we'd used before leaving England was not designed for use in tropical waters where barnacles grow so much more quickly than they do in the colder, more saline water of northern Europe.

# 26

# Birth and Tragedy

Our next stop was Martinique, the French island I'd visited so many times before. We arrived just before Christmas and experienced the sumptuous French hospitality of my many old friends. I was proud to introduce them to my elegant and beautiful Chinese wife. We both liked Martinique and stayed there long enough to realise that we were going to have a sibling for Thomas. We'd waited so long that we were overjoyed at the prospect of a new baby, something which would seal our marriage even closer.

Thomas didn't share our enthusiasm at all and probably resented the fact that he'd no longer be the centre of attention and have to share everything with a new brother or sister.

While I was in Martinique, I got a firm offer from a man for the plans for the 40-footer Ann had suggested I design. It took me two months to make all the drawings, working full-time every day but Sundays. That might be surprising to some people, but I couldn't simply reduce the drawing I had for *L'Artemis* to the shorter length. Regardless of the desired length of the boat, the size of the skipper, his wife, and everybody else remained the same. Headroom inside the cabin had to remain the same and so did the length of the beds.

Another reason not to reduce the scale of a drawing when changing the size of a boat is because the stability of the boat is a function of its size and wind force must be taken into account. In other words, a whole new design had to be made. I still sold the set of drawings for $500, emphasising that the copyright remained my property, and retaining my right to resell the same design to oth customers. I enjoyed sitting and drawing in the peace of our snug salon with Ann sewing clothes for the new baby beside me.

We had a good life in Martinique and might have stayed there longer, but I was getting homesick for the United States and wanted to show the country to Ann. Unfortunately, due to red tape, she was never to see America. We sailed to Antigua and visited the American consulate there. We were informed that, although Ann was my wife, it would be a lengthy procedure for her to get a permanent residence permit to the States. They did say that they could give us a visitor's visa good for a year with no problem.

But, when we entered American territory by sailing to the American Virgin Islands, we were told that, although our visa was good for a year in the sense that we could enter the United States at any time during that period, it gave us the right to remain on U.S. soil for only 20 days starting from the day we entered the Virgins! When I asked for an extension so that we could visit the continental U.S., we were informed that only a consul could do that, preferably the one who had issued the visa in the first place.

As Antigua was dead to windward in the opposite direction of where we wanted to go, we decided to see the American consul in the Dominican Republic instead, since it was on the way. When we entered the country, the ship, Thomas and I were cleared with no problem, but since they had no diplomatic agreements with Malaysia they wouldn't allow Ann to go ashore. I pointed out that she was my wife and I was an American citizen and that we needed to go ashore to see the American consul. But they stood firm and refused her permission to set foot ashore.

I called the consulate and asked permission to fill out the forms for my wife, but they refused, saying "the applicant has to come and sign in person." I tried everything I could think of for two weeks until I got so disgusted with the red tape that I hoisted the sails laying a course back to Europe. Ann had been admitted everywhere there without any hassle.

We stopped in the Azores on the 15th of July, 1983, and liked it so much that it wasn't until the beginning of September that we found the will power to leave. At that time full gales had begun. Indeed, halfway to Portugal a vicious gale forced us to heave-to under the storm canvas for three days. On the 12th of September, we finally arrived safely and with no damages at Sagres, on the south coast of Portugal. We'd been luckier than a few other yachts that had rolled over and become badly damaged in that same gale just a couple of hundred miles north of us.

From Sagres we sailed along the coast of Portugal all the way to Spain and fell more and more in love with that beautiful and friendly country. We especially liked the Guadiana River, which forms the border between Spain and Portugal. People still live there nearly as they did one hundred years ago. They still use donkeys and horses, kerosene lamps and candles, fetch water at the village well, and wash their clothes in the river. Most of all we were seduced by the friendly smiles we were met with everywhere. We bought food directly from the farmers, got homemade goat cheese at half the regular stores' price, and were always invited to sit down and have a chat with people going about their unhurried ways.

But regardless of how much we liked it in the river, we had to start thinking about our baby's birth, which would happen soon. We would have liked to have the birth onboard, provided of course that this time we could be assisted by a midwife. But we were warned that we would run into a lot of red tape if a child were born on a foreign boat, even if it was within their territorial waters at the time. In other words, we'd have the same problems I'd had with Thomas. If we went to a Portuguese hospital for the birth, the baby would be given Portuguese citizenship and it would be easy for me to get dual citizenship when I returned to the States.

But progress had also sneaked in to this part of the world. Upon trying to make a reservation in the tiny local hospital, we were informed that they were no longer delivering babies. We had to go to a fancy new hospital in Faro, far from where we were.

"But this is ridiculous," I said. "Suppose labour begins and we come to you here. You couldn't possibly refuse to deliver the baby."

"In that case, we'd put your wife in our ambulance and drive her to Faro. They handle all the births in the region."

"How far is it to Faro?" I asked. "Suppose the baby arrives before the ambulance reaches the hospital?"

"Oh, it wouldn't be the first time," the doctor replied, completely unconcerned.

We couldn't find a single midwife—apparently they'd all gone to the fancy new hospital in Faro. We decided that if they would deliver the baby there, at least we were going to make sure that it didn't happen in the ambulance on the way to Faro. We decided to sail to Faro and wait for the birth. We arrived in Faro on the 30th of September and anchored in a well-protected lagoon, about a mile from town. With our dinghy, it was no problem to row right into the centre of town and tie the dinghy in the basin by the park. We liked Faro immediately. It was a beautiful old town, with many streets reserved for pedestrians only. It would be no strain to wait for our baby's birth in these surroundings.

On the morning of October 14th, Ann complained of pains in her abdomen and back. I wanted to row immediately to shore and get her into the hospital even it we still had two weeks according to our calculations. She thought it was a false alarm and didn't want to be like so many women who alert everybody at the slightest sign, only to learn after admittance that the birth is still a long way off, and have to go home again.

The pains subsided after a while, so we disregarded it all. After lunch, I suspected that Ann was in pain again, but she didn't want to tell me about it for fear I'd force her to go to the hospital prematurely. All afternoon she insisted she wasn't having any pains. I realised that she was in pain, but just didn't want to go to the hospital. Finally, a little after six o'clock in the evening, she admitted that perhaps it would be a good idea to go to the hospital.

Never before nor since have I rowed a dinghy so fast. We entered the inner basin where I tied the dinghy and told Ann not to move until I could run to the fire station to fetch an ambulance. When I came back, she'd managed to get out of the dinghy herself and was waiting for us ashore. She assured me she was quite all right but she did agree to lie down on the stretcher without protest rather than try to enter the ambulance on her own.

We arrived at the hospital a few minutes later, and after a hasty examination the doctor said it was indeed a good idea that we hadn't waited any longer. She was rushed into the delivery room where I was permitted to stay and comfort her. Less than half an hour later, the baby was born. She screamed instantly, even before her feet were out making me marvel again at the miracle of birth. She was beautiful and of average weight, which is quite big enough for an 85-pound mother. Ann never showed the least bit of pain and never complained, although at one point she whispered to me that maybe one baby would be enough.

We had been a bit concerned about the policies of a modern and spotless hospital. We were afraid they would force bottle feeding on the baby and keep her isolated from her mother in a special, sterilised nursery. We were relieved and very happy when, after the birth, mother and child were wheeled into a private room with just two other mothers. Each mother's child lay in a tiny bed beside her own.

Before leaving us, the doctor and nurse told us with a friendly smile that they hoped Ann and the baby would be happy there. Ann could feel free to nurse or bottle feed the baby and, if she needed any help, all she'd have to do was ring and they would come instantly.

Visiting hours were twice a day. Each time I looked forward to seeing them again, but I was a bit nervous the day I took Thomas along to meet his baby sister. I thought it best if he got to know her in the hospital rather than have a strange baby suddenly intrude on his territory on the boat without warning.

As he entered the hospital, he looked a bit shy and uncomfortable. He seemed glad to see Ann again, but his face changed completely when we showed him the baby. He didn't utter a word or smile. It was all too evident that she was not welcome in his heart, and it was to remain that way for a long time.

On the fourth day I was told all was well and I could take both mother and baby back home. When I went to the office to check them out, I was a bit worried about the bill from such a fancy hospital. But to my surprise, all births in Portugal are completely free. When the friendly office girl saw my surprise and hesitation, she guessed my thoughts and said, "Yes, all births are free, even for foreigners." Thinking it over, she added, "Besides, your daughter is not a foreigner—she's Portuguese, like all babies born in our country."

I heard some good-natured laughs around me. Certainly our baby didn't look Portuguese, especially with a Chinese mother and tall, blonde father, neither of whom spoke a word of Portuguese. Yet the law said she was Portuguese, so a few days later I obtained a Portuguese passport for our new baby. We were now a family of four, but with four different passports. The baby had her Portuguese one, Thomas still had his French passport, Ann had a Malay passport and I had an American one. (A couple of years later I obtained dual citizenship for my two children. On their 18th birthdays they will have to decide for themselves which one they want to keep.)

It was so nice to have a new baby onboard and she knit our family even tighter together. But a few weeks later, the winter settled in. On the 16th of November, a gale blew so hard that, despite being in a well-protected lagoon, we were unable to reach shore for two days. When the gale let up and I could go into town to do some shopping a friend asked why I didn't enter the inner basin where I could tie up along the wall facing the street. I could even hook up electricity there.

"But that's quite impossible," I said. "There is a railroad bridge that's too low blocking the way, and it's not the opening type."

"You're only partially right," my friend said. "If the rails are dismantled, it's possible to get the bridge to open up with a special crew of workers. Go to the railroad station and explain that you have a newborn onboard and that it's too much of a hardship for your family to lie in the lagoon in the middle of winter. He's a nice man. I bet he'll let you in."

I could hardly believe it, but both the harbourmaster and the chief of the railroad station readily agreed to open the bridge for me despite all the inconvenience it would cause. They told me to enter after the last train had passed at midnight and they would wait for me with their crew. True to their word, as soon as the last train had passed, the seven- or eight-man crew went to work with big crowbars and wrenches. After about half an hour, the bridge opened and they signaled for me to go through, which I did, quickly warping the boat over so they could swing the bridge back and align and screw back the rails in safe time before the first morning train.

We made fast along the quay next to the telegraph pole and got electricity onboard. I doubt a safer, more convenient port could be found anywhere in the world. Within a five-minute walk through beautiful pedestrian streets were a baker, butcher, grocery, hardware store, bank, post office and a school for Thomas. The most unbeliev-able thing was that it didn't cost us a cent except for electricity.

Yet no matter how good a place is, sooner or later a sailor gets the urge to feel the life of his ship beneath him as she cuts her way through the waves again.

When spring came and the winter gales had faded in our memories, we went back to the stationmaster and thanked him for letting us stay in such a safe basin all winter. We told him we were ready to leave, so once again in the middle of the night they opened the bridge for us. By dawn, we were again in the open sea, rejoicing at our newly restored freedom.

From then on we tried to make up for the long winter months. We sailed back and forth along the south coast of Portugal, which we loved. The wind was from the north most of the time so we had a beam wind from shore with a smooth sea. We had perfect conditions for sailing and plenty of places to anchor. We were never bored. We also sailed up and down the Guidiana River as far as the little village of Foz, where the streets were laid with cobblestones and the houses painted white with chalk, just like in the postcards.

We wanted to see some of Spain and what better place to see than Seville, which evokes so much history. Seville has an historic castle from which the queen saw Columbus leave on his famous voyage. It also evokes memories of the opera *Carmen*, for which we had named our little daughter.

We had a beautiful sail up the Guadalquivir River, disregarding the usual warnings that it couldn't be done without a motor and arrived in Seville on September 2nd.

Seville is a beautiful town which is kept in immaculate shape. The very palace where the queen received Columbus after his renowned voyage to the new world stands in perfect condition today, its well-kept park stretching almost all the way to where we were moored. Not far away in the other direction is the tobacco factory where Carmen, the heroine of the famed opera, is supposed to have worked.

At night in the many small nightclubs we watched the flamenco dancers. There were not only professional dancers in shows for the public. In many of the clubs, the customers danced flamenco with burning eyes and trampling heels—quite a contrast from the dull, reserved dancing styles of northern Europe and the States.

One morning we awoke to find our boat engulfed in a cold morning mist rising from the water. It was a chilly reminder that another winter was approaching. However much we liked this part of the world, one winter had been enough. We lost no time in hoisting the sails for the south again. On November 22, we sailed down the peaceful river but we had delayed our departure too long and the winter gales had already started. We had to wait several days at the mouth of the river before a southerly gale would let up enough to allow us to set to sea. But after a very short let-up, the wind blew up again, making the trip very rough. We finally managed to arrive in the Canaries without any damage and moored in the safe Santa Cruz de Tenerife harbour on December 2.

I met up with many old friends including Fred Bo, who was on the Norwegian gaff ketch *Eye Seraye*. Bo was a traveling soul like I was and had lived in so many countries and spoke so many languages that he was no longer quite sure which nationality he should claim. *Eye Seraye* was an old, converted Norwegian fishing boat, but was in very good shape. Like my own, it was rigged without a main boom. In addition to his normal ketch sails he also had a square sail.

When he saw that I had a telegraph pole and was adzing it down to make a main boom, he came over and strongly insisted that I was making a mistake.

"Don't put a boom on your main," he suggested. "It's so much nicer to be free from all that trouble. Instead make a square yard out of it. Close-hauled you don't need a boom on your main and, while running when a boom would be useful, just lower the whole sail and hoist the square sail instead. You'll never regret it."

I didn't listen to his advice and was to bitterly regret it just a few weeks later. We had sailed on December 31st, headed for Grenada in the West Indies, and everything had gone quite well. After all, it was my seventh crossing of the Atlantic and it ought to have become merely routine. The trades blew fresh and Ann gradually overcame her seasickness.

By January 26 we had arrived quite close to Grenada. After breakfast, Ann and I sat relaxing and talking together in the saloon while the children played in the forward cabin. A little later, Ann went on deck to wash the diapers and I went forward to keep the kids company. Perhaps half an hour had elapsed when I noticed from the movements of the ship that we were getting off course. I wondered what could be the reason. The winds seemed steady and the automatic self-steering device had always been reliable. When I reached the deck, I instantly saw the problem. Ann had put the clothesline so close to the vane that it was hindering its free motion. That brought the boat more and more off course—so much so that the boat was already sailing by the lee and threatened to jibe all-standing. I rushed over to the pilot to clear it, but it was too late. The heavy new boom was already swinging over. I shouted to Ann to duck, but before she could react, she was hit and flung far overboard by the tremendous force of a heavy, gybing boom.

In despair, I disconnected the pilot, threw the tiller over and sheeted in all the sails so I could come back to where she had fallen. Thomas came on deck, having heard all the commotion, and looked on in awe. Neither he nor I could see any trace of her.

I knew that I had to find Ann immediately, as our chances of finding her would disappear rapidly since she didn't know how to swim. Minutes passed and neither Thomas nor I could see any trace of her. After a few minutes, I realised that our prospects for finding and saving her had become nil, but I continued to search, sailing back and forth for hours. We'd had it so good together and we'd expected to have so many more years ahead—it simply could not end like this!

Six hours after the accident, Thomas spotted something in the water, floating between two waves. My heart stood still as I steered towards the spot. He had not been mistaken. There was something there. But it wasn't Ann, just a plastic bucket floating upside down. The trapped air must have kept it from sinking. It was our bucket. Ann must have been using it for washing and it must have fallen in the water with her.

I now lost all hope. Finding that bucket floating between those waves proved that we had been looking in the right place. Had she been able to keep herself afloat, she should have been there. After searching in vain in the right spot for hours, I had to surmise that she'd drowned.

On the 29th of January, I anchored in St. George's Harbour in Grenada, alone with two small children. Thomas was not yet eight years old and Carmen was just a little over a year.

I felt desperately lonely.

# 27

# Without Ann

he days dragged on in sorrow and discouragement. On June 5th, I finally hoisted the sails and headed for North Carolina in hopes of settling into a new life for myself and my kids. Sailing into the crowded harbour of Beaufort in a very fresh breeze without Ann wasn't easy. The boat was rigged to be sailed by two—most of the sheets didn't lead back to the afterdeck.

After I lost Ann, I had managed by just running back and forth between the sails, their sheets and the tiller, but now in the strong wind it was out of the question to let go of the tiller, for even a second. We were going along at great speed between all the moored boats, so Thomas was my only hope. He assured me he could handle the tiller and grabbed it enthusiastically.

The boat was well balanced so it didn't need any undue force on the tiller, but nevertheless the sight of that little boy steering a 50-foot boat (counting the bowsprit and the bumkin it was actually closer to 70 feet), racing through a crowded anchorage must have made it all too obvious that part of the crew was missing. Later everybody asked me where his mother was. A journalist came over and wrote a long article about the lone sailor and his two small children.

The story led to several offers from women who wanted to come and crew for me and help with the children, but I couldn't stand the thought of having a strange woman on the boat where I'd shared so many memories with Ann.

Beaufort was a nice, friendly little town. Perhaps I should have been satisfied to stay there and start a new life with my children. But

I thought it would be better to go to Annapolis, where I could sell the boat and settle in a house, as everybody had been trying to convince me to do for years.

I hoisted the sails and headed north towards Annapolis through the intercoastal waterway. Each night we moored along the shore to sleep, so the trip was very restful. Thomas was fascinated by all the wildlife and, indeed, I was surprised to see such long stretches of jungle-like vegetation in a super-civilised country such as the United States. We still had all the conveniences of civilisation. The dense vegetation would clear at a small village and we could buy whatever we needed. Sometimes the water was as wide as a Norwegian fjord, while at other times it was as narrow as a canal, but it was always well-marked, safe and easy to navigate.

After a week we neared Norfolk, Virginia, and I stopped by a town with the strange name of Great Bridge. I was to get no further north and our lives were to take a new turn from there.

It started when the Belgium yacht *Emilie* moored alongside us for the night. It was a 40-footer with a father and daughter onboard. I heard them speaking French with Thomas and they soon invited us for dinner. We were served the best food we'd had for months. Both Thomas and I were very impressed that the daughter, who didn't appear to be more than 15 or 16, could make such good food. She seemed so shy, having said little since we came onboard.

But with her father, the conversation flowed easily and he sounded like a first-class sailor. Among his other exploits, he'd run a sailing school in the North Sea for 12 months a year! When he asked me what kind of engine we had, I confessed we had none. His daughter, Florence, suddenly became interested in the conversation.

"Is your motor broken, or do you mean you don't have a motor?" she asked, rather surprised.

"I have designed and built my boat as a true sailboat," I answered.

"Even if I now wanted to put a motor in, it would be difficult and rather unsuitable."

The father seemed stunned. "But how in the world have you managed to get here without a motor through all these canals? And what about the bridges? They don't always open when it suits us. Or did you get a tow?"

I laughed and said that sailors have managed without motors for thousands of years, so it was no worse for me, although I admitted that a crew certainly would have made it easier.

After a long silence, Florence, whom I'd thought so shy, surprised me by taking over the conversation.

"Dad always uses his big diesel engine. It makes a lot of noise, it stinks, and worst of all, it's right in the middle of my cabin. It sure would be nice to sail without a motor. Could I sail with you tomorrow and we could meet my Dad later on? I could help you with the boat and the kids. I have two years experience as a nanny."

"How old are you?" I asked a bit surprised.

"I'm 18," she declared, a bit annoyed.

I was not too keen on having anybody onboard, and certainly not such a young girl who seemed like potential trouble to me. Hurriedly I searched for an excuse which would not seem like an insult. I said I was too poor to pay wages for a nanny or even buy extra food to feed another person. But she was not about to be discouraged. She said she would come as a friend and didn't expect a salary at all. In fact, she said she was perfectly willing to foot her share of the food bill.

The father, who seemed to have already gotten used to the idea, confirmed that she was no longer a minor and had the right to "fly on her own wings." He said that she indeed had the money to pay for her share, as she'd recently sold her own boat, a little 21-footer that she'd bought with her savings from her work as a nanny.

I didn't want to hurt them by saying that I simply didn't want her onboard, so I searched desperately for a plausible excuse. Florence unknowingly came to my aid when she lit up a cigarette.

"It would be very pleasant," I said, "but unfortunately it is completely impossible for me to have a smoker onboard. I'm allergic to cigarette smoke."

She hesitated perhaps a second, then threw the lit cigarette into the water, followed by the entire pack she held in the other hand. "I was a smoker, but I'm not one any longer," she said. "So if you have no more excuses, I'll come tomorrow and fix breakfast for us all."

Before I had a chance to protest, she said goodnight and turned and disappeared into her cabin.

"I wonder what is going on with that girl?" her father said. I tried for years to get her to stop that horrid habit and now she just throws her cigarettes into the water. Well, if you can continue to have such a good influence on her, you're welcome to take her onboard!"

I found out later that he was expecting his new fiancee in a few days, so it must have suited him to get his daughter out of the way.

In the days that followed, Florence was to prove that she was not just a beautiful young woman. She was also an excellent cook and a good nanny for the children. She also pulled her weight onboard in all respects. It wasn't long before all thoughts of selling the boat had vanished and we decided to set course back to the West Indies. Florence had liked it when she had been there with her father.

We had a rough trip over, which was to be expected, since it was now the height of hurricane season. On September 21 we arrived in San Juan, Puerto Rico, just in time to avoid hurricane Gloria, one of the worst ever registered.

Four days later, Florence and I married. It was a great relief for Thomas, who no longer had to suffer my rather poor cooking. The following year, on October 11, 1986, Thomas and Carmen got a new sister, whom we named Virginia, after the state where Florence and

I had met. She was born on the same settee where Thomas had been born on that stormy night, ten years before. This time, however, we were securely anchored in a calm bay in Puerto Rico.

We realised, of course, the advantages of delivering a baby in a modern hospital, but in Puerto Rico, the father was not allowed to be present at the birth. Florence panicked at the thought of giving birth alone among strangers, so we decided to do without them and have the baby in the warmth and peace of our cabin.

Since we were free from the regulations of a hospital, we also decided to let Thomas and Carmen be present at the birth. In this manner, we hoped to avoid the jealousy so common among older siblings at the arrival of a new baby which apparently has been purchased in some unknown hospital without their consent.

Thomas was given the responsibility of cutting the cord—a task he managed with pride, squeezing the big scissors with both hands. Carmen also helped by leading the baby's head toward her mother's breast. Since that day, they have always been proud of their little sister, whom they always call "our baby."

I was soon to realise that not everybody shared our views on births when one day Thomas, looking rather troubled, asked me, "Papa, why do you think my teacher looked so surprised when I told her about the birth of my little sister?"

# 28

# The Present and Future

*F*lorence, despite her very young age, had proven to be the perfect wife. Not only was she young, beautiful and a wonderful lover; she was also an excellent cook, a good housekeeper and a loving mother to all three children. I was the happiest of men, expecting it to last forever. Unfortunately, it lasted for only three years.

I have never seen Florence again, nor my youngest child, Virginia, whom she took with her. I was so depressed, I was on the verge of a nervous breakdown. I decided to sail back to my beloved tropics and back to the life I'd become adjusted to—back to moonlit sails, palm trees and eternal summers, back to a land where we are greeted with smiles and welcomes instead of "NO TRESPASSING" signs.

When I made it known that I intended to sail back, good friends all protested, telling me that I was showing inexcusable irresponsibility. "In your state of health, how can you consider going out to sea alone with two small kids? Suppose you die at sea? Have you considered what a situation you might put your kids in? They could be drifting around helplessly with a dead man onboard!"

Those were not exactly the words a depressed man wants to hear. I was undecided about what I should do until my bright little boy of only 11 overheard some of the conversations and said, "Papa, it would be just as sad for me to see you die here ashore in the hospital as it would far from help and alone in the boat. I think you'd have much less chance of dying if we sail back towards the tropics where you'd be happy, rather than stay here. You'd get more and more depressed here. Should the worst happen, I'll know what to do. You know that I'd be able to bring the ship back to port."

Tears came to my eyes—my own little boy was the best friend I had. He and my little Carmen were my most precious treasures. Nobody was ever going to take them away from me. Both their mothers were dead and I was their only family.

I made the boat ready for sea immediately and the next day we sailed back towards Puerto Rico. We arrived in good shape after a very rough 20-day crossing. We left at the end of August and arrived in mid-September, right at the height of the hurricane season! But we were back and, in fact, I was in better shape after the crossing than I had been in Florida.

That was three years ago and, although it's said that time heals all wounds, I still miss my wife.

I have my boat and something invaluable, which only a few fortunate people ever attain—freedom. I'm my own skipper on my own boat. I don't have a big bank account, but I also don't have a single debt. I have a very small income, but the important thing to me is that I've organised my life to be comfortable and happy within my budget. I am never troubled by getting into the red, which is more than I can say when I was a "successful" businessman many years ago. I had the latest model Cadillac, a swimming pool and a fur-clad wife . . . and suffered sleepless nights.

I am free to sail anywhere in the world. I get so many questions about why I sail without a motor. Some think the only reason is because I'm a diehard sentimentalist and a purist who doesn't mind making life hard on myself in order to live up to my ideals. Nothing could be further from the truth. I would be a fool if I made life harder than necessary for myself. I sail without a motor and other modern gadgets for practical reasons—none of them are really necessary. They all cost a lot of money and are subject to regular breakdowns and maintenance and require a bigger budget than I have.

In order to manage my life on such a small budget, it's imperative that I be as self-sufficient as possible. If I were to depend on various spare parts and the mechanics and specialists required to keep them going, there would be no limit to the amount of money required.

Sailboats have sailed the oceans of the world for centuries, managing quite well with none of these modern inventions. "But what about all those accidents and shipwrecks?" some might ask. I wonder if there were any more than today. What we've gained in technology, most of us have lost in seamanship. I can't count the number of yachtsmen who've lost their ships because their motors, their modern navigation equipment or other gadgets failed at the wrong moment and the skipper was caught unprepared and helpless.

There is no substitute for good seamanship. In the old days, a man had to serve five years' apprenticeship before he could be considered a seaman. Today, a man who can sign a check and press the starter button considers himself well able to handle his own ship with just a couple of weekends of sea trials and reading manuals.

Those who might criticise me can't understand how I've been able to sail for so long without a motor, yet suffering no accidents. They don't realise that a true sailboat has been designed not to rely on a motor and is an entirely different proposition. The engine-less boat will sail much better under sail because it doesn't have the weight of the motor, fuel tanks, batteries and all the accessories and the drag of the propellers.

The skipper who has gone to all the expense of buying such equipment will take advantage of it, not just when the sea is becalmed, but also in manoeuvering in and out of the various anchorages and ports. The trouble is that, by doing so, the skipper never gets the proper experience to handle the boat under tricky conditions. Then one fateful day, the motor refuses to start and the skipper is in trouble because he has no experience in handling the boat without a motor. A manoeuvre that would be routine for an experienced skipper on a finely tuned engine-less sailboat could become reason for a mayday call or even a shipwreck for the inexperienced skipper.

Disregarding the practical reasons, I must confess that there is a lot of satisfaction to be gained by sailing a true sailboat from anchor to anchor solely aided by the forces of nature. In my case, I have the added satisfaction of knowing that the ship I've sailed all over the world was assembled piece by piece by my hands alone and from my own drawings and dreams.

Another question I often get is about my children's schooling, since I never stay in one place for very long. School-age children do present problems for live-aboarders and there are no really satisfactory solutions. The first and most obvious solution would be to choose a suitable school and anchor as close as possible to it during the school year and go sailing only during vacations. That is an entirely unsatisfactory solution, to my mind. Another way would be to use a correspondence school, as the majority of cruisers do, which can give very good results.

But it all depends on the kids, the parents and the mail service in the countries being visited. In my case I gave up. Mail was often slow and would force us to wait, sometimes in places we were impatient to sail away from. Worst of all, Thomas found those programmed lessons a real bore. He would sit in front of them all day, just staring into empty space, despite our urging him on and trying to help him. It got on our nerves so much that both I and my wife, who really did her best in the beginning, ultimately gave up.

We then tried to teach him ourselves with lessons which might interest him. I tried, for example, to make him read books, newspaper articles, or anything he would like, then asked him to put it aside and rewrite it in his own words. That seemed to me to be a complete exercise, one that would teach him to concentrate, remember and choose his own words.

But he showed little interest in rewriting those stories. Tired of nagging, we decided to put him in school whenever there was a school in proximity and take him out when we were ready to sail. Sometimes that amounted to several months, but all too often was just a matter of days before we would move on. Each time there would be a new teacher, new books and, sometimes, even new languages. Thomas has been in Italian, French, Portuguese, English and Spanish schools. It couldn't have been as easy for him, or later, for Carmen, as it was for the other children, but Thomas generally earned all A's until last year. When he turned 14 he refused to go to any more schools and I would literally have to drag him there and enroll him by force. He still got the last word, because at the end of the trimester he came home with nothing but F's.

Thomas has been tested and found to have an IQ of 148, so there was no excuse for him suddenly to be earning F's. I had a long talk with him, man to man, and he explained that he was bored in school. Everything he'd learned, he said, he'd picked up from listening to my grownup friends when they came onboard and from his many books. I can't vouch for that, but I do know that he had learned one thing in school—bad manners!

I tried to impress upon him that, whether he learns in school or outside of school, he will need the diploma— the paperwork—to get a proper job. But when I tried to explain that without a diploma he could only get a job sweeping floors, he was quick to point out that you don't need a diploma to be president of the United States, and added that Onassis had been a success in life without a diploma.

So, I gave up. After all, there are other schools in life than the prescribed ones and, except for the proper credentials, results are what counts. Thomas is trilingual, speaking perfect English, French and Spanish. He can add up to a half dozen purchases in his head as fast as a cashier can knock them out on her machine so he can be sure he'll never be overcharged. I defy anyone to catch him on any geographical knowledge. More than once I've caught him looking at me with a sign of exasperation when grownups can't quite follow his discussions of faraway places. And certainly not too many people know more about the stars than he does.

He even surprised me the last time we crossed from Florida to Puerto Rico and he wanted me to check on his navigation. After a couple of weeks at sea, he had figured out how many miles remained for us to go. His mark on the chart was only about 15 miles off, which, after traveling over a thousand miles through the water including tacking, wasn't bad. I asked him how in the world he could have calculated it that close and he said," Well I used Stella Polaris and this sextant I made." He showed me a large plastic disk on which he'd installed a long, rotating pointer with all the degrees marked in. He lined up the star to the pointer and the base line of the disk towards the horizon to get the North Star's height.

"That can't be very accurate," I protested. "Besides, the North Star is not exactly over the Pole."

He looked at me, rather hurt at my underestimating him, and replied, "I've got good eyes and I sighted very carefully. I'm sure I can stay within one degree, which would amount to about a 60-mile error, but with a little luck I should do much better. As for the Stella Polaris, I know it wanders around the Pole with a one-degree offset, but by its position in relation to the rest of the constellation, we can easily eliminate that error within just a very few miles."

At that time, Thomas was not yet 12. No wonder he was getting bored with school.

He also started to study naval architecture and borrowed my books, sometimes appropriating my more precious ones. Soon he could calculate a boat's displacement and had learned about prismatic coefficients, stability factors and relationships, as well as the wetted surface-to-sail area. When he started to make sailing models to test his theories, he discovered that his models were sailing much faster than anyone else's. Since he won all the races, he could sell his models at good prices, and with the money he set aside from their sales, together with money he made working on other yachts and giving sailing lessons, it was possible for him to buy his own yacht, which he called *Spartan*. The name was certainly appropriate, as a more spartan boat would be hard to find.

He moved onboard the very day he bought the boat, but he never fails to come back onboard *L'Artemis* at mealtime. The *Spartan* is modest, but very salty-looking and businesslike. It's a 22-foot gaff sloop designed by Howard I. Chapelle, the American historian and designer who loved America's workboats of the last century.

I think, for the immediate future, we will remain on the water. I love Puerto Rico, but I feel the time has come for us to move on. The world is big and there is so much more to see. Besides, as Lord Nelson said, "Ships and men rot in harbour."

Thomas and I will sail together and rediscover the world together whether or not he or I should get a crew. I can adjust the speed of *L'Artemis* so that we can stay together. Many claim that it will be difficult not to lose each other in the open sea. But Christopher Columbus kept his fleet together without any radios or other modern navigational instruments or electronics. It's just a matter of adjusting our speeds and keeping a regular lookout. And, of course, you should never fail to have a good, bright light at night.

Where are we going to sail? I don't know yet. I am still deciding between a half-dozen different routes and destinations. Maybe we'll just island-hop down the chain of these wonderful West Indies, as well as the islands of the Bahamas. Perhaps we'll go back to Europe with its old world charms, or perhaps towards Panama, the gate to the Pacific and the romantic South Seas Islands.

Perhaps I shouldn't make up my mind yet. Carmen knows that Panama is one of the stops we have to make if we're going to China, and that's where she wants to go so I can find her a new mommy.

Carmen wants a mommy who looks like her. At the tender age of eight, she is already painfully aware that she looks "different," due to her Chinese mother. She can't remember her mother, but thinks of her as a sort of mysterious, invisible and certainly unreachable fairy. She often cuddles up to me and worries that we look so different. "Why is my skin darker than yours?" she asks.

"Some people have darker skin than others. Some people have longer noses than others. What does it matter?" I tell her.

"I'd prefer to look more like you," she insists.

I laugh and assure her that I would prefer to look more like her— and be 59 years younger in the deal.

"Why couldn't I look more like Thomas? He's my brother and only seven years older?"

"You do look a bit like him," I said. "But primarily you are yourself. You are Carmen and you are beautiful the way you are. Why would you want to be any different?"

My little Carmen is both beautiful and modest. And certainly everybody she meets loves her. In fact, I have lost track of all the offers I've had for adoptions, sometimes accompanied by sizable offers of money. At first these offers insulted me and made me feel inadequate as a lone parent. Now I realise that people can't get used to the idea of a male single parent, especially one so much older. They fall in love with that beautiful little girl, who, except for me, is all alone in the world with no family.

She is the most important woman in my life for now. In a few days, when the ship is stocked up we'll see where our course will go.

It will be soon enough to decide, for a truly free man doesn't have to make up his mind until the last minute.

Indeed, I've left port cleared for the next one and then, halfway there, changed my mind and set a course to an entirely new place. Perhaps this is one reason I always follow the old-timers' habit of never saying I'm sailing "to" a place but "towards" it. Thus I feel entitled to change my mind without having to account for it.

Freedom is a treasure that is enjoyed by fewer and fewer people in this world of increasing rules and regulations. Most people obey so they can blend in with the system and have a chance at being "successful." I have found a way of life which suits me so well that I can think of no one I'd like to trade places with.

I haven't forgotten the inscription on that ashtray in my parents' home which so intrigued me as a child:

*Whoever lives without folly is not as wise as he thinks.*

# Epilogue

At 2 o'clock Thursday afternoon, we left Puerto Rico, bound for Bonaire in the Dutch Antilles, *L'Artemis* towing my own 22-foot *Spartan* on the end of 300 feet of nylon rope. My Dad and I had agreed that it would be necessary for me to stay in my boat to be sure the open cockpit did not fill with water, which would then flood the cabin, leading to instant sinking.

After three nights of bothersome close reaching, the wind went to just behind the beam, making my boat surf and also throwing a lot less spray, so I didn't have to bail every three hours anymore. I managed to shout to my Dad, "Are we going to see Bonaire tonight?" to which he nodded his head up and down.

I woke up for the third time, uncurled from my fetal sleeping position and splashed through the three inches of seawater above the floorboards and into the cockpit where the water was only ankle deep. A bright lighthouse stood off my starboard stern, quite high on the horizon. I stood up and looked forward. Right off our starboard beam was a loom and straight in front, a fairly dim lighthouse.

I started bailing the water out, first port, then starboard, then inside. I stood up, thinking about anchoring amidst the yachts at dawn, meeting new people, cleaning my boat out. I felt good. I worked out, from my father's chart, that the loom was Kralendijk. The big lighthouse was the easternmost one and the dim lighthouse, the southernmost. I saw the south lighthouse first on one side of *L'Artemis,* then on the other and back again as the boat yawed under self-steering. I felt the seas stack up as they approached the shore.

"Gosh, he's passing awful close," I thought. "He's probably inside looking at the chart and any moment now he's going to change course, which will be quite necessary because we are now heading straight for the lighthouse."

Already feeling slightly anxious about it, I suddenly saw three rocks jutting out of the horizon and thought, "Oh, no! This must be Aves!" (A dangerous coral atoll some 30 miles to windward of Bonaire.) Then I saw the broad white line, the boiling foam of relentless, charging waves crashing onto the shore.

In seconds *L'Artemis* was on it, the bow plunging down and the stern rising with such violence as to knock all the wind out of the main. "Non! Non!" I screamed, as if it were going to make any difference. It can't be real, I thought, it must be a particularly large wave. But when I noticed the limp towline, I knew this was the real thing. I looked at my Dad's 50-foot boat being tossed about like a piece of driftwood in the surf. The boat set itself parallel to the coast. The next instant the rig snapped off with a crack audible above the thunder of the roaring waves.

I rushed inside, fumbling with the knot, frantically trying to untie my surfboard in complete darkness, for there was no moon at all. Once free, I shoved it in the cockpit and groped for a pair of pants, found none and gave up, leaving in only a wool shirt and rain jacket. I jumped in the water with my surfboard, paddling for Dad's boat, wanting to be with them and to scramble ashore together. But when I got closer, I was afraid of getting crushed by the boat. (Two days later I learned that was probably what had happened to my father.)

I stayed as close to *L'Artemis* as possible, waiting for a break in the waves to dash in and jump onshore. Under the light of the stern lamp, I could see the boat being destroyed with ghastly efficiency. She would leap up in the air with the rising water and, as the water went back out, the boat would drop 10 feet onto the sharp coral with the sickening noise of cracking wood and my sister's hysterical screams coming from inside. For a minute or two, I saw my Dad sitting in the companionway shining a flashlight out to sea and then across the reef. I put my surfboard up in the air, but I don't think he saw me.

Then *L'Artemis*'s stern lamp went out from the successive shocks, leaving her completely in the dark. I paddled out and away from the breaking waves. After a little while, I didn't feel panic at all. Instead it was a lot like a dream. I figured I just had to keep paddling to stay warm, and wait until sunrise when I could climb the coral and find them both waiting for me.

After some three hours, the sun finally came up and I could see the coast. It was Bonaire, after all. Edging closer to the reef, I spent another two hours trying to get in, timing it so I would reach the coral as the wave went down. But there was a current pulling me away from the coast. The important thing wasn't timing, the idea was to get in. As I headed north again, I saw something on the reef. It was the remains of *L'Artemis*—part of the stern here, a bit of dagger board there, fenders floating around, millions of little bits of teak.

At around 9 o'clock, I finally got on shore without too many scratches but, after staying six hours on the surfboard, I had massive friction burns. Immediately I set about searching for my father and sister—but they weren't there.

— Thomas Tangvald
August 1991
Andorra

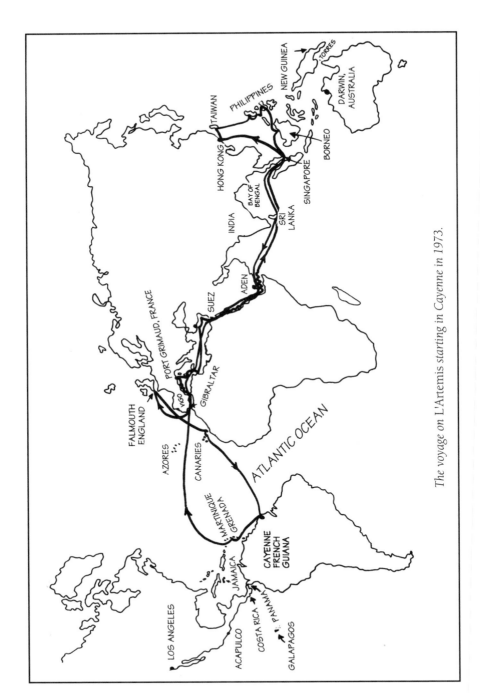

*The voyage on L'Artemis starting in Cayenne in 1973.*

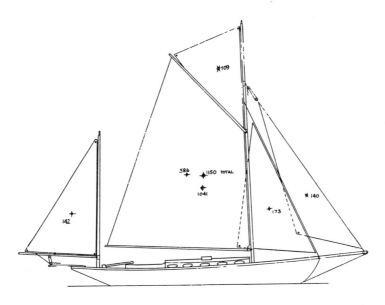

*"Windflower," the 45' yawl sailed from England to California in 1957 and 1958,
built in England in 1928 out of oak and teak.*

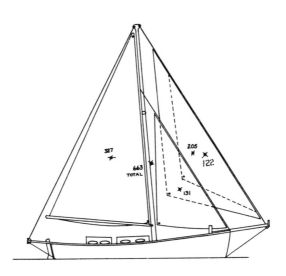

*"Dorothea," which I sailed around the world from 1959 and thereafter to the West
Indies and French Guiana before it sank in the Atlantic. She was built
in England in 1934 and was 32' long.*

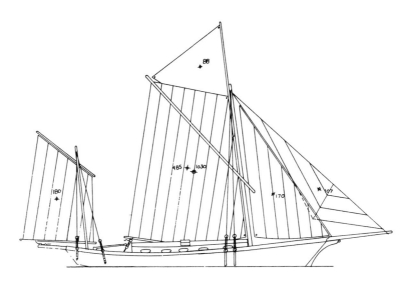

*The yawl* L'Artemis de Pytheas *with sprit mainsail amd lug mizzen. Despite very short masts, she was very fast as it was easy to trim the boat to suit the various wind conditions. I often sailed past various "racing machines" much to their crews' surprise. Once I was even accused of cheating with my motor—-they thought I was joking when I told them I had no motor onboard.*

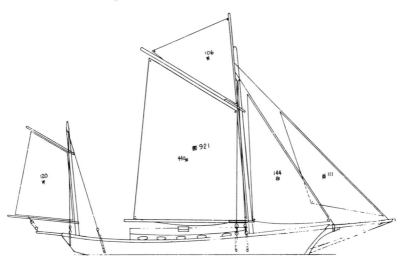

L'Artemis *gaff-rigged, the way I sailed her from France to Taiwan in 1976. The boat was not as fast as with the sprit rig but safer to handle without the long heavy sprit.*

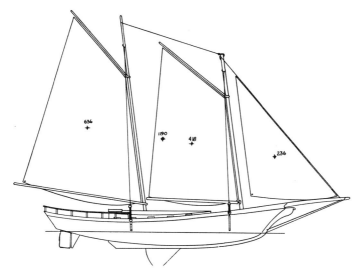

When L'Artemis *was damaged by the typhoon in Taiwan, I used the opportunity to rerig the boat entirely as a schooner, mainly because I had always admired the schooner rig for its beauty. It was to prove exceptionally fast when reaching, but slightly slower closehauled. The rig's big weakness was running. The boat then was very slow and almost impossible to steer. The big mainsail far back blanketed the rest of the sails making the boat under-rigged.*

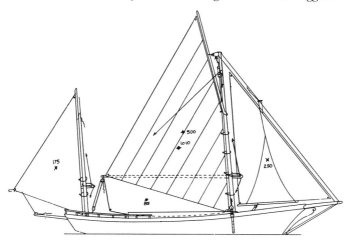

*The winter 83/84 I rerigged "L'Artemis" back to a yawl. This time I used only one headsail on a shorter bow sprit and the mizzen got a sprit boom and no shrouds. This proved very successful. The high boom was mainly to avoid accidents like the one which killed Ann. The empty space under the mainsail can be filled with a "watersail" in light airs.*

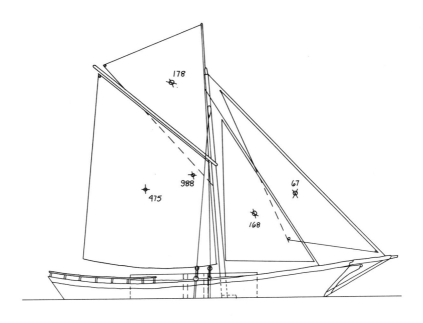

L'Artemis *the way she looked most recently under her loose-footed gaff cutter rig. I rerigged her again as I wanted the advantages of a modern windvane, and for that the mizzen sail was in the way. I had to rerig her as a single sticker, but this proved to have the added advantage of reduced maintenance in port while giving me a very fast boat to windward.*

## A Note from the Publisher . . .

No one really knows what happened that tragic night off the coast of Bonaire. Peter Tangvald's health was not good. He had suffered a massive heart attack in 1988, and also incapacitating attacks of kidney stones. We can only surmise that a heart attack or some other malady caused him to sail his yacht and his family into such a perilous situation. Peter carried that secret with him. However, I feel quite certain that Peter knew he would eventually meet his end on the seas and wouldn't have had it any other way.

— *Nancy Scott*